SUCCESS
THROUGH
DIVERSITY

SUCCESS THROUGH DIVERSITY

WHY THE MOST INCLUSIVE COMPANIES WILL WIN

CAROL FULP

Beacon Press · BOSTON

BEACON PRESS
Boston, Massachusetts
www.beacon.org

Beacon Press books
are published under the auspices of
the Unitarian Universalist Association of Congregations.

21 20 19 18   8 7 6 5 4 3 2 1

This book is printed on acid-free paper that meets the uncoated paper
ANSI/NISO specifications for permanence as revised in 1992.

Text design and composition by Kim Arney

Library of Congress Cataloging-in-Publication Data

Names: Fulp, Carol, author.
Title: Success through diversity : why the most inclusive companies will win
    / Carol Fulp ; foreword by Deval Patrick.
Description: Boston : Beacon Press, 2018. | Includes bibliographical
    references and index.
Identifiers: LCCN 2018018020 (print) | LCCN 2018019797 (ebook) |
    ISBN 9780807056295 (ebook) | ISBN 9780807056288 (hardback)
Subjects: LCSH: Diversity in the workplace. | Strategic planning. | Leadership. |
    BISAC: BUSINESS & ECONOMICS / Strategic Planning. | BUSINESS &
    ECONOMICS / Leadership. | BUSINESS & ECONOMICS / Workplace Culture.
Classification: LCC HF5549.5.M5 (ebook) | LCC HF5549.5.M5 F85 2018 (print) |
    DDC 658.3008—dc23
LC record available at https://lccn.loc.gov/2018018020

To all of the business and organizational leaders
who are committed to a more diverse workplace in America

CONTENTS

Foreword by Deval Patrick · ix

Introduction · 1

CHAPTER 1   From "Nice to Have" to "Do or Die" · 14

CHAPTER 2   Recruiting Like Rooney · 39

CHAPTER 3   Building a Better Board—and a Larger,
More Vibrant Organization · 57

CHAPTER 4   Connecting with Community at John Hancock · 77

CHAPTER 5   Marketing Outside the Box · 98

CHAPTER 6   Innovating a More Colorful Company · 119

CHAPTER 7   Supplying for Success · 142

CHAPTER 8   A New Age of Business Ethics · 161

Epilogue · 181
Acknowledgments · 185
Notes · 187
Index · 213
About the Author · 221

FOREWORD

OUTSIDE OF LAMONT LIBRARY in Harvard Yard sits a large brass statue by famed British sculptor Henry Moore. Up close, it's unremarkable: a bunch of lumpy golden shapes where small children often climb. But walk out of the Yard by way of Quincy Street, take a sharp left, and gaze back through the railing about fifty yards down the block. Suddenly you will see a gorgeous and voluptuous work, once meaningless metal transformed into a majestic human figure in repose. For Jeremy Knowles, late professor of chemistry and longtime dean of Harvard's Faculty of Arts and Sciences, this experience contained a powerful lesson for incoming students. If they didn't understand a scientific theory, a passage from a classical text, a Schoenberg trio, or their roommate's politics, Dean Knowles would tell the freshmen, try a new perspective.

Dean Knowles's story might seem quaint today, as our college campuses—not to mention our political parties—grow ever more polarized, unyielding, and rancorous. But his wisdom is timeless. There is a transformative power in trying a different perspective. Surely, it is the source of both understanding and progress.

I grew up in the tough neighborhood of Chicago's South Side, where poverty and crime were much too familiar. At age fourteen, with the blessing of a full scholarship, I was jettisoned to Massachusetts to the world of Milton Academy, then on to Harvard College—worlds of manicured lawns, ivoried towers, and the advantages of wealth and privilege. After graduating from Harvard, my perspective was again upended by a year living and working in Sudan on a Michael Clark

Rockefeller Traveling Fellowship, where I exchanged manicured lawns and hoary traditions for arid desert, the ordered chaos of the *souk*, and subsistence living. All that before I entered the professional world back in the States.

My early experiences exposed me to some of the vagaries and injustices that divide us, and the many yearnings we have in common. But above all they taught me the power of seeking perspective. And that perspective has, among other things, enabled me to sustain my own high expectations of myself and others, and my drive to perform and leave whatever I can better. This very spirit of optimism infuses my friend Carol Fulp's book.

As you'll discover in these pages, Dean Knowles's lesson is a point of departure. She teaches that we must assume different perspectives to understand one another, and we must also celebrate these differences and strategically mobilize them to forge a better future. Our workplaces must encompass and nurture a broad spectrum of human difference if they are to overcome the forces of market disruption and flourish. In the chapters that follow, you'll learn how we must harness the power of difference—be it racial, gender, class, perspective—to power our companies' marketing capacities, innovative potential, recruitment possibilities, and performance. While corporate greed and malfeasance may dominate the news headlines, this book reminds us that our most admired companies harness the power of difference to create innovative, vibrant, and dynamic organizations.

Success Through Diversity: Why the Most Inclusive Companies Will Win tells how we can do well by doing right.

Deval L. Patrick
Governor of Massachusetts (2007–2015)
Bain Capital Managing Director (2015–present)

INTRODUCTION

AT A CIVIC EVENT YEARS AGO, as a young African American just starting out in my career, I had a chance to sit next to Jim Coppersmith, then the president of Boston's ABC-TV affiliate, WCVB. I struck up a conversation with the personable white CEO and advised him that I was serving as the fund-raising chair for a valued African American social service nonprofit. Our organization, I related, would welcome CEOs at our civic events, as we were trying to garner support from the business community. Unfortunately, we weren't having much luck appealing to corporate executives. I had assumed that CEOs weren't interested in our cause or that they perhaps felt uncomfortable attending events where most attendees were people of color.

"You know," I said to Jim, "we're having a fund-raiser soon. Why don't you come?"

Smiling, Jim said, "You always hold your fund-raisers on weekends. If you want CEOs, you should hold your events during the week. Then I'd happily come and help bring my colleagues." He advised me that scheduling issues had prevented him and probably some others from attending in the past. Weekends were when they preferred to spend time with their families and friends, not attend to civic activities related to their corporate roles.

I began to schedule fund-raising events on weekdays. Sure enough, with Jim's help, business executives began coming. I never would have learned about the importance of weekday scheduling had I not had a frank conversation with a white CEO. And that was only the

beginning. Within a year, this same CEO hired me when the human resources manager position at WCVB came open.

If you're trying to raise money, land a job, or achieve some other professional goal, interacting with people who are different from you will prove valuable. The cultivation of difference helps organizations too. During the 1980s, when I worked at WCVB, I found the station to be decades ahead of most businesses in the country when it came to difference. The entire organization, including management, didn't simply tolerate people from diverse backgrounds. It *valued* difference. Delivering on its charter, WCVB was a true community station that served all of Boston's neighborhoods, ethnicities, and religious groups. Members of *all* communities were represented on the organization's staff and its on-air programming. And the station's award-winning show *CityLine*, hosted by well-respected director of public affairs and community services Karen Holmes Ward, an African American media veteran, today continues to serve as the voice of Boston's diverse communities.

Whenever I go on a job interview, I arrive early to watch people and learn about the organization's culture. When I arrived at WCVB for my initial interview, I spotted a man wearing pink fuzzy slippers. He seemed completely at ease and happy at work, as did his colleagues around him. Can you imagine what it meant to an African American woman during the 1980s to see a man in the workplace wearing pink fuzzy slippers? If WCVB could welcome a man who dressed in such an unorthodox fashion, I felt it would embrace my difference as well.

It was such a contrast to an experience I had while interviewing for a community relations manager position at a financial services institution. There, my three interviewers were all tall white men with blue eyes and blond hair, dressed in blue pin-striped suits. It was clear that they represented the institution's "picture" of success, and that this picture didn't look like me. At Channel 5, however, I saw people of color, women, those with physical disabilities, and, of course, my favorite—the man with pink fuzzy slippers, who attended to his work as I waited in the reception area. During those fifteen minutes prior to the interview, I observed a culture in which individuality, creativity, difference, and even eccentricities were accepted, fostered,

and prized. I knew immediately that I could do my best work in this environment. Sure enough, when I came on board, I found that WCVB wholeheartedly valued me not only for my job skills, but for the unique perspectives I brought. In fact, my colleagues viewed my difference as an asset.

WCVB's culture of diversity and inclusion enabled it to create an array of award-winning programming. In 1985, for instance, the station unveiled its "A World of Difference" public service campaign. Joining forces with the Anti-Defamation League (ADL), the campaign was designed to promote democracy, undermine prejudice, and strengthen multiculturalism. ADL subsequently evolved this campaign into the World of Difference Institute International, which provides diversity education programming to businesses, educational institutions, community organizations, and government agencies throughout the country and around the world. To date, this diversity initiative has nurtured and trained nearly three hundred fifty thousand teachers and fourteen million students—and again, it all started at WCVB.

WCVB not only cultivated diversity in its own organization, but also advocated for it publicly. And WCVB's culture of advocacy was so strong that it spawned many efforts beyond the station. The station's vice president of community programming, Donna Latson Gittens, oversaw the World of Difference campaign. Mobilizing her incredible talent and breadth of experience, this African American woman subsequently founded her own company, Cause Media Marketing (later MORE Advertising). It was WCVB that first brought Donna and me together. After we moved on from the station, we continued to collaborate on inclusion initiatives with the Democratic National Convention, the Red Sox Foundation, the *Boston Business* Journal, The Partnership, Inc., and others.

Through the World of Difference campaign I also met philanthropist and longtime ADL leader Esta Epstein, and we further supported many diversity-related causes over the years together. We also both fund-raised vigorously for President Barack Obama's campaigns.

During my eleven years working for WCVB, I realized that the station's commitment to diversity didn't just make people like me comfortable and promote inclusion in its programming—it also drove

business results. WCVB was considered the country's best local network affiliate, with the ratings and awards to match. Many factors contributed to that success, but as I saw it, inclusion was the energizing ingredient. *Everyone* in the organization had the freedom to be him- or herself—to be creative, to dress in ways that felt natural, to speak his or her mind, and to bring his or her best self to work. With so much difference on open display, WCVB was *buzzing* with creative and intellectual ferment. We learned from one another, we trusted one another, we innovated in our jobs, and we enjoyed the environment of freedom and self-expression. We were motivated to excel and felt proud to work for a company that prided itself on its interesting and open culture.[1]

By authentically valuing personal differences, WCVB anticipated the changing face of diversity and inclusion in the twenty-first century. During a recent conversation with Scott Martin, who at the time served as the digital marketing and social media manager for the YMCA of Greater Boston before becoming director of strategic coalitions for Governor Charlie Baker's relection campaign, and Keenen Grooms, assistant director for strategic partnerships at the Massachusetts treasurer's office, I was reminded of how the term "diversity" has expanded in meaning over the generations.[2] As African Americans born in the 1990s, Scott and Keenen are millennials who learned from their parents how to navigate predominantly white business climates. Since their childhoods, they have seen diversity transition from being thought of principally in terms of race or gender to encompass the staggering diversity of our nation's many cultures, lifestyle and sexual orientations, skill sets, religious and spiritual inclinations, viewpoints, and experiences.

Keenen oversees the state treasurer's college savings accounts directed toward low-income communities across Massachusetts. Working closely with five cities that comprise mostly low-income people of color from predominantly Latino, first-generation, and immigrant communities, Keenen surrounds himself with as many different types of people as possible. He can't create effective financial programming without truly diverse input. As Keenen told me, Treasurer Deborah Goldberg, who hired him to oversee the project, makes it a policy "to

hire people that not only look, talk, and think like our target communities, but are also willing to bring different strategies and perspectives to the table so we can develop ways to engage and market to very diverse communities." As a result, Keenen and his colleagues recently developed a financial education program in thirteen languages. Thirty years ago, a progressive treasury department might have created a Spanish-language program for the state, but not something of this scale.

At the YMCA of Greater Boston, Scott doesn't just work to market swimming pools and gym facilities to children and families. The YMCA is also the largest provider of early childcare in Massachusetts. To market to diverse needs, Scott must consider everyone in his community. As he related, "Men, women, gay, straight, bisexual, black, and more, you need a diverse workforce because through that you're creating a true representation of the community and a better understanding of services you need to offer that will impact everyone." That includes people living in rural areas such as western Massachusetts. Massachusetts has a national reputation for being cosmopolitan, Scott says, but outside metropolitan Boston, this isn't necessarily the case. As Keenen observed during our talk, a team of five Ivy League–educated African Americans could create a strong business strategy, but it wouldn't be truly reflective of the diverse community or clientele in today's marketplace. It wouldn't be an *inclusive* strategy. "Even if you have black people from all different backgrounds," he qualifies, "you're definitely limiting what ideas you may or may not come up with." The same applies if you have a group of racially mixed people who are all male: "You're not going to be able to grasp the full spectrum of ideas that are out there," Scott observes. And as we'll explore throughout this book, you're not going to have the same type of lively, challenging, and productive debate that leads to innovation and drives business results.

Unlike Scott and Keenen, I came of age during the civil rights era, when my family and community struggled against race-based segregation and discrimination not only in our workplaces, but in housing, schools, lunch counters, and polling places. For much of my career, diversity has been synonymous with the promotion of historically disadvantaged groups, particularly African Americans. While my views

have evolved to reflect the broader way that many people in Scott and Keenen's generation think about inclusion, I remain ever so cognizant that unless African Americans have parity in our society, no group will have full equality. Although I do give voice to the views of younger people on diversity and inclusion, many of the narratives in this book reflect my own background and the sense that the struggle of African Americans remains sadly unfinished.

If anything, recent developments have only intensified my sense of the road African Americans still have to travel. In December 2017, the *Boston Globe* published a seven-part series titled "Boston. Racism. Image. Reality." The series "examined whether Boston still deserves its longstanding reputation as an inhospitable place for blacks."[3] Its conclusion: "In the corridors of power, blacks have failed to gain commensurate economic and political clout in a city where they make up nearly one-quarter of the population."[4] Elsewhere in America, blacks have achieved significant power, both economically and politically. In Boston, however, "inequities of wealth and power persist, and racist attitudes remain powerful, even if in more subtle forms."[5] As the *Globe* noted, a mere 1 percent "of board members at publicly traded firms" in Massachusetts were African American and "only two of the roughly 200 companies."[6] Law firms, unions—almost everywhere you look in the Massachusetts economy, blacks are grossly underrepresented in the leadership ranks.

In Boston and elsewhere, we must still fight for African Americans to experience the same economic and political privileges that members of other demographic groups do. On a brighter note, however, the tide is starting to turn. A small group of leading-edge businesses are starting to appreciate the manifold benefits afforded by the full spectrum of diversity. They're recruiting and promoting more people from underrepresented groups and taking many more steps to inject inclusivity into their organizations because they understand the main argument of this book: in the years ahead, companies won't survive if they cannot attract and retain diverse talent. And foremost among the talented staffers they'll need to attract and retain are African Americans. If black people don't find an organization hospitable, members of many other groups likely won't either.

One firm that understands the business value of diversity better than most is the insurance company Liberty Mutual, where Dawn Frazier-Bohnert serves as senior vice president and chief diversity and inclusion officer.[7] In 2013, she began to create the company's first enterprise-wide diversity and inclusion strategy. The following year, in anticipation of the national program's launch, she embarked on what she termed an "impact tour," a two-year educational and awareness campaign in which she traveled throughout the country to connect with the company's forty thousand employees. Dawn promoted the business case for diversity, demonstrating how a global organization, operating in a changing demographic landscape, absolutely needs to embrace diversity to attract new customers and talented employees and to strengthen its bottom line.

Dawn was especially concerned with developing a common understanding of diversity across the company. One of the first things she encountered on the tour was a bewildering number of definitions of diversity, many of which struck her as narrow and limiting. "There was not a lot of individual or even collective ownership around why both diversity and inclusion were necessary. Nor what it meant and why it was important for Liberty Mutual as an organization," Dawn recalled. Generally, people thought diversity meant race and gender, but as Dawn explained, race meant *every race*, not just black and brown people but white as well. Gender included males and females as well as other forms of identification.

During her campaign, Dawn helped Liberty Mutual employees see that diversity referred to all the differences and similarities that exist among individuals and groups, including age, race, ethnicity, gender, disability, sexual orientation, religion, and more. Some people countered Dawn, making statements such as, "I don't care what someone's gender is, nor their race, color, age, or physical ability. I don't care if they are purple or polka-dotted. That's not something I see." As well-intended as such statements might have been, Dawn explained, they didn't represent the most productive way of approaching diversity or cultivating inclusion. "Take me as an example," Dawn would tell her audience. When you look at Dawn, you can't help but see an African American woman. There are also elements of diversity that

you don't see, like Dawn's international sensibility (as a "military kid," she grew up traveling the world, learning to thrive in different environments). "I want you to recognize all of these things that make me Dawn," she'd say. Her message was: "Diversity is about all of us, and inclusion requires all of us." And it requires seeing and valuing all aspects of each individual.

Dawn gave Liberty employees the permission to recognize and celebrate diversity. And that message energized her company. "There was not an office where I felt like people weren't excited," she told me. "Wow," someone declared during her tour, "we've been waiting for this message. You're talking about me."

Liberty has also evolved as an organization since the national program's launch. In employee opinion surveys, respondents express a renewed sense of empowerment and gratitude for how their particular uniqueness is not only accepted but celebrated. Among its many awards and accolades, the company received a perfect 100 rating on the Human Rights Campaign's 2018 corporate equality index—a dramatic increase from its 0 score the year Dawn joined the company.[8] As she concedes, there is room for improvement, and Liberty is looking to address gaps in the representation of certain ethnicities, genders, and geographic backgrounds in its workforce. But with a changed company culture, it is well positioned for continued success.

Like Dawn, I believe in the energizing and transformative power of difference, both in our businesses and in the world more generally. That's one of the reasons why wherever possible I have not used the term "minority" in this book. The term "minority," after all, is increasingly obsolete as we approach 2042, the year the census bureau forecasts that Caucasians will lose their demographic majority in the United States. In an increasingly global marketplace, I chose to focus on the fact that people of color *are* the majority, and a dynamic one at that. Difference *is* energizing. It spurs innovation and creativity. It makes workplaces more enjoyable and interesting.

As inspiring as Liberty Mutual's story is, it remains an outlier in America today. African Americans, Latinos, and other underrepresented groups still face daunting economic obstacles, and it's the rare organization that embraces difference as fully as WCVB and Liberty

Mutual did. As we'll see, it's rare to find diverse corporate boards, or people of diverse backgrounds occupying executive leadership positions inside companies. If you walk the lobbies of large American corporations, you won't see many portraits of leaders of color or women. In some companies, you might see none at all.

Talented leaders of difference do exist, of course, but the vast majority—blacks, Latinos, Asians, women, gays and lesbians, Muslims, the disabled, and others—hit a glass ceiling long before they reach the C-suite. White men continue to dominate the executive ranks of our country's leading companies. As of 2016, Caucasians occupied more than 85 percent of Fortune 500 board seats while African Americans/blacks held only 7.9 percent, Hispanic/Latinos 3.5 percent, and Asian/Pacific Islanders 3.1 percent.[9] Looking beyond corporate America, blacks occupy only 8 percent of nonprofit board positions, and only 7.9 percent of college or university presidents are black.[10] Notwithstanding these numbers, many in our country suffer from diversity fatigue. As a 2016 *Time* magazine feature on the diversity backlash sweeping the nation commented, "The idea of diversity seems to have worn out its welcome. It is now like a house guest who has stayed too long."[11]

Why have we made so little progress? It's simple: companies talk about diversity and inclusion, and they invest in diversity initiatives and sensitivity training, yet many haven't fully internalized diversity's *value*, the way my friends Scott, Keenen, and Dawn have. Companies still largely perceive diversity as an ethical imperative or a legal requirement, or as something businesses are obliged to do because customers are clamoring for it. Organizations fail to perceive diversity for what it truly is: a fundamental and strategic business asset, something companies *must* do to fulfill their fiduciary responsibilities to shareholders and to maintain the vibrancy and dynamism of their organizations. As a result, many companies don't pursue diversity deeply and don't embed diversity throughout their operations—in recruiting, board deliberations, marketing strategy, innovation, the supply chain, and so on. Companies close themselves off without even knowing it, forgoing much of the advantage that might otherwise become available to them.

Diversity is in fact a business imperative, and companies must make rapid progress—not in ten years, but now. Long before 2042,

demographic shifts will put unprecedented pressure on the operating models of most businesses. Organizations like WCVB that proactively embrace diversity in all areas of their operations will see their fortunes rise, while those that ignore this shift and maintain business as usual will find it more difficult, even impossible, to compete. They'll fail to recruit the best talent, they'll miss opportunities in global markets, they'll lose grassroots support, and they'll fail to innovate when it comes to their products and services. Diversity is rapidly taking on a whole new importance, transforming from a "nice to have" option to a make-or-break requirement.

A look at the numbers reveals that diversity is already quite valuable. A study by the management consulting firm McKinsey & Company found that companies with the most diverse boards averaged returns on equity (ROE) *more than 50 percent higher* than those with the least diverse boards—a result that held true across countries.[12] Similarly, a *Forbes* study linked corporate performance and diversity: "Among companies with more than $10 billion in annual revenues, 56% [of survey respondents] strongly agreed that diversity helps drive innovation."[13] And another large research study reported in the *Harvard Business Review* found that respondents at more diverse companies were "45% likelier to report that their firm's market share grew over the previous year and 70% likelier to report that the firm captured a new market."[14]

It's one thing to be able to recite numbers like these, but it's another to keenly understand how diversity improves businesses internally and externally. That's where this book comes in. In the following chapters I'll explore how personal differences of all kinds comprise vital assets for companies in our era of demographic change, detailing several key ways companies can integrate difference into the core of what they do—and reap the rewards. Firms, I suggest, can hire in new ways, encourage employees to embrace differences, frame marketing strategies with an eye toward difference, take ethical stands related to diversity, and galvanize consumers and other constituencies outside the company around diversity issues. Only by adopting diversity in these ways—as a *central part of their business and operating strategies*— can firms truly prepare for today's marketplace realities. They must

internalize and actualize the business value of difference as never before. Otherwise, they will fall behind.

In my role as president and CEO of The Partnership, Inc., a professional services diversity leadership development firm with national reach, I've been fortunate to encounter a number of corporations that understand the business imperative for diversity. Consulting directly with large organizations on diversity and inclusion issues, I've seen firms that once struggled to incorporate individuals of difference reorient themselves so that inclusion now strongly informs their corporate strategy. This book will highlight these companies and more, offering in-depth, insider case studies from organizations such as Liberty Mutual, the NFL, Eastern Bank, American Express, Highmark Health, and John Hancock The case studies in turn present specific best practices that the organization in question has embraced to make inclusion a core part of its mission and operations.

Beyond case studies, I will relate a number of personal stories, including some from my own career. Prior to joining The Partnership, Inc., I rose through the ranks in the consumer products, communications, and financial services industries. I experienced unconscious bias firsthand—seemingly innocuous comments, gestures, and microaggressions that confirmed that "people like me" were relegated to the periphery of the organization. On some occasions, executives would ignore my suggestions but applaud the exact same recommendations when they came from a white male colleague. Or they would assume that, as a black woman, I should focus my career solely on diversity programs rather than on core parts of the business, such as marketing or operations. Such treatment would have severely limited my career had I not also had the support of enlightened CEOs.

I'm not the only one with stories like these. The Partnership has helped develop more than four thousand executives and professionals of color, and each of these ambitious, high-potential individuals has come up against the limits of today's corporate cultures. This book weaves their stories into its arguments, reminding us that diverse executives such as American Express's Ken Chenault, Xerox's Ursula Burns, PepsiCo's Indra Nooyi, and Merck & Co.'s Kenneth Frazier can rise to lead some of America's greatest companies. Going inside

firms, I reveal what life is really like for people of color, women, and other professionals of difference, despite the best intentions of those presently occupying leadership positions. I also convey what corporate life becomes in those inspiring instances when companies do get diversity right, embracing it as a central part of their business. As we'll see, difference can function as a firm's greatest asset when enlightened leaders truly believe in it and reorient their businesses around it.

Lately, the specter of demographic change has sparked an ugly blowback. Around the world we've seen resurgent xenophobia, racism, sexism, anti-Semitism, homophobia, and discrimination of every kind. In our own country, some people want to build walls instead of tearing them down. They want to revel in their own identity and stem the tides of multiculturalism. As Moises Velasquez-Manoff wrote in the *New York Times*, research suggests that "merely reminding whites" of the reality of 2042 "increased their anti-minority bias and their preference for being around other whites."[15] As a white business leader, you might feel disinclined to infuse diversity into every part of your strategy and operations. You might question your company's existing diversity initiatives. Reading my words may initially make you uncomfortable and resistant to advancing diversity.

If that's the case, I implore you to read on, for your own benefit as well as your company's. Although populist politics may be ascendant for the time being, the underlying demographic trends remain clear and unstoppable. People of color in our country are becoming, collectively, the majority. We are entering a new age of diversity. One response—the comfortable one—is for companies and leaders to resist change and protect the status quo. Over time, this response will prove fatal. Far better to adopt for your company a vision similar to the one Barack Obama famously articulated for our country in 2004: "There's not a black America and white America and Latino America and Asian America; there's the United States of America."[16]

I've seen this vision translated into reality, and I'll never forget it. In 2010, my husband, Bernie, and I first stepped inside the soaring, modern offices of the US Mission to the United Nations, housed in a building named for the deceased African American Secretary of Commerce Ron Brown. President Obama had appointed me to serve as our

country's representative to the 65th General Assembly, and I was there for my swearing in. As I entered the lobby, I immediately came upon an expansive, glistening white wall that featured portraits of President Obama, Vice President Joe Biden, Secretary of State Hillary Clinton, and UN Ambassador Susan Rice, a remarkable African American woman. I stopped, stared, and cried tears of joy. As an African American woman, I was so moved by the inspiring impression these images evoked—the sense that true American leadership is open to individuals from myriad ethnicities, cultures, genders, and ages.

To thrive in the years ahead, we must make our business organizations similarly diverse. We must not content ourselves with just talking about difference or creating an isolated initiative around it. Above all, we cannot give in to fear and turn our companies backward. Instead, we must challenge ourselves to broaden our organizations like never before and help our workforce understand the business case for embracing differences. We must create an environment that welcomes talented leaders of difference and helps them shatter the glass ceiling. We must build difference into a winning strategy. We cannot do this ten years from now. We must get ahead of the trends. If our businesses are to be competitive in the future, the time to prepare is now.

FROM "NICE TO HAVE" TO "DO OR DIE"

ON JANUARY 27, 2017, only a week after his inauguration, President Donald Trump issued a presidential order restricting the influx of refugees and immigrants from seven Muslim-majority countries.[1] The political outcry was swift, sending ripples through the economy. New York City cab drivers staged a strike, and immigrant-owned bodegas, eateries, and other businesses throughout the country shuttered their doors in solidarity with immigrants.[2] The world demonstrated its distaste for the new policy with its pocketbooks and passports. Airline ticket sales to the US declined almost 7 percent in the week following the new order, and hotel and tourism companies slashed their prices, preparing for a lean year to come.[3]

The corporate world reacted as well.[4] The technology industry, which maintains a workforce heavy with immigrants, came out in strong opposition, with Expedia, Amazon, and Microsoft actively supporting the ban's reversal. Large banks expressed caution and neutrality, with Wells Fargo suggesting it was "reviewing" the immigration proposal and Morgan Stanley declaring it was "closely monitoring developments." Giant media and telecom companies, along with heavy metals and oil conglomerates, were largely silent, refraining from discussing specifics; many instead circulated statements to employees expressing respect and solidarity. As the then chairman of the Motion

Picture Association of America, Chris Dodd, reassured his associates, "We firmly believe our country can both protect its national security and be a welcoming place for those who respect our values."

Some corporate reactions, however, stood out from the rest. In the direct aftermath of the order, then Uber CEO Travis Kalanick adopted a conciliatory tone, emphasizing that the company needed to focus on its core mission and work with any global partners who could help: "We'll partner with anyone in the world as long they're about making transportation in cities better, creating job opportunities, making it easier to get around, getting pollution out of the air and traffic off the streets," Kalanick stated to his workforce.[5] As the New York taxi system waged its strike in protest of the new immigration policies, Uber filled the void, its vehicles crossing an invisible picket-line perimeter at the airport to ferry travelers to their final destinations. To customers, as the *Washington Post*'s Faiz Siddiqui put it, it looked as if "the company was trying to profit off of striking workers."[6] The weekend following the executive order, people registered their indignation, deleting Uber mobile phone applications in droves. The hashtag #DeleteUber began trending on Twitter and Facebook, with Lena Dunham, Susan Sarandon, and other celebrities furthering the cause. Inundated with two hundred thousand requests to delete its app, Uber was forced to create a new system to process the volume, further angering customers who thought their requests weren't being honored.[7]

According to TXN Solutions, which tracks consumer spending through credit- and debit-card transactions, Uber had an 83 percent market share in ride-hailing services early in 2017.[8] But following the #DeleteUber social-media campaign, it shed brand image, market share, and customers to its closest rival, Lyft.[9] Spending on Uber declined in its major metro markets—New York; Washington, DC; Los Angeles; and San Francisco—with overall sales the month following the scandal slumping 2 percent (and Lyft's sales increasing 30 percent in the same period).[10] To help those harmed by the travel ban, John Zimmer and Logan Green, Lyft's cofounders, donated $1 million to the American Civil Liberties Union.[11] Capitalizing on its new position as a "friendlier" ride-hailing service, Lyft attracted $500 million in investments, with Reuters increasing its overall valuation by $2 billion

compared to the year prior.[12] The company continued to experience staggering growth, reporting that halfway through 2017 it had already delivered more rides than during all of 2016.[13] Lyft has since redoubled its commitment to diversity and the power of difference, appointing African American Valerie Jarrett, a senior adviser in the Obama administration, to its board of directors.[14]

When the #DeleteUber campaign began trending on social media, Travis Kalanick was immediately apologetic, assuring customers that Uber opposed Trump's executive order and pledging $3 million to help any drivers negatively impacted by the ban.[15] Kalanick insisted, furthermore, that he hadn't intended for Uber drivers to cross any picket lines. After all, the company had disabled its "surge price" feature, which typically activates during high-volume times, so as not to profit from the strike.[16] But these belated attempts to mitigate the scandal smacked of insincerity and did little to help Uber's image. In the racially and ethnically diverse America of 2017, corporate commitment to inclusion is important and must be proactive as well as principled and sincere.

It's worth noting that the anti-Uber public backlash didn't permanently damage the company, which as this book goes to press remains one of the most profitable private tech firms in our nation's history.[17] After several high-profile scandals involving sexual harassment, verbal assault, underpaying of employees, and patent infringement, stakeholders and investors forced Kalanick's resignation in June 2017. Media magnate and wellness expert Ariana Huffington, the only woman on the company's board, helped fill the leadership void and create a more hospitable culture, as did former US attorney general Eric Holder, whom the company hired to help investigate sexual harassment allegations and make recommendations for improvement.[18] Investors and corporate partners, however, remained leery of Uber's long-term success. "The amount of dislocation at Uber is almost unprecedented," said Mark Mahaney, an analyst with RBC Capital Markets. "I would assume that Uber has materially pushed back whatever IPO [initial public offering] date they had."[19] As one automotive executive, speaking under condition of anonymity, said, "We've had internal discussions, and we don't think Uber is a major player after 2020."[20]

We'll let the tech experts debate whether Uber, Lyft, or another ridesharing outfit, such as Via, will ultimately dominate as the industry prepares for its next major pivot toward autonomous vehicles. More importantly for our purposes, the Uber controversy serves as a harbinger of shifts related to diversity and inclusion. As 2042 approaches, customer discontent over a company's diversity and inclusion missteps won't just manifest as a short-term marketing or public-relations blip. Issues of inclusion and difference will loom much larger than they do today, affecting companies in even more dramatic ways, both day to day and in moments of crisis. Already, a firm's posture toward diversity yields a range of important business impacts, determining a company's power, effectiveness, capacity to innovate, profitability, and future viability. Sadly, most companies haven't come to grips with this reality, an oversight that in the years to come will dramatically impede their capacity to compete.

THE DAWNING OF THE AGE OF DIVERSITY

Many companies today claim to understand that diversity and inclusion are important. Visit most corporate websites, and you'll see descriptions of diversity initiatives and outreach projects, along with images of people of color and women proudly featured on the covers of annual reports and in brochures and other marketing materials. And it's not all for show.

Consider the expanded reach we've achieved at The Partnership, where I serve as president and CEO. In 1987, when the organization began, Boston's diversity pipeline was modest and shallow, and the organization mentored a cohort of thirty-one midcareer professionals in the local area. Following the city's struggle with desegregation and federally mandated busing (1974 to 1988), Boston developed a national reputation for being inhospitable to African Americans, a reputation that still haunts us today.[21] Still, the pipeline of talent has improved markedly. This is in large part due to the visionary leadership of the former president and CEO of The Partnership, Bennie Wiley, who brought the organization to prominence. This nationally recognized African American woman led the organization from 1991

to 2005. Today, more than four thousand professionals of color have participated in The Partnership's leadership-development programs. We've also worked with more than three hundred businesses, helping them to attract, develop, and retain multicultural professionals at all stages of their careers, including those occupying the C-suite. Beverly Edgehill, an African American woman, began her career as part of that initial 1987 cohort. In 2005, she assumed the position of president and CEO at The Partnership, bringing the organization to a new stage of growth by designing and implementing the Next Generation Executive Development Program. A major speaker at our Thirtieth Anniversary Leadership Summit, held on Martha's Vineyard in 2017, she announced to the four hundred attendees that "The Partnership in Boston is now an institution on par with the Museum of Fine Arts, Massachusetts General Hospital, and the Red Sox."[22]

Beyond New England, corporate executives increasingly acknowledge diversity's contribution to their companies' success. Marillyn A. Hewson, chairman, president, and CEO of Lockheed Martin, credited her company's major energy innovations to diversity: "These developments are possible because different people with unique perspectives looked at the challenges in new ways. The biggest breakthroughs come from individuals and teams that actively seek out different points of view. In short, innovation is powered by diversity and fostered by inclusion."[23] Jill Macri, the global director of recruitment at Airbnb, actively seeks to secure business contracts with female-owned and diverse supply companies and hosts national outreach events to increase the diversity of its workforce. "Our hosts are 55 percent women," Macri acknowledged, "so there's an obvious connection between our mission and our diversity."[24] Some companies are paying top dollar to increase the number of women and other underrepresented individuals they hire. In 2015, Brian Krzanich, CEO of Intel, pledged $300 million to diversify that company's workforce; Apple allocated $50 million; and Google elevated its diversity line item to $150 million.[25]

Still, diversity in corporate America remains shadowed in secrecy. While the Bureau of Labor Statistics collects diversity data from all US organizations and publishes global diversity and gender trends in the American workforce, data about individual companies is not

publicly available.[26] That means that while we know the rough composition of most of our country's corporate boards and leadership teams, only 3.2 percent of Fortune 500 companies voluntarily reveal their full diversity data.[27]

Most companies that voluntarily disclose their diversity markers are clustered in the technology industry. Bowing to public and shareholder pressure, Google published its diversity numbers in May 2014, with other tech giants such as Yahoo, LinkedIn, Facebook, Twitter, and eBay following suit.[28] But years of these public disclosures, which the *New York Times* referred to as "Tech's Small Diversity Parade," have done little to move the needle.[29] "Does releasing the numbers alone catalyze change?" queried the *Atlantic* in a feature. After scrutinizing the data, it concluded: "The answer is no."[30]

Take Twitter, the social media platform with a section some refer to as "Black Twitter" because of its popularity among African Americans. After the company publicly reaffirmed a commitment to diversity and inclusion, it published its 2014 diversity statistics, which revealed that it employed a mere *forty-nine* African Americans, representing 1.7 percent of its US workforce of 2,910.[31] "There's a big gap between their talk and their implementation," Jesse Jackson lamented.[32]

Based on what we do know about US corporate diversity, we can safely say that most firms are anything but diverse. African Americans account for 13.6 percent of the population but only 2 percent of the entire US workforce; Latinos constitute 17 percent of the population but occupy only 5 percent of America's jobs.[33] Among all American companies with at least one hundred employees, the number of black men occupying management roles increased by only 0.3 percent between 1985 and 2014, while women's participation in such roles has stalled since 2000 (stagnating at 29 percent).[34] Like many sectors, the financial services industry remains a white male bastion. The number of women in the finance industry actually declined during the first decade and a half of the twenty-first century. When it comes to executive positions in finance, whites occupy 80 percent, men approximately 66 percent, and African Americans less than 3 percent.[35]

The entertainment industry fares little better. The roughly six thousand members of the Academy of Motion Picture Arts and Sciences are

predominantly older white men, with nonwhites accounting for only 6 percent.[36] And then there's the notoriously insular Silicon Valley. Despite the bold pronouncements, grand gestures, and diversity-oriented recruitment efforts, blacks and Latinos occupy 5 percent of executive positions in technology companies, and they experience much higher turnover than their white male counterparts.[37] Every year, almost 20 percent of all computer science graduates are black and Latino. Only 5 percent, however, occupy "technical roles"—positions requiring specialized coding and data analytics knowledge—within the technology industry.[38]

Diversity has progressed so little in part because firms tend to limit their efforts to formal diversity programs, and as a 2016 *Harvard Business Review* cover article revealed, these simply haven't worked. In fact, after considering thirty years of data, interviews, and the experience of more than eight hundred companies, the authors of the article demonstrated that diversity programming often *triggers* bias instead of ameliorating it.[39] Another 2016 *Harvard Business Review* article concluded the same with a provocatively titled headline: "Diversity Policies Rarely Make Companies Fairer, and They Feel Threatening to White Men."[40] This piece concluded that diversity programs and policies have either failed to promote diversity or, in some instances, reversed the gains we've seen over the past few decades.

Consider the latest, trendiest diversity-training programs that even T-shirt-clad Silicon Valley engineers volunteer to take. I refer here to unconscious-bias trainings—Diversity Training 2.0.[41] Tech giants such as Google and Facebook have embraced these programs, hoping to create more sensitive managers and inclusive company cultures. Rooted in rigorous social-science research, the programs acknowledge that unconscious biases are part of the human condition. Indeed, we are inundated with millions of stimuli every second, and absent unconscious strategies to quickly sort and categorize this information, we could barely survive. Unfortunately, these evolutionary adaptations pose problems in the workplace, where they might be used to unfairly stereotype people and influence hiring decisions. To sensitize people to these cognitive dynamics, participants in unconscious-bias

workshops undergo "implicit-association" tests. A facilitator asks them to associate words (son, English), career paths (chemistry), and concepts (liberal arts, family) with certain genders and races. Crucially, seminar attendees can't reflect on or ponder these associations but instead must register their immediate, knee-jerk reactions. Because of the way we've been socialized, these tests almost always reveal an unconscious bias of some sort. The association of "family" with female words and "career paths" with male ones, for example, is common.[42]

Seminar participants aren't chided for exhibiting such bias. In fact, they're reassured that if they exercise vigilance, they can overcome unconscious associations in the workplace and create a more equitable corporate culture. But as Liza Mundy, senior fellow at the think tank New America and author of *Code Girls* notes, "Though the approach is much more congenial than the 'sensitivity training' popular in the 1980s and '90s—in which white men were usually cast as villains—it suffers from the same problem: People resent being made to sit in a chair and listen to somebody telling them how to act."[43] Furthermore, rehearsing these biases serves to normalize and reinforce them. As a 2015 study by Michelle M. Duguid of the Olin Business School at Washington University in St. Louis and Melissa C. Thomas-Hunt of the University of Virginia's Darden School of Business demonstrated, "telling participants that many people hold stereotypes made them more likely to exhibit bias. . . . When you say over and over that women come up against a glass ceiling, people begin to accept that, yes, women come up against a glass ceiling—and that's just the way it is."[44] The same normalization occurs when you associate a graduate degree with white people and blue-collar jobs with people of color.

Aside from problems with design and execution, traditional diversity programs tend to become marginalized within companies, commonly siloed in the human resources and corporate social responsibility departments. As C-suite executive and innovation expert Glenn Llopis has remarked, such programs are "viewed as cost centers (expenses) rather than profit centers (investments) to drive influence in the workplace and growth in the marketplace."[45] Sociologists Frank Dobbin of Harvard University and Alexandra Kalev of Tel Aviv University further

note that diversity programs remain anchored in the past: "companies are basically doubling down on the same approaches they've used since the 1960s—which often make things worse, not better."[46]

Also, diversity programs sometimes hurt the cause by providing companies with fodder for warding off legal challenges that might have forced sorely needed change. When employees bring discrimination claims against companies, firms often respond by pointing to the existence of diversity programs or policies as evidence of nondiscrimination. In a 2011 Supreme Court case, Walmart did exactly that to defend against allegations that it had discriminated against women.[47] Walmart won its case, and other companies have since mobilized this "diversity defense," making diversity programs actively detrimental to the cause of diversity and nondiscrimination efforts.[48]

My friend and fellow Partnership board member Javier Barrientos, who is Latino, is an inclusion and diversity management consultant who now serves diversity executive at Charter Communications on the West Coast. He understands that most diversity programs do more harm than good.[49] That's why when advising companies how to make workplaces more inclusive, he begins by identifying and working on overcoming structural bias. Unconscious bias initiatives focus on changing the inner workings of the individual worker's mind, whereas structural bias assessments address the policies, practices, codified behaviors, and other physical manifestations of unfairness at a workplace itself—such as portraits only of white men. During his time as a diversity consultant, Javier undertook comprehensive environmental assessments of organizations, which included everything from evaluating human resources policies to assessing condiment vendors and artwork. These exercises proved illuminating, revealing, for example, that a company's 401(k) plan excluded LGBTQ partners from survivor benefits.

Javier once discovered that every table in a company's large cafeteria had a ketchup bottle with a label that depicted a man in a business suit eating pasta and a woman in an apron. "Not now!" the pasta eater snips at the lady, extending the palm of his hand into her face. This depiction understandably offended female employees and represented a physical manifestation of structural bias. "People were bothered by it, but they hadn't vocalized it," Javier recalled. Not until Javier's as-

sessment was completed, that is; after which, everyone agreed that the company needed to contract with a different ketchup vendor. In another instance, a woman approached Javier and said, "Why do we have a wall with the history of the company that lacks a single woman?" The individual who had designed the picturescape certainly hadn't intended to overlook women, but this decision nonetheless marginalized women at the company, and made it appear that they hadn't contributed to the company's history.

As Javier told me, it's only once these structural biases have been remedied that companies can begin to address unconscious bias. But as we noted above, when it comes to human thoughts and behaviors, it's very hard to reprogram out unconscious biases because many of our tendencies are based on millennia of evolution. Human beings, like their counterparts in the animal kingdom, developed mechanisms to quickly distinguish whether someone was inside or outside of their group.[50] These immediate associations could prove lifesaving, allowing animals to avoid harm from hostile outsiders and take safe haven in their insider group.[51] "It's a feature of evolution," says Harvard psychology professor Mahzarin Banaji, referring to such hardwiring.[52] But what helped us in prehistory has led to detrimental outcomes in the modern business world. In fact, unconscious bias assessments reveal that we often have deep-seated racial and gender associations that our conscious selves would find unfortunate and even offensive. Still, Javier believes that video, artificial intelligence, robotics, predictive algorithms, and gamification technologies hold great promise for helping us overcome our evolutionary obstacles.[53]

Some technology companies are already helping organizations improve their bottom lines by using technology instead of seminars to root out unconscious bias. Take Talent Sonar, a firm that helps organizations focus on specific qualifications and competencies during the hiring process. Among the services it offers is résumé disaggregation, under which hiring managers can choose only from a menu of candidate competencies, rather than allowing a person's name, address, or any other identifying information to trigger an unconscious mental association. Another company, the artificial intelligence startup Pymetrics, offers neurologically based competency tests and bias-free

simulations, allowing firms to measure a candidate's capacity to perform against a benchmark or predetermined skills profile (once again, not permitting unconscious associations on the part of hiring managers to color their assessments). Javier told me that many organizations that administered these assessments found that some candidates with no formal college education scored higher than others with PhDs or other advanced degrees. Such results are startling and could disrupt standard recruitment models, allowing companies to cast their nets beyond educational institutions and consider nontraditional talent sources such as freelancers, gig workers, and other skilled individuals.[54]

Eliminating both structural and unconscious bias is firmly in a company's best financial interest. As the *Wall Street Journal* put it, "Candidates today often seek out the employer rather than the reverse, so it's important for companies to actively manage their employment brand and reconsider how they communicate their value proposition to the workforce."[55] If your workplace denies survivor benefits to certain employee spouses or features misogynistic ketchup bottles in the cafeteria, you can expect word to get out and talented recruits to look elsewhere.

Bear in mind, employee turnover is extremely expensive. Most new hires at US companies are unsuccessful in the first year and a half. In fact, 20 to 46 percent of company hires qualify as a mismatch (with employees possessing the right skills but not the right company fit), and the Center for Law and Social Policy and the Center for Economic and Policy Research document that it costs more than $26,000 to replace a worker earning $100,000. That means that large corporations hiring a thousand new workers could pay nearly $5.5 million in bad hiring costs.[56] Perhaps this is why forward-thinking global corporations are changing course, using Pymetric-style solutions to transform their hiring practices. "While the process is still in its early stages," notes the *Wall Street Journal*, "recruiters are reporting significant benefits" following the implementation of these technologies in the hiring realm.[57] To remain financially competitive and credible in the changing demographic landscape, companies will need to take decisive action to overcome unconscious and structural biases in the hiring process and in the workplace.

SCANDALOUSLY OUT OF TOUCH

For further evidence that mainstream diversity programs are failing us and that companies like Talent Sonar and Pymetrics are sorely needed, we can also look to the many diversity-related public relations scandals that have embroiled entire industries. Comedian Jimmy Kimmel, host of the 2016 Emmy Awards, began his opening monologue trying to make light of Hollywood's persistent diversity problem: "This year's nominees are the most diverse ever. And here in Hollywood, the only thing we value more than diversity is congratulating ourselves on how much we value diversity."[58] But most viewers didn't think the problem was very funny. When the 2014 blockbuster *Selma*, dramatizing the forward march toward civil rights in this country, did not receive any nominations for its black director and actors, the #OscarsSoWhite hashtag wound its way through social media, spreading awareness about the lack of diversity among our country's entertainment elite.[59] In 2016, after another disappointing showing for people of color and women in the Oscar nominations, the hashtag resurged and became even more powerful, with high-profile celebrities such as Jada Pinkett-Smith and Spike Lee boycotting the ceremony in protest.[60]

The academy responded with action that was drastic and, unfortunately, ill-conceived. In an emergency meeting, the academy's board decided to alter the voting membership structure, replacing older, whiter members with younger, more diverse cohorts.[61] This left many older members and concerned outsiders crying "ageism." The hashtag #OscarsSoAgeist made the rounds, as people reflected on how the shedding of older members corresponded poorly with the broader graying of America's population.[62] The decision also represented a sad loss of true diversity in the academy. People such as seventy-eight-year-old Dolores Hart, who had starred opposite Elvis Presley in several movies during the 1960s before turning to a religious life, was the only nun who sat on the committee. She spoke for many when, after receiving a note saying she'd been elected a nonvoting "emerita" member, she said, "I'm not going to go down screaming. But I think if they cut off too much of the elder community, they're going to clip the *wisdom* dimension of the Academy."[63] Replace "elder community" with "people of difference" and her critique is just as powerful. In trying to appease

public opinion and maintain its relevance, the academy exhibited a shortsighted view of true diversity and inclusiveness. Rather than jettisoning older existing members, why not add new ones with diversity and inclusion in mind?

The technology industry fares much worse in diversity than Hollywood, and it is becoming increasingly disconnected from the young and diverse Americans who buy its products. In 2016, when Facebook's global director of diversity, Maxine Williams, publicized the company's annual diversity statistics, the reaction was poor.[64] Unsurprisingly, people of color and women had made little headway in the tech giant. And though we were heartened when retiring American Express chairman and CEO Ken Chenault was named to Facebook's board of directors in 2018, becoming the company's first African American board member, the question remains: why would the world's premier social media platform, designed to build community and forge human connection, be so noninclusive in its hiring?[65]

When Williams suggested that part of the problem was that not enough talent lay in the tech pipeline, a firestorm erupted. The *Wall Street Journal* published an article titled "Facebook Blames Lack of Available Talent for Diversity Problems," and people of color and women executives in the industry publicly chastised the company for "passing the buck" to America's faulty education system.[66] African American engineering student Kaya Thomas published an essay called "Invisible Talent," which coursed its way through social media and caught the attention of the tech world. In her final year studying computer science at Dartmouth, Thomas was offended and got teary-eyed when she read Facebook's diversity release, feeling discounted by the industry before she even joined the workforce. "There are thousands of other Black and Latinx who graduate every year with computer science Bachelor degrees," she notes. "Most of us don't get hired into the tech industry."[67] Kaya Thomas and the *New Yorker*'s Anna Wiener know that the real problem doesn't reside in a faulty educational system. The problem is bias and inadequate recruiting strategies. Silicon Valley's hiring practices remain an old-boys' network of word-of-mouth referrals and dubious "cultural fit" tests (such as going on a cruise with current employees and seeing how everyone

meshes). Such methods, pervasive in the tech world, favor candidates who resemble the educational, racial, and sexual profile of those already present.

Corporate diversity initiatives are often so out of touch that even when well-meaning and progressive companies attempt to promote diversity, their efforts strike many Americans as inappropriate. Consider Starbucks' 2015 "Race Together" initiative, in which baristas were encouraged to engage customers in discussions about race and inclusion over their morning mocha lattes. The backlash was swift, with people taking to Twitter to express their distaste. Some tweets pointed out the lack of sincerity, with the #RaceTogether promotional materials featuring only white baristas, and others noting the disparity between the initiative itself and the corporation's executive complexion (perhaps, as one observer tweeted, "Starbucks: Nothing Says #RaceTogether Like Only Hiring 3 People of Color Out of 19 Executives").[68] After Corey duBrowa (a white man), then Starbucks' senior vice president for communications, was inundated with tweets asking him to explain the reasoning behind the initiative, he disabled his Twitter account, seemingly perplexed by the reaction to the "respectful conversation" he and CEO Howard Schultz had tried to initiate.[69]

The global soft-drink giant Pepsi also ran into trouble. In March 2017, the company attempted to reach the politically conscious millennial demographic with an advertisement depicting a fictional Black Lives Matter social protest.[70] The ad features streets filled with young people chanting, dancing, singing, and carrying signs. The two protagonists are the Pepsi product itself, which protestors enjoy throughout the advertisement, and the white model and reality-television celebrity Kendall Jenner. As people of difference peacefully clamor for change in the background, Jenner leaves a glamorous photo shoot to join the protestors, shedding her lipstick and cocktail dress for appropriately rugged and hip street attire. The advertisement climaxes when Jenner hands a Pepsi can to a police officer, and the crowd erupts in applause—apparently for Jenner's Pepsi "olive branch."

After a resounding collective outcry that the soft-drink corporation had appropriated the struggles facing people of color in order to sell more product, the company responded: "Pepsi was trying to

project a global message of unity, peace and understanding. Clearly, we missed the mark and apologize. We did not intend to make light of any serious issue. We are pulling the content and halting any further rollout."[71] Bernice King, the daughter of Martin Luther King Jr., took to Twitter with a picture of her father in a real protest saying, "If only Daddy would have known about the power of #Pepsi."[72]

GAUGING THE BUSINESS IMPACT

Although embarrassing, these public relations gaffs on the part of Facebook, Pepsi, Uber, and the Hollywood elite might seem relatively minor. Millions of customers still drink Pepsi every day and then hop in an Uber to go catch a movie, right? Not so fast. Even if these and other companies aren't permanently damaged, the persistent scandals reveal the presence of an underlying diversity gap that is quietly costing them. If nothing else, many organizations today are missing out on the many *business benefits* that diversity brings. As we'll explore throughout this book, diversity contributes to greater employee retention rates, the ability to engage increasingly global and diverse markets, higher employee morale, enhanced innovation, and an even better bottom line.[73] Consider, for instance, the following statistics that link financial performance with diversity:

- Racially and ethnically diverse companies are 30 percent more likely than their less diverse counterparts to earn "financial returns above their respective national industry medians."
- Companies with strong gender diversity perform better, having a 15 percent greater chance than their less diverse counterparts of garnering "financial returns above their respective national industry medians."
- Nondiverse companies, measured in terms of ethnicity, race, and sex, underperform the average company in their sector (to paraphrase McKinsey's *Why Diversity Matters* report, such companies "are lagging rather than merely not leading").
- There is a strong correlation between diversity in management and financial outcomes in the United States. Every 10 percent

increase in management's diversity yields a 0.8 percent increase in earnings prior to taxes and interest (in the United Kingdom it yields a 3.5 percent increase).

- Diversity is a "competitive differentiator," as it helps predict industry market share, with more diverse companies distinguishing themselves from their competitors based on their diversity rates.[74]

As we learned in grade school, correlation is not causation. So, what *causal forces* underlie these findings, driving better performance in more diversified companies? One is recruitment. We know that a more talented and skilled workforce yields increased profits. As new technologies transform the workplace and consumer behavior, a company's ability to locate and secure increasingly scarce talent translates into improved profitability. As McKinsey's "Diversity Matters" study suggested, "Diversity in leadership can help a company secure access to more sources of talent, gain a competitive recruitment advantage, and improve its global relevance."[75]

A 2017 Deloitte study further underscored how inclusive companies attract and retain the best talent. Of the more than 1,300 people polled, 80 percent registered inclusion as important for selecting a workplace, 39 percent expressed willingness to leave a noninclusive workplace, and 23 percent indicated they already had left a noninclusive organization for a more hospitable environment.[76] Inclusiveness was of particular concern to the polled millennials (those born from 1980 to 1995), who by 2025 will represent three-quarters of the global workforce.[77] Executives are eager to retain these individuals, because as the study notes, "millennials are the most likely generation to switch jobs, with their turnover costing the United States economy approximately $30.5 billion annually."[78] Forget the days of career-long company employees! On average, millennials switch jobs once every twenty-four months, with nearly two-thirds expressing an openness to leave their current job.[79] Perhaps this helps explain the country's dismal employee engagement numbers—as Gallup reports, a scant 32 percent of people are actively engaged at their jobs, while the majority lack engagement, and 17.2 express feeling "actively disengaged."[80]

As this Deloitte data demonstrate, inclusive environments, where people can bring their authentic selves to work and interact with a diverse team or workforce in an environment of trust and mutual respect, will go a long way to keeping workers happy, and in the process reining in company costs associated with high turnover and lack of engagement.[81] "Inclusion is an essential component for attracting and engaging today's workforce," concludes the study. "Our respondents have told us that inclusion is not a nice-to-have but often a critical factor in determining whether they will stay or leave an organization."[82]

Diversity also drives better performance by enhancing a company's marketing capability. Diversified companies can respond to the changing needs and desires of an increasingly diverse consumer base, which controls larger amounts of wealth and spending capital than ever before. Employees are also happier in more diverse employment settings, feeling enhanced support and camaraderie. A diversity of races and cultures likewise yields an increased diversity of thought, leading to productive dissent, creativity, and innovation. Would diverse advertising teams at Pepsi and Starbucks really have suggested that people discuss race over morning coffee or depict social-protest movements in a soft-drink commercial? As my millennial friend Scott Martin told me, definitely not! "I can guarantee that was not a diverse group of people coming up with that Pepsi ad," he said. "A lack of diversity was responsible for that."[83]

When we examine specific industries and economic sectors, we can spot the business impact of diversity even more clearly. In 2014, UCLA's Department of African American Studies began investigating the relationship between diversity and revenue, trying to understand a baffling contradiction they had observed. As the lead scholars framed it, "The Hollywood industry is woefully out of touch with Americans' increasing diversity, despite increasing evidence that diversity is good for business."[84] As they discovered, racially homogenous creative content served neither the film and television industry's consumers nor its own financial well-being. Despite this, Hollywood continues with the nondiverse status quo. While the nation is becoming increasingly diverse, women and people of color, from the executive ranks to entry-level

positions, continue to be underrepresented, under-rewarded, and/or under-recognized in Hollywood.

As the 2016 version of the UCLA study confirmed, Hollywood's rank and file, spanning directors, producers, broadcast show creators, theatrical film creators, and actors, continues to exhibit a marked lack of diversity.[85] And this is not what the audience wants. In 2013 and 2014, people of color bought the majority of movie tickets and patronized films with more diverse casts. Those films earned more at the box office than those with homogenous casts and had a greater return on overall investment. The study also found that viewers ages eighteen to forty-nine, inclusive of all races, preferred television shows with diverse casts and articulated this support with greater frequency on social media. Because people of difference now constitute the majority of television audiences and movie patrons, the report concludes, "Hollywood's business as usual is a model that may soon be unsustainable."[86] To see how diversity yields success, one need only look at Disney's 2018 breakthrough film *Black Panther*, based on the Marvel comics superhero. Featuring an all-star black cast in a groundbreaking celebration of black culture, *Black Panther* has grossed more than $1 billion worldwide at the time of this writing, making it one of the highest-earning films of all time. This indeed is an example of success through diversity.

The tech sector must also come up with innovative solutions to succeed in the future. With people of color set to outnumber Caucasians within decades, how will Silicon Valley's predominantly white and male companies fare? Mitch Kapor, who is white and chairs the Kapor Center for Social Impact, says that while Silicon Valley likes to think of itself as a meritocracy, it actually resembles a "mirrortocracy."[87] The very structure and logic underlying the northern California constellation of technology corporations only serves to reinforce this. Silicon Valley's founding myth is that any newcomer with a bright idea and some seed capital has the capacity to generate windfalls. But its network-driven hiring culture, with people self-selecting others of similar race, pedigree, and credentials, could impact the bottom line. How could such insular hires possibly create the next big sensation,

the next Facebook, if they are increasingly out of touch with American demographics, Kapor wonders. "I bet we'll be able to do some really interesting business case studies in ten years and see what companies did and didn't make it—and who had the most diverse teams from top to bottom," noted Eric Kelly, president and CEO of the San Jose–based data-protection company Overland Storage.[88] Owen Grover, iHeartRadio's general manager and senior vice president, echoes these concerns when he notes that "Silicon Valley is still too white, too male, and too focused on solving the problems of the young, single, and wealthy."[89] While the tech industry continues to enjoy profits, the future innovation curve is not likely bending in its favor.

The finance and banking industries know they must diversify or lose profits in the years ahead. And this isn't just because discrimination in the field leads to costly lawsuits (Morgan Stanley settled a racial discrimination case for $16 million in 2008, while Merrill Lynch paid $160 million to settle a racial bias suit in 2013).[90] Because the field is so dominated by white men, women and minorities have faced strong barriers to entry. But as business journalist Elizabeth MacBride suggests, "That lack of racial diversity among financial advisers has a growing cost for the profession and the people it serves."[91] A homogenous finance and investment sector likely will be unable to reach an increasingly diverse consumer base and will also lack the minority-fueled innovation driving popular investment products.

Exchange-traded funds (ETFs) are a case in point. Containing a diversity of bonds, commodities, mutual funds, and stocks, an ETF is an attractive investment vehicle because of its built-in financial diversification. It's also a lot cheaper and has fewer fees than stocks and mutual funds, making it a more democratic and accessible investment tool for a broad segment of the population. As it turns out, the ETF industry is demographically diverse as well, with more women and people of color serving on finance teams and in senior management positions. According to the "Godfather of ETFs," Reggie Brown, who is African American, every ETF company or unit boasts, at minimum, one woman or person of color in its leadership ranks.[92]

Since their creation in 1993, ETFs have taken the world by storm. "One of the fastest-growing investment products in history," accord-

ing to an *Atlantic* feature, ETFs have more than $2.5 trillion in assets, which means "they now control more money than hedge funds do."[93] But it wasn't always this way. In the 1990s, ETFs enjoyed less favorable trading advantages and prestige. Men shied away from the vehicles as a result, allowing women to fill the ETFs' nascent ranks. Marie Dzanis, one of the women who got in on the ground level, describes the opposite pipeline situation from a company such as Facebook: "My boss was a woman, and my boss's boss was a woman, and her boss's boss's boss was a woman!"[94] Bastions of female leadership and mentorship from the beginning, it's hard not to suspect that ETFs' demographic diversity helped to fuel their economic success. Not plagued by an incestuous, network-driven hiring culture, employees and executives were free to express themselves most creatively and freely. "There is more opportunity," notes Sue Thompson, an ETF executive, "for the smartest, the brightest, those with the most interesting visions."[95]

As ETFs become more profitable and popular among the financial services industry, some experts fear they'll be absorbed by less diverse financial services behemoths such as Wells Fargo and Merrill Lynch. That doesn't appear to be the trend, though. Financial services experts understand that diversity produces better results and many financial managers reward such diversity. In 2016, the financial services holding company State Street Global Advisors debuted "SHE," an ETF tracking only companies with women in top leadership and board positions. SHE forms part of a cluster of diversity-minded impact investment funds, joining other financial products such as Denver Investments' Workplace Equality Portfolio ETF and Barclays' Women in Leadership exchange-traded note (or ETN).[96] SHE, however, has risen in prominence since the California State Teachers' Retirement System (CalSTRS), the nation's largest teacher retirement fund, announced it had purchased $250 million of the ETF for its pension funds, with a forecast of an addition $500 million in the future.[97] CalSTRS is likely attracted to the charitable component of this fund (a first for State Street), in which some of the money generated from the small annual fees, known as expense ratios, will go to SHE Impacts, which helps empower future female leaders.[98] But charitable causes aside, CalSTRS saw SHE as the best investment for its money because it

understands how corporate diversity is a great predictor of financial performance. This isn't anything new. The investment world has always promoted financial diversity as the true path to capital gains. What ETFs demonstrate is that *talent* diversity drives investment gains and promotes more creative, innovative businesses.

If financial services must diversify, so too must the field of professional economics, or we risk another implosion of our global financial and economic system. Lisa Cook, an associate professor in the department of economics at Michigan State University, reminded me of this during a conversation we had in the fall of 2017.[99] Lisa, who is also my husband's cousin, was on the White House Council of Economic Advisers with Janet Yellen, the first woman to serve as chair of the Federal Reserve. After surveying the chief predictions made during the 2009–2012 financial crisis, the *Wall Street Journal* (in an article that was a finalist for the Pulitzer Prize for national affairs reporting) declared that "the most accurate forecasts overall came from Ms. Yellen."[100]

Yellen was also right about another consistent message: a lack of diverse thinking drove the bad decisions that helped precipitate the financial and economic crisis that began in 2008. "There's just too many people who look exactly like each other, have the same education. Without having the benefit of different thinking or diversity of thought it was difficult to pick up the nuances of the market and what was shaping up. They weren't asking the right questions at the right time," Lisa said, confirming Yellen's observations. And how could our country's lead economists make bold, creative, and novel predictions? Of the 134 people who had held the post of president of any of our country's Federal Reserve banks as of 2016, none was Latino or African American, and eight of the twelve regional banks never had a female occupant to speak of.[101] As a Brookings Institution article observed, such lack of diversity extends far beyond gender and race: "A lack of diversity of background, experience, and vantage points can lead to group-think and collective misjudgments."[102]

A specialist in the economics of innovation, Lisa has uncovered other ways in which a lack of diversity harms our country's economy. As her research found, 1 percent of all venture capital funding on average goes to African American–owned firms, while roughly 5 percent

goes to female-owned firms (as of 2010). This "pink and black" funding gap is alarming to many economists, including those staffing the National Science Foundation and the Washington Center for Equitable Growth, which funded Lisa's influential 2010 publication on the topic.[103] One reason for concern is that women live longer and have a greater need for financial security throughout their extended lives. Since marriage rates are rapidly declining and single women are beginning to outnumber their married counterparts, such wealth disparities threaten our economy's social safety net.

Lisa's research on patents found that the economic productivity of patented inventions, furthermore, was greater when they were produced by coed teams rather than by single-sex ones. And, as Lisa told me, if there were more women and African Americans participating in the fields of science, technology, engineering, and medicine (STEM), our country's GDP would be an estimated 0.8 to 4.4 percent greater. Lisa's provocative and pathbreaking research findings have been corroborated by work in the fields of sociology, psychology, and economics, demonstrating the imperative of diversity to our country (and globe's) economic stability and vitality.

DEMOGRAPHY IS DESTINY

We can now appreciate how companies lose out when they inadequately engage with diversity. We can likewise understand how much businesses strongly benefit when they diversify. And that's just as of this writing in 2018. As we inch our way toward 2042, diversity will loom even larger, determining a far greater range of business outcomes.

America used to be a white nation peppered with a black population. In 1960, whites constituted 85 percent of Americans. By 2060, their ranks will decrease by almost half, to 43 percent.[104] Asians and Hispanics now compose less than 25 percent of the American population; they are forecast to be 40 percent by 2060.[105]

In large part, these shifts are due to immigration. America absorbs more than four times as many immigrants as any other country in the world. As demographer Joel Kotkin documents, "In 2005 the United States swore in more new citizens than the next *nine* countries put

together."[106] As of 2014, seventy-nine million people of "immigrant stock" (i.e., immigrants and their offspring) inhabited this country. If immigration trends continue, first- and second-generation immigrants will account for more than two-thirds of all US population growth by the mid-twenty-first century.[107] As Paul Taylor, also a demographer, notes, "Based on current mortality-fertility-immigration trends, roughly 90% of the growth in the US labor force between now and mid-century will be from new immigrants and their children."[108]

These immigrants are skilled. "More than half of all skilled immigrants in the world," Kotkin documents, "come to this one country."[109] Businesses are, unsurprisingly, among the most vocal proponents of liberal immigration systems because they benefit so directly from the entrepreneurial strength, work ethic, and specialized knowledge of immigrant workers.[110] Here's something even more important: nine of ten immigrants coming to America today hail from outside Europe.[111] "Immigrants in the twenty-first century are doing more than replenishing our labor force and electorate," Taylor says. "They're changing our complexion."[112]

These nonwhite, skilled immigrants will determine our economic survival. Like other Western European countries, America will either absorb an increasingly diverse cast of immigrants into its ranks or become by midcentury what Joel Kotkin calls "a granny nation-state."[113] Absorbing immigrants carries huge potential rewards. As Paul Taylor notes, "Immigrants are strivers. They have energy, ingenuity, tolerance for risk, an appetite for hard work, and a faith in the future. Few if any countries have been more enriched by immigrants than ours."[114] Compare America to Europe, which has experienced similar immigration trends but has nonetheless proven, according to Kotkin, "far less able to absorb them." Immigrants in Europe often live in "exclusionary ghettos," suffering higher unemployment and experiencing alienation from the host country.[115] "Overall, the integrative process in the United States, which over the past century has experienced the largest influx of migrants in history, generally has proved more successful than that of Europe," Kotkin notes.[116]

But successful integration doesn't mean it's seamless. Massive transformations always produce resistance and backlash. As Americans

took to the streets in the 1960s, campaigning for equality for African Americans and women, there was a pushback. It came in the form of the so-called "silent majority" that catapulted Richard Nixon to the presidency in 1968.[117] We see something similar under way today. Donald Trump's anti-immigration policies and pronouncements reflect the "nativist" sentiment we have seen throughout our increasingly diverse industrialized world. The backlash, however, didn't arrest the forward march of the civil rights and feminist movements of the 1960s and '70s. And no backlash today will forestall the demographic trends currently transforming America. "Most demographers agree that sometime around 2050, if not sooner, non-Hispanic whites will be in the minority," Kotkin says. "Even if immigration were to slow dramatically due to harsher economic conditions, America's racial and ethnic die is already cast."[118]

AT STAKE: OUR VERY SURVIVAL

America is changing, and it's time for everyone—including our businesses—to prepare. This change is so epochal and fundamental that we must adjust the way we understand the country itself. In the twentieth century, the melting pot was the predominant metaphor of difference in America. It suggested that people of difference meld themselves together, shedding their particularities into one common American stew. In the twenty-first century, the melting pot has yielded to the mosaic.[119] The mosaic metaphor suggests the very opposite of the melting pot—the preservation of difference amid manifold diversity. In a mosaic, everyone's singularity remains intact; but when viewed from a distance, the mosaic comes to resemble a unified picture. The mosaic is a fitting metaphor for contemporary America, and as I will argue in the following pages, it's the ideal representation of twenty-first-century American companies.

The message of this book is simple. Whether businesses embrace it, celebrate it, fear it, or reject it, diversity is increasing and it's here to stay. Embracing and cultivating diversity has therefore gone from being a twentieth-century business nicety to a matter of economic survival. The following chapters explore the manifold benefits

of diversity across a number of operational and functional areas of a business. I'll introduce you to individuals and organizations who, more presciently than most, are aggressively making their leadership ranks, boardrooms, supply chains, marketing functions, community outreach strategies, and cultures more welcoming of diversity. I'll describe the challenges they face and suggest tactics and strategies that will allow diversity to flourish in these parts of your organization. As you'll see, these individuals and organizations all take for granted that fostering diversity is the right thing to do for the good of society. But they know something else: If they don't diversify their businesses, those businesses will perish. And if they do diversify, they'll thrive.

One of the most obvious and important ways a company can diversify is in its workforce. Some organizations and industries have made great progress recruiting employees from historically underrepresented groups. But very few have channeled diversity up to where it really counts: the management ranks. One exception is the National Football League, where the "Rooney Rule" requires that teams interview diverse candidates for coaching and front-office positions. For years before the Rooney Rule, named for the recently deceased Pittsburgh Steelers' owner, Dan Rooney, the NFL had many players who were black but precious few black coaches, a disparity that caused grave concern among players and prevented the NFL from broadening its appeal. Clearly, more needs to be done, and the NFL certainly has its challenges, such as penalizing players for silently acknowledging injustice on the field while the national anthem is played. However, the Rooney Rule has brought change and, with it, business advantages. Let's explore this pioneering rule and its implications for corporate America, taking the perspective of a former player who saw it up close and then went on to break through barriers in the business world.

RECRUITING LIKE ROONEY

THE GAME OF FOOTBALL runs in Arnold Garron's blood. During the early 1960s, his dad, Larry, became one of the original members of the Boston (now New England) Patriots.[1] Arnold and his brother Andre in turn both fell in love with the game. The two enjoyed stellar high school careers, followed by spectacular collegiate careers at the University of New Hampshire, which honored them with induction into its football Hall of Fame. Arnold went on to play professional football for the Washington Redskins (1984) and the Patriots (1986–88).

As Arnold's playing career drew to a close, he faced the question of what to do next. His first choice was coaching. Why not leverage his professional background and try for a coaching position in the NFL? Back in the 1980s, that wasn't likely—African Americans didn't become NFL coaches. As Arnold told me, "I just didn't see the path."

Arnold went on to a successful business career at John Hancock Financial Services and as a financial services executive elsewhere. Today, he sees that progress has been made as African Americans and others of diverse backgrounds can reach the NFL's coaching ranks. When I interviewed Arnold in the winter of 2017, the San Diego Chargers had recently announced the appointment of Anthony Lynn as their first African American head coach.[2] Many NFL teams had been interested in Lynn, and the Chargers secured his appointment the day after making public the controversial decision to relocate the franchise from

San Diego to Los Angeles. Lynn was not alone: in the NFL there were now African American general managers, assistant coaches, senior vice presidents, heads of marketing, and directors of social media. In 2015, the NFL crossed the gender line and hired Sarah Thomas as its first full-time female game official, something Arnold had thought he'd never witness.[3] "It's just great to see," he told me. "Should my son or daughter opt for a career in the NFL, there is now opportunity for them both."

The NFL's path to leadership diversity started on January 15, 2002, on what would have been Dr. Martin Luther King Jr.'s seventy-third birthday.[4] That morning, football aficionado and prominent Iranian American labor lawyer Cyrus Mehri opened the *Washington Post* sports section, searching for the latest football news. To his consternation, Mehri discovered a headline declaring, "Dungy Out."[5] But how could this be? In 1996, Tony Dungy became one of the first African Americans to become an NFL head coach. Following the historic appointment, Dungy transformed the lackluster Tampa Bay Buccaneers into one of the league's most impressive franchises.[6] Mehri's dismay quickly yielded to indignation when he recalled that only two weeks earlier, Dennis Green, another African American who'd performed superbly at the helm of the Minnesota Vikings, was similarly sacked. For Mehri this seemed to confirm his long-standing suspicion that in the NFL, African Americans were the "last hired, [and the] first fired."[7] Though Mehri knew that the most egregious racial discrimination of Dr. King's era had significantly dissipated, he had devoted his career to fighting the subtler discrimination that still limited the advancement of African Americans.

A decorated class-action litigator, Mehri understood that he would need more than anecdotal evidence and newspaper headlines to confirm racial bias in the NFL. He reached out to Johnnie Cochran, an African American, and a football fan and acclaimed attorney, known for his successful defense of O. J. Simpson. Mehri and Cochran collaborated with labor economist and statistician Janice Madden to determine whether the "last hired, first fired" pattern stood up under rigorous scrutiny. Their 2002 report, *Black Coaches in the National Football League: Superior Performance, Inferior Opportunities*, confirmed

their suspicions, demonstrating what it referred to as a "dismal record of minority hiring into NFL head coaching positions."[8] While roughly 70 percent of NFL players were African American, a mere 6 percent of head coaches were nonwhite. In the eighty years leading up to the study, six of the NFL's more than four hundred head-coaching hires had been of African Americans, a scant 1.5 percent.[9] This was a major injustice because, as the study also revealed, these NFL minority coaches averaged 1.1 more victories per season than their white counterparts and made the playoffs at a much higher rate.[10] Despite their superior performance, black coaches were woefully underrepresented.[11]

Mehri and Cochran wouldn't abide this racially homogenous and unjust status quo any longer. Their position was simple: either the NFL would extend more leadership opportunities to African Americans or the two attorneys would take the league to court.

It never came to that. Instead of using its considerable resources to fight charges of discrimination, the NFL chose to address the problem. On October 31, 2002, it assembled a Committee on Workplace Diversity. Steelers owner Dan Rooney presided over the committee, which also consisted of the Tampa Bay Buccaneers' general manager, Rich McKay; the Baltimore Ravens' vice president, Ozzie Newsome, an African American; the Indianapolis Colts' general manager, Bill Polian; and the Atlanta Falcons' executive vice president, Ray Anderson.[12] McKay zeroed in on the problem immediately: "I remember the discussion, and it focused on three things. We needed to create a system that requires a process for hiring. There were too many times where the hiring was done based on whom someone knew from the past or one recommendation."[13] He could have been speaking about the corporate world today, and the rush to fill positions. The Committee on Workplace Diversity made its pitch to individual team owners, who agreed with the committee's recommendations and promptly made the "Rooney Rule" mandatory for all teams in the league. Per the rule, each NFL team must consider at least one candidate of color for every head-coaching vacancy.[14]

The results of this rule were not long in coming. Four years following its instatement, the NFL went from having two coaches of

color in the entire league to having two coaches of color square off at the Super Bowl. In 2007, the Indianapolis Colts, led by Tony Dungy, triumphed over Lovie Smith's Chicago Bears. From Mehri's perspective, everyone won that day. "It couldn't have happened to two finer people and two finer coaches," he said, commenting on the historic game. "We're on cloud nine. We couldn't be happier. We came into this to change America's game. . . . Sunday gives us a chance to have America's game change America's consciousness."[15] During the ten years prior to Mehri and Cochran's study, less than 10 percent of head-coaching hires went to people of color (seven of ninety-two vacancies).[16] Following the new rule, this number increased to 20 percent (seventeen of eighty-seven vacancies). Assessing the Rooney Rule and the progress it achieved in its first few years, Mehri concluded, "Everything we're doing has exceeded our best expectations. We really have had a cultural change."[17]

Since that landmark 2007 Super Bowl, the Rooney Rule has continued to spur progress toward a more inclusive NFL. While originally applying only to head coaches, the rule now extends to general managers and some other executive vacancies.[18] In 2016, NFL commissioner Roger Goodell extended the rule to encompass women applying for senior management jobs in the league. As Robert Gulliver, the NFL's chief human resources officer and an African American, explained, "Forty-five percent of our fans are women, so it only makes sense for women to be involved in all levels of our sport. It just makes us better as an organization."[19] And yet, despite this progress, the NFL still has work to do. With roughly 70 percent of the league consisting of players of color, parity would dictate a far greater number of coaches, general managers, and owners of color. And when a talented young player takes a stand on issues of civil rights in this country (and starts a movement), as Colin Kaepernick did by kneeling during the national anthem, he should not be blacklisted from playing in the league. Nor should other players who similarly protested be ostracized for being allegedly "unpatriotic."

Many companies over the past few decades have recognized the strategic importance of diversifying their workforces. It's fundamental: if you don't have diverse people on your team, you're drastically

limiting the talent pool your organization can call upon, and you're making diversity in virtually every other part of your business more difficult to achieve. Yet the work these companies have done is incomplete in one critically important respect: *most sectors have successfully diversified only their entry-level and middle ranks*. That's unfortunate because diversifying the entry and middle ranks isn't enough to let organizations reap the many benefits that diversity provides. We need diversity at all levels, especially within the leadership ranks. The NFL has taken important steps toward leadership diversity. Now it's time for many other organizations across industries and geographies to do the same.

MISSING IN ACTION: DIVERSE LEADERSHIP

Now you might wonder: after so many years and so many diversity initiatives, does the American workplace still have a problem with diversity at the top? Absolutely. Consider the field of law. At the turn of the twenty-first century, the legal profession knew it needed to diversify its ranks and endeavored to do so. In 1999, approximately five hundred chief legal officers signed "Diversity in the Workplace—A Statement of Principle," signaling their commitment to the value of diversity and their dedication to increasing it.[20] The statement was analogous to Mehri and Cochran's 2002 study—and a clarion call to diversity that influenced an entire industry. Several years later, the Supreme Court further assisted these efforts by increasing the pipeline of minority candidates. In *Grutter v. Bollinger* (2003), the court ruled that law school admissions committees could use race as a consideration in evaluating applicants. Sandra Day O'Connor, who authored the 5–4 majority opinion, recognized that generating "a diverse student body" was in society's best interest, helping to ensure that diversity was present in future leaders.[21]

As my mentor and friend Wayne Budd relayed to me, however, progress has since been slow. In 1969, Wayne, an African American icon in the legal and business world, founded the law firm Budd, Reilly and Wiley, which became the largest minority-dominant firm in New England. One of the cofounders, Tom Reilly, later became attorney

general of Massachusetts. Another, Flash Wiley, went on to help lead PWRT, one of the country's largest minority businesses. Budd has occupied a series of distinguished posts ever since, including New England president of Bell Atlantic (now Verizon Communications). He also served as senior executive vice president and general counsel at John Hancock Financial Services, where I worked for him overseeing community impact programming at the company.[22] When Wayne began his legal career, in the late 1960s, there were only a handful of diverse candidates who made partner at Boston-based law firms. As he recalls, his was a nontraditional career path for African American men at the time; they gravitated instead to opportunities in the ministry, teaching, or the military. "Whenever you went into a court of law," Wayne reflects, looking back to his early career, "you always felt that the bar, no pun intended, was set fairly low" for people of difference. If Wayne would accompany a white colleague to make a business pitch, he found that all of the questions would be directed to his white counterpart. One friend even took him aside one day and asked for a recommendation for a solid *white* attorney.

As our country has changed and become more equitable over the course of Wayne's career, the number of diverse corporate lawyers hasn't kept pace. "I would almost guess that there are certainly no more partners today than there were when I began," Wayne suggests. Wayne's intuition is, unfortunately, right. Of the 716 equity partners in Boston's leading legal firms in 2013, a mere four were African American equity partners. That actually represented a significant loss (of about one-third) since 2008.[23] And Boston isn't an exception. In Houston, which boasts an especially large population of African Americans and Hispanics, the *Dallas Morning News* reported in 2013 that "not only is diversity not improving at the city's biggest firms, it is getting worse. . . . Only 1 percent [8] of the 799 equity partners at the largest law firms in Dallas are African-American. Thirteen of the 19 firms have no African-American partners and five of the firms only have one." Hispanic partners were similarly scarce, representing just 2.5 percent (or twenty) people.[24]

While making partner at any big law firm is tremendously difficult, people of color face unique challenges. My friend David Wilkins, who

is African American and the well-respected director of the Center on the Legal Profession at Harvard Law School, has identified several such barriers. Like technology companies, law firms tend to fashion themselves as meritocracies, creating a "mirrortocracy" effect, with lucrative contracts and hires flowing to insiders who resemble the racial and gender profiles of those already present. Wilkins also identifies implicit bias as a major problem, "because high-stakes decisions often need to be made quickly, with limited information."[25] As of 2014, 93 percent of the partners at 1,127 law firms belonging to the National Association of Law Placement (NALP) were white, and Caucasians occupied 84 percent of in-house counsel positions.[26] This means that diverse lawyers have a built-in disadvantage, having a harder time attracting the type of blue-chip clients that can afford to pay for expensive billable hours. Ultimately, this makes diverse lawyers less likely to generate the lucrative client portfolio necessary to make equity partner. As Wayne can tell you, securing billable hours and collecting on them is one of the many pressures in the legal world—but the pressure is even greater for people of difference.

When Wayne was general counsel at John Hancock, he fought against these disparities, notifying law firms that wanted to do business with Hancock that they needed to have diverse teams. Since that time, others have sought to reduce the homogeneity of Big Law. In 2016, city council members in Chicago, home to many of the nation's largest law firms, openly criticized Chapman and Cutler for lacking diverse employees, particularly in leadership positions. The city had paid the firm handsomely in billable hours and fees, and according to caucus member Leslie Hairston, it expected to see "a workforce [among city contractors] that reflects what the city looks like."[27] That was hardly the case: Chapman's workforce was nearly 90 percent white, and 91 percent of its partners were white.[28] Hairston understood that Chapman wasn't an outlier. In the profession as a whole, less than a quarter of junior attorneys are nonwhite, and only 8 percent of nonwhites ascend to the highest levels of leadership. But like many, Hairston was hungry for change. According to *Crain's Chicago Business*, this episode represented "a public display of what some companies tell their law firms in private: Improve diversity within your ranks or lose our business."[29]

Looking more broadly across sectors, we find another, perhaps even more fundamental reason why businesses routinely fail at diversity, especially when it comes to leadership. Business journalist Glenn Llopis presented a group of senior business leaders with the following hypothetical scenario:[30] Imagine that your business is poised to expand to the West Coast, where it lacks any prior footprint and brand recognition. You must hire a leader responsible for overseeing this expansion. This hire must find a way to connect with new clients, community members, and vendors within an increasingly diverse regional market that includes significant populations of Pacific Islanders and Chinese Americans. After your in-depth and rigorous talent search, you settle on two highly competitive finalists: a Chinese American woman who has spent her life on the East Coast and lacks any familiarity with the new market area and a white woman who has spent her life and career in California. Who gets the position?

If you are like most survey respondents, you chose the Chinese American. Only 20 percent of these senior business leaders chose the white candidate (and a stunning 95 percent of diverse leaders also elected to go with the Chinese American candidate!). Wrong choice, Llopis says. In choosing the minority candidate, "you were thinking about diversity, *not* inclusion." This hypothetical scenario reveals that companies still approach workforce diversity in terms of quotas and compliance instead of with an authentic spirit of inclusiveness and growth. Llopis has experienced this in his own life. As a Cuban American, he is constantly approached by companies asking for advice about expanding into the Miami market. But he's an American who has no familiarity with Miami and therefore would be as little help expanding into that market as the Chinese American woman in the hypothetical scenario would be expanding into the California market.

America is changing so drastically that we can't rely on the same outdated, compliance-driven approach to diversity. It's behind the times. Millennials in particular view diversity less in a strictly visual or representational way, and instead value inclusive environments, where they can interact in a respectful way with people from a diversity of viewpoints, cultural experiences, and backgrounds.[31] That's what makes the NFL's Rooney Rule so powerful. It doesn't mandate

hiring decisions or enforce hard quotas. Rather, it's a soft policy that extends opportunity to groups that have historically been denied it. The Rooney Rule, according to public policy expert Cynthia (C. C.) Dubois, "changes the composition of the candidate pool, rather than the criteria used during the hiring process."[32] And that allows managers the maximum latitude to select the best candidate from a deep and talented pool.

Think back to the leadership hire in our hypothetical job search. This person was responsible for the company's growth in an entirely new regional market and business ecosystem. The nondiverse California native was, for Llopis, this company's "path to long-term growth and sustainable inclusive leadership." That's because while the candidate herself lacked certain diversity markers, she brought geographical diversity to her position that would help nurture diversity of thought. Unlike her hypothetical East Coast counterpart, she possessed the knowledge and wisdom to connect with California's customer base and meet its particular needs. Such needs would entail making more Chinese American hires among people also attuned to this regional market. That, in turn, would more likely result in sustainable growth for the company in the new area. This short story illustrates the pitfalls that come with prizing compliance-driven diversity instead of prizing inclusiveness. It's also an endorsement for the Rooney Rule.

A TALE OF TWO DIVERSE COMPANIES

To understand the inherent value of diversity in leadership, and to also gain a sense of what it takes inside companies to bring more underrepresented groups into the managerial ranks, let's look at two brief case studies. We start with Xerox.[33] In 1964, when race riots broke out in Rochester, New York, the home of Xerox's corporate headquarters, CEO and founder Joe Wilson arranged meetings with black leaders to gain insight about their discontent. As he discovered, African Americans rioted because they couldn't secure jobs. Wilson pledged to hire more African Americans, and his company made significant headway. By 1991, 9 percent of Xerox's top managers were black, a stunning increase over the national average of 0.5 percent.

Such leadership-driven diversity has created a strongly cohesive corporate culture at Xerox, increasing loyalty and decreasing job turnover. Instead of instituting ineffective "diversity programs," Xerox did something purposeful to help support people of color within the company. It created a peer-based caucus system. The "black caucus" has proven to be highly effective in helping to create a sense of community, loyalty, and mentorship among black Xerox workers. Particularly striking was that members of the black caucus pledged not to compete with one another. Within a cutthroat corporate environment in which everyone jockeys for a handful of select jobs, such a move was unprecedented. The pledge created bonds of solidarity instead of a climate of mutual suspicion. Over the decades, more caucuses or affinity groups emerged within the company. According to former CEO Ursula Burns, "We have one for women, we have one for African American women, for Asians, for Hispanics, for Hispanic women, for gays and lesbians, all kinds."

As the black caucus nurtured an inclusive corporate environment at Xerox, Burns herself was making her way up the company's pipeline, joining Xerox in 1980 and becoming CEO in 2009. She succeeded Anne Mulcahy, an extremely successful diversity trailblazer, making Xerox the first Fortune 500 Company to have successive female CEOs (a feat made more remarkable by the fact that Burns is an African American woman). Shortly after assuming the position, Burns came to the following realization: African American men were thriving at the organization, while women of all backgrounds had fallen behind. In manufacturing operations, in particular, women were nearly absent from the roster of plant managers. When company executives investigated why that was, they discovered that the company offered zero work flexibility, enforcing stringent 9-to-5 schedules. Women needed more flexibility, so Xerox created a "job sharing" program in which people could divide their hours or even split a full-time job to meet their lifestyle needs.

After Burns's intervention, not only did the manufacturing portion of Xerox's workforce become more diverse, but its leadership ranks did as well. When Burns was CEO in 2011, eight other women served as top executives at the company, and 25 percent of Xerox's corporate

leaders were women (compared with only 15 percent among other Fortune 500 companies). This is a prime example of diversity in leadership enabling other types of diversity to flourish inside a company.

In addition to creating a lively and loyal corporate culture, Burns believes that diversity helped save the business. When Xerox debuted its copy machine in 1959, it created an entirely new industry, catapulting the company to amazing growth.[34] For most of Xerox's corporate life, it relied essentially on one core product: machines that allowed people to make paper copies. By 1991, when Xerox claimed the twenty-second spot on the Forbes 500 list, it had become practically synonymous with copying. In common parlance, "to Xerox" meant to make a copy. "That was 100 percent of our revenues," Burns says.

Afterward, the rise of digital imaging threatened to make the company's singular product irrelevant. But because of the company's diversity, Burns notes, Xerox was sufficiently strong, resilient, and forward-thinking to transform itself from a machine-maker to a product-services company. E-ZPass, call centers, and toll collection currently account for half of all corporate revenues. To be sure, Xerox's corporate makeover remains ongoing as of this writing. But in Burns's estimation, "Our business changed, and we were strong enough, fast enough, and confident enough to actually reposition the entire company and the brand toward a whole big set of opportunities that are different than they were before." It is remarkable that, despite the digital revolution, Xerox is still on the Forbes 500 list—a marked contrast with another legendary company headquartered in Rochester: Kodak. Burns believes that Xerox, "the leading diversified service company in the world," is a much more innovative and prosperous company than it was in the 1990s when it occupied a much higher rung on the Forbes list. Leadership-driven diversity not only saved Xerox—it made the company *better*.[35]

We find a similar story of business success when we turn to another, very different company: IKEA, the world's largest furniture and home goods chain. In addition to ranking among the most profitable retail companies in the world, IKEA also ranks on the Forbes list of the fifty most powerful brands.[36] Company executives will tell you that diversity and inclusion in the leadership ranks contribute significantly to

that success. As CEO Peter Agnefjäll puts it, "We are a diverse group of people working together to create an inclusive and humanistic culture. Our values, such as humbleness, simplicity, togetherness, and enthusiasm are the foundation of our work and form the unique IKEA culture."[37] One of Agnefjäll's hallmark initiatives to make the company more inclusive focuses on women. Nearly half of all of IKEA's seventeen thousand global managers are women, and 40 percent of the company's top 240 managers are also female. The company's goal is gender parity in leadership, reflecting global gender distributions. As Agnefjäll explains, "That our business is equally led by men and women is essential for our future growth and for being a great place to work. Diversity opens new perspectives, creativity and innovation."[38]

The global retail giant takes a comprehensive view of its responsibility to its diverse employees and customer base. It's not enough to merely hire diverse workers. The company must also be flexible in dealing with the many needs of such a diverse workforce. To that end, IKEA has created day-care centers, paternity leave policies, job-sharing arrangements to further accommodate parents, and up to six months of paid salary to allow employees who've relocated a chance to settle into their new cities. This deep, authentic spirit of inclusiveness and responsibility also shapes IKEA's advertising and product lines, allowing it to connect to an increasingly diverse consumer base. Take the company's "We Help You Make It" campaign. Instead of appealing to the increasingly elusive desire for wealth, the advertisement depicts, according to journalist Martha C. White, "the way the American dream has evolved to fit a post-recession economic reality."[39] Advertisements feature an overcrowded living room where a man struggles to balance his living and work spaces, parents tiptoeing around their sleeping infants, and two brothers figuring out how to share a room. The American Dream, telegraph the ads, belongs to everyone. "It's an inclusive message," White says, "that, in this fraught political climate, could be a campaign slogan just as easily as a pitch for floor lamps and futons."[40]

Since this advertisement campaign reflects a common reality, White notes, it is necessarily inclusive, "emphasizing a panoply of ages, ethnicities and family living situations: A middle-aged woman makes a face when she opens up a compost bin in her kitchen; a bride

flings herself onto a sectional sofa and digs into a carton of ice cream; a mixed-race same-sex couple cuddle up on the couch to watch TV."[41] Not only is everyone represented and included in the campaign, it also has the advantage of appealing to millennials. That's because the ad foregrounds experiences over commodities, a hallmark value of this generation. Of course, this is not to say that putting a few young people, people of color, and same-sex couples into ads is a panacea, but it does represent a company aware of the need to broaden its audience and working on various strategies to achieve that.

As we near 2042, more companies like Xerox and IKEA will rise to the top of their industries. With their diverse management teams, these companies will drive more diversity into the middle ranks of the workforce. They'll also better drive diversity into other strategically important areas of operation that we'll discuss in this book, such as innovation and marketing. Simply put, diverse leadership teams understand the global marketplace. They can appeal to the widest range of communities, ethnicities, races, and genders to imagine and execute entirely new business strategies. On the day-to-day level, they can think more creatively and make their organizations nimbler and more adventurous. Xerox added years and perhaps even decades onto its corporate lifespan. Many more companies will find that their fortunes rise or fall based on the diversity (or lack thereof) of their leaders.

THE ROONEY RULE AND *YOU*

What should your company do to extend leadership opportunities to a broader pool of candidates? The Rooney Rule provides a good starting point. It's worth considering for a moment how that rule has benefitted the NFL financially. During his career as a professional player during the 1980s, Arnold Garron remembers that some teams weren't able to always fill their seats. The game, however, was tailored to a very particular type of consumer. You didn't see many people of color in the stadiums.

Arnold is convinced that it is diversity in the managerial ranks that has allowed NFL franchises to connect to a broad array of consumers, including people of color and women.[42] And Arnold should know.

Following his professional football career, he attended Harvard Business School and then worked for John Hancock in sales management. "As more and more diversity crept into the NFL, things changed," Arnold says. Football now boasts as much as $13 billion a year in revenues. As it continues to expand into lucrative markets such as China, those numbers are projected to swell to $25 billion by 2027.[43]

Since its implementation in the early twenty-first century, the Rooney Rule has emerged as a "best practice" for diversity and inclusion. In 2011, Robert Johnson, CEO of RLJ Companies, cofounder of Black Entertainment Television (BET), and the country's first black billionaire, called on all Fortune 1,000 companies to voluntarily adopt the Rooney Rule when filling new leadership vacancies and selecting suppliers, vendors, and contractors. This NFL-inspired policy, which he renamed the "RLJ Rule," would allow companies access to a talented and undertapped workforce and help lower the country's black unemployment rate, which at the time was 16 percent. "The RLJ Rule is principally designed to encourage companies to voluntarily establish a 'best practices' policy to identify and interview the tremendous talent pool of African American managers and African American companies that are often overlooked because of traditional hiring or procurement practices," said Johnson when announcing the policy.[44] By addressing employment disparities between whites and people of difference, he insisted that these new recruitment and hiring strategies would be in every company's financial best interest. "This is not a mandate and this is not a program that attempts to appeal to the better angels of anyone's nature," Johnson said. "We've tried that. We are making the business case for fixing this problem."[45]

Several years later, when President Barack Obama urged the tech sector to diversify, companies heeded the call by following the rule when filling leadership positions.[46] Social media giants Facebook and Pinterest, along with smaller companies such as Box, a cloud content-management and file-sharing services firm, all committed to implementing various versions of the Rooney Rule when faced with managerial vacancies.[47] For every leadership vacancy at Pinterest, one woman and one diverse candidate is now considered.[48] Intel ranks

among the most ambitious and successful tech companies following Obama's challenge. In addition to implementing the Rooney Rule and publishing the firm's diversity hiring statistics, Intel CEO Brian Krzanich committed to having his workforce more accurately reflect the complexion and composition of the American and global marketplace by 2020.[49] Always a leader in diversity, Xerox has implemented the "Wilson Rule," named in honor of its first CEO, Joe Wilson, which mandates that people of color and women constitute at least one of three interview finalists for every US management opening.[50] Damika Arnold, Xerox's global diversity and inclusion leader, made diversity and inclusion part of every manager's annual performance review.[51]

The Rooney Rule is also invoked when large corporations are floundering. In June of 2017, Uber CEO Travis Kalanick resigned amid corporate and personal scandals involving intellectual property theft, sexual harassment, a customer's rape by a driver, and transportation and safety violations.[52] Former US attorney general Eric Holder, who was hired to consult for the company, suggested a dramatic overhaul of what some deemed to be the "generally toxic environment" that prevailed at the company. Among his suggestions was instating a version of the Rooney Rule so that women and people of color, underrepresented in the management ranks, could assume leadership roles.[53] Uber's board agreed unanimously to adopt all of Holder's recommendations.[54]

Local governments are also adopting the rule. Diversity rates in municipal governments and agencies are just as challenging as in corporate America. Ferguson, Missouri, presents a famous—or perhaps infamous—example. About 66 percent of the population is African American, while a staggering 95 percent of its police officers are white. This measure places Ferguson slightly above the national average: the United States is currently 64 percent white and has a 75 percent white law enforcement workforce (blacks make up 12 percent of law enforcement personnel; Hispanics, 10.3 percent).[55] But these numbers might soon change. Following Dan Rooney's death in 2017, Pittsburgh mayor Bill Peduto implemented a Rooney Rule for his city.[56] Per Peduto's executive order, the city would "create and

implement a policy that ensures purposeful recruitment of diverse candidates and requires the City to interview at least one external and one internal diverse candidate before the final selection of a candidate for any supervisory position in City government, such as directors, deputy directors, managers, and supervisors."[57] With the Rooney Rule's help, Pittsburgh's governmental agencies—like the workforce at Intel—might soon more closely resemble the demographic makeup of America. And, as I discussed in the opening chapter, they'll make themselves much more competitive by doing so.

Don Bell, former president of the US Senate's Black Legislative Staff Caucus, would like to see the Rooney Rule implemented on Capitol Hill. Less than 5 percent of Washington-based legislative staffers are African American.[58] And yet, our senators and congressional representatives need advisers who represent the diverse racial, socioeconomic, and geographic communities in the United States. Failing that, Bell notes, the most democratic body in the United States won't actually be very democratic at all. "In football," Bell said, "the Rooney Rule is vital in trying to bridge the gap between the league's robust majority of minority players [72.6 percent] and its scarcity of minority head coaches [18.7 percent] and general managers [15.6 percent]. In Congress, we need a Rooney Rule to begin bridging the gap between the staffs that influence lawmakers' policy choices and the diverse body politic that Congress represents."[59] And let's not forget our political leaders themselves. America's federal legislature has steadily diversified over the twenty-first century, with the 115th Congress boasting 19 percent nonwhite members—the most diverse cohort of lawmakers yet. This progress is laudable, though there is a long way to go before the two chambers reflect the diverse makeup of the country.[60]

The Rooney Rule is hardly perfect. Ten years after the rule's instatement in 2003, scholars, commentators, and fans alike began noticing a diversity progress plateau in the NFL's leadership ranks. As *New York Times* sports reporter David Waldstein noted, some feared the Rooney Rule resembled "merely tokenism in a league that is dominated by black players but has relatively few members of minority groups in leadership positions."[61] In 2013, Earl "Butch" Graves Jr.,

president and CEO of Black Enterprise and a retired basketball player, surveyed the numbers of African Americans in NFL leadership positions and called the Rooney Rule a "sham."[62] That year there were five African American general managers and three head coaches in a league where 65 percent of the players were African American. Even more upsetting, all fifteen open leadership positions that year went to whites. As Harvard Law School professor Charles Ogletree commented, "There is a big difference between interviewing and hiring." Given how talented minority coaches are, Ogletree believes that "There is no acceptable reason for this underrepresentation."[63]

More recently, the NFL has improved its record. There are currently eight nonwhite head coaches in the league, tying 2017 with 2011 for the most diverse coaches at the start of a season.[64] Still, the Rooney Rule isn't a magic bullet. Organizations can't just enact a hiring policy and assume they're "done." Instead, they must make an enduring and authentic commitment to leadership diversity. Even a league as forward-looking as the NFL must remain constantly vigilant to ensure that its rule doesn't become a mere formality, bereft of its initial spirit and intention.

Overall, the Rooney Rule is justifiably a "best practice" as well as a welcome first step in many organizations that so sorely need more diversity in the C-suite. My hope is that the Rooney Rule, combined with even more robust diversity measures, will help forge business cultures that truly value inclusion. John Wooten, a former player and current NFL executive and chairman of the Fritz Pollard Alliance, points us toward the ultimate goal. "I am not an affirmative-action guy," he said. "I don't believe 70 percent of the coaches should be black, or any percentage. I believe the best man should get the job, and for years, that wasn't always true. In this case, it is. The hope is that one day we won't even need a rule."[65]

Even if organizations succeed in recruiting a diverse workforce at all levels, their path to preparing for 2042 is hardly complete. In fact, it's just beginning. Energized by the spirit and reality of diversity at the top, companies must go on to inject diversity into virtually every area of their operations. One critically important place to start is with the

board of directors. It's hard to commit an organization to becoming more inclusive if the body overseeing executive leadership doesn't itself reflect diversity. The board is a critical part of a company's public face. Boards also set strategic agendas and guide executives as they make decisions. To thrive with diversity and secure their future success, companies must send a strong message to all stakeholders by making their boards diverse. As we'll see next, companies that do this wind up with sharper strategies that drive both profits and sustainable growth.

BUILDING A BETTER BOARD— AND A LARGER, MORE VIBRANT ORGANIZATION

DURING THE MID-1990S, only a few socially conscious shareholders were clamoring for board diversification. One of these mavericks was Doris Gormley, who served as director of corporate social responsibility for the Sisters of Saint Francis of Philadelphia.[1] Sister Doris's convent in Ashton, Pennsylvania, belonged to the medieval Franciscan order, which embraced the values of social solidarity and radical inclusivity. In line with the order's teachings, Sister Doris analyzed the proxy information of companies in which her religious order invested its money, determining if women and people of color were represented on the board. Should an organization fail to achieve such representation, she sent it a brief letter detailing her commitment to board diversity and graciously explaining why—when no diverse candidates were on an election slate—she chose to abstain from voting on new board members.

Typically, her missives elicited simple responses, with some managers politely acknowledging her comments and others casually indicating that they were (or weren't) actively diversifying their boards of

directors. When Thurman John "T. J." Rodgers, the founder and then CEO of tech heavyweight Cypress Semiconductor, received her letter, however, he responded with a blistering six-page epistle of his own.[2] Variously characterizing her letter as "immoral" and special-interests driven, he suggested she dismount her "moral high horse." After all, he explained, "choosing a Board of Directors based on race and gender is a lousy way to run a company."[3] And furthermore, he argued, diversity lends no intrinsic value: "Bluntly stated, a 'woman's view' on how to run our semiconductor company does not help us, unless that woman has an advanced technical degree and experience as a CEO."[4]

Rodgers was a gruff, outspoken leader whose penchant for strongly worded op-ed pieces on sensitive political issues earned him a reputation for being "The Bad Boy of Silicon Valley."[5] Still, his letter to Sister Doris appeared especially venomous, and members of his board and executive team weren't thrilled about his decision to distribute it to all of the company's shareholders. But even more startling than the letter itself was the outpouring of support he received for it! Of two hundred letters directed to his Silicon Valley corporate campus in the immediate aftermath of the controversy, only fifteen expressed any criticism. Many of Rodgers's executive peers, such as the chairmen of Advanced Micro Devices, Inc., and Hewlett-Packard Co., applauded his stance, while economist Milton Friedman called his antidiversity manifesto a "splendid letter."[6] Even progressive journalist and peace activist Colman McCarthy took Sister Doris to task: "I'm pained to say," he reflected in the *Washington Post*, "that the unsaddled nun had it coming. She was outmatched and had no prayer against the experience-based arguments of Rodgers."[7] Likeminded investors were inspired to buy more Cypress stock, and some suggested that Rodgers turn to politics.[8]

Today, at least some business leaders understand the positive financial impacts a diverse board engenders. In a 2016 public statement, a group of white male top executives at American companies, including JP Morgan Chase's Jamie Dimon, General Electric's Jeff Immelt, BlackRock's Larry Fink, Berkshire Hathaway's Warren Buffett, and ValueAct Capital's Jeff Ubben, did the opposite of Rodgers and advocated for greater board diversity. As their statement read, "Diverse

boards make better decisions, so every board should have members with complementary and diverse skills, backgrounds and experiences. It's also important to balance wisdom and judgment that accompany experience and tenure with the need for fresh thinking and perspectives of new board members."[9] Research has repeatedly confirmed their position, particularly as it concerns gender. As the Catalyst Research Center has found, "Companies with the most women board directors outperformed those with the least on return on sales (ROS) by 16 percent and return on invested capital (ROIC) by 26 percent."[10] A McKinsey study of European companies found that those with at least two female board members and high proportions of female leaders "outperformed industry averages," including a "10 percent higher return on equity."[11] Most European countries acknowledge this value and enforce board diversity quotas, while leaders of other advanced economies, such as Japanese prime minister Shinzo Abe, have strongly advocated board gender diversification for all their national companies.[12]

Notwithstanding the public stances of a few progressive leaders, however, American business in general has made little progress in board diversity since the mid-1990s. BoardSource, which specializes in nonprofit governance and leadership best practices, has been tracking board demographics for the past two decades. As the firm's CEO, Anne Wallestad, noted in 2017, "We've moved the needle only very slightly when it comes to the racial and ethnic diversity of boards."[13] In fact, nonprofit board diversity is getting worse. BoardSource's 2015 study, for example, documented that "89 percent of chief executives and 80 percent of board members were Caucasian, and 25 percent of boards were 100 percent white."[14] In the 2017 study, the numbers of Caucasians had increased to 90 percent (chief executives) and 84 percent (members of the board).[15] Corporate boards fare little better. In 2014, men occupied more than 80 percent of the boardroom seats at S&P 500 companies, as did whites.[16] The twenty-five least diverse Fortune 250 companies had *no* board seats held by people of difference, and only 3.2 percent held by women.[17]

Lagging on board diversity, or approaching it in a disinterested, superficial, compliance-driven fashion, is increasingly dangerous for companies. It will negatively impact profitability and harm the ability

to connect with customers, local communities, and stakeholders. By pursuing board diversity deliberately, diligently, and energetically, by contrast, companies can sustain a powerful, long-term competitive advantage. In the face of demographic shifts and technological disruption, firms in even the most risk-averse industries can thrive by creating boards with a multiplicity of backgrounds and points of view. Sister Doris's words were progressive in the 1990s, but now they represent common sense. Draw on this country's increasingly diverse talent and elect some fresh faces to your company's board. It's a powerful strategy to drive profits and future-proof your company.

THE EASTERN ROUTE TO DIVERSITY

When you think of dynamic, innovative, high-performance organizations, your local community bank doesn't usually come to mind. But if you live in New England, it might. Founded in 1818, Eastern Bank is the country's oldest and largest mutual bank, serving communities throughout Massachusetts, New Hampshire, Rhode Island, and beyond. It's also one of the country's most progressive banking institutions. Eastern provides fairly priced banking, investment, and insurance products and services for consumers, businesses, and underserved communities. Since 1999, on average Eastern has donated at least 10 percent of its net income—seven times the national average—every year to charity and local organizations working on causes such as advancing women in the workplace, supporting immigrants, and advocating for social justice.[18]

Doing good has also been part of a winning growth strategy for the bank. Eastern as we know it today took shape through an acquisition strategy that has spanned decades. Beginning in the 1980s, Eastern began acquiring small savings institutions in its local area (including a bank founded by my husband, C. Bernard Fulp, who also was the first African American executive vice president in the New England banking industry). In the 2000s, Eastern continued to expand, and in 2017, it had over 120 locations and crossed $10 billion in assets. Eastern achieved record financial results in 2017, which included an increase of nearly 40 percent in net income.[19]

Despite its growth, Eastern is small compared to the banking industry's primary players. In 2016 the top four US banks—JP Morgan Chase, Bank of America, Wells Fargo, and Citigroup—managed a combined $8.1 *trillion* in assets.[20] Still, $10 billion was enough to make Eastern the 120th largest bank in the country—out of 6,000.[21] And in one respect, Eastern is way ahead of these four massive banking behemoths (and many smaller financial institutions too). I'm talking about diversity. As of 2018, 50 percent of its officers and 33 percent of its management committee—a group comprising the company's twelve most senior executives—were women, people of color, and/ or those considered diverse, such as members of the LGBTQ community. Eastern's main subsidiary, Eastern Insurance Group, is the largest insurance agency led by a woman in the US. About one-fifth of Eastern's employees are people of difference. If you brought all of the company's 1,900 employees together in one place, you would hear a number of sounds that might be unfamiliar. That's because they speak more than fifty languages and dialects.[22]

In contrast to most of its industry counterparts, Eastern has an extremely diverse board, with 50 percent composed of women, people of color, and/or others considered diverse. In the banking industry, women occupy only 9 percent of all board seats—despite holding the majority of professional jobs in the country and making the vast majority of all consumer decisions.[23] The boards at the regional Federal Reserve Banks were overwhelmingly populated by white men as well.

Unlike many publicly traded companies, Eastern spawned three separate governing bodies over the past two centuries. Back in 1818, when a group of wealthy philanthropists founded the bank, they formed a group of corporators to oversee the running of the organization. In fact, the bank's first customer, Rebecca Sutton, was a woman, a true sign of diversity and inclusion at a time when women were not permitted to have bank accounts. Through the years and given the bank's many acquisitions, the number of Eastern's corporators grew greatly. As a result, a group of trustees was chosen from among the corporators to serve as an executive committee. It eventually became apparent that Eastern also needed a group of directors to handle governance matters—individuals who could devote more time and

provide specific expertise. A board of directors was formed, typically composed of twelve to fifteen members.

Fast-forward and since 2003, Eastern has placed great importance on diversity and inclusion among its directors, trustees, and corporators. It has gone from having an overall board that was previously composed of 92 percent white males to having, as of 2018, 50 percent of the 140 members represented by people of color, women, or individuals from the LGBTQ community. In addition, all members of the boards reflect a vast array of professional backgrounds, skills, and expertise.[24]

Does a connection exist between Eastern's unique board diversity and its rapid growth? As a member of the Board of Trustees, I believe the answer is an unambiguous "yes." Board diversity has allowed Eastern to "punch far above its weight" compared to much larger local competitors such as Citizens, TD Bank, Santander, and Bank of America. Specifically, it has helped Eastern improve its strategic decision-making, recruiting, innovation, and connection with the community.

Eastern's board diversity didn't just materialize on its own. It evolved thanks to sustained commitment from senior leadership, in particular the bank's current chair and CEO, Robert "Bob" Rivers. Upon Rivers's arrival in 2006 as vice chair and chief banking officer, he saw the opportunity to diversify the bank's governing boards.

Given the bank's roots in Salem, Massachusetts, and long history serving Boston's North Shore, its board reflected those primarily white communities. In addition, as is typical in corporate board recruitment across industries, board members tended to recommend individuals from their own networks for board posts. Eastern's board makeup also reflected its history of acquisitions of other banks in which some of the acquired banks' board members moved onto one of Eastern's governing bodies. Most often, the acquired bank board members were white men.

When Rivers joined Eastern, the bank's board of directors did feature several individuals from traditionally underrepresented backgrounds but not the trustees and corporators, the two other governing boards. The disparity puzzled Rivers. As he recalls, "I tried to reconcile why the make-up of the directors was so different from the trustees' and corporators'—and not just in terms of diversity but different

in every way imaginable, especially in engagement and connectivity to our customers. The resulting diversity of thought elevated board conversations, and innovative ideas and creativity flowed."[25]

Building on the existing commitment of immediate past Eastern CEOs Richard Holbrook and Stanley Lukowski to boost diversity among the bank's customers, employees, leadership team, and board of directors, Rivers made it a priority to add people of many races, genders, sexual orientations, and backgrounds to Eastern's boards of trustees and corporators, and also to have the bank advocate more aggressively on issues related to inclusion. "We had been pursuing 'diversity light' up until then," he notes. "We had it in our employee policies and we had included people with nontraditional backgrounds on our board of directors. But we had never really injected it into the entire organization and governing bodies. We were conscious of the changing demographics, but it hadn't fully crystallized for us. I was determined to change that."

Born in the Greater Boston area, Rivers is named after former attorney general and US senator Robert F. Kennedy, and he shares Kennedy's commitment to racial equality and equal opportunity. Yet Rivers also saw the trustees and corporators, the two larger boards, as untapped business assets that could help Eastern in its future growth plans. "For me, it was all about how we could have the most robust collective thinking to address increasingly complex challenges in a more rapidly changing world. The way to do that was to have as many people with different backgrounds and experiences as possible. And that didn't simply mean putting more people of color or members of the LGBTQ community on the board. It meant diversity across a number of dimensions." Rivers was excited about the prospect of an entire board that could energize the bank and drive innovation. He also saw board diversity as a way to help spread and embrace differ-ence across the entire organization: "I knew that if we have diversity on the board, it would not only help us increase our cultural com-petence and understanding, but it would also send a very important signal that we're serious about it."

As directors, trustees, and corporators retired, Rivers considered diversity as a primary factor when considering their replacements. To

embrace diversity and the best talent of all kinds, he first looked at building diversity on the nominating committees for new trustees and corporators. Since the bank at the time had few people of color on these governing bodies, Rivers began by recruiting more women to join these committees, believing that women would be eager to have more diverse governing bodies, and for all the right reasons.

From the outset, Rivers and other leaders at Eastern were adamant that board diversity could never come at the expense of overall excellence and fitness for the post. Says Rivers, "Our mantra in the nominating committee was first and foremost to find the best, brightest, most strategic people we can get to join our board. It was to aim high, considering those that we weren't sure we could even attract. Our second criterion was to look at *anybody* as a potential candidate but particularly identifying candidates who are women, people of color, and members of the LGBTQ community."

Eastern's lead director at the time and a longtime board member, African American businessman Wendell Knox, agrees: "We were very strategic in trying to add people who not only were the right gender or the right color but also who brought expertise, knowledge, and connectivity to the community in concrete ways that were consistent with what we were doing. We actually demonstrated that you can achieve diversity and add a ton of value, rather than compromise on your standards."[26]

With the goal of more diverse nominating committees for trustees and corporators in place, the bank secured the participation of many more people with underrepresented backgrounds, while also continuing to appoint white males to its governing bodies. By any standard, the quality of these recruits has been impressive. Appointments during Rivers's tenure have included Dr. Myechia Minter-Jordan, an African American woman who is CEO of the Dimock Center, the leading health and human services provider for Boston's urban neighborhoods; former US senator William "Mo" Cowan, vice president of legal policy and litigation at General Electric who is also African American; Vanessa Calderon-Rosado, a Hispanic woman who serves as CEO of Inquilinos Boricuas en Accion, a critical Boston-based community-building

organization; and Gunner Scott, a Massachusetts-based activist and the first openly transgender individual ever elected to a bank board in the US (the board has had two transgender members as of this writing, including one who transitioned while serving as a sitting corporator). "If you look at the new board members we brought on over the last several years," remarks Knox, who served as lead director from 2009 to 2017, "there is a very concrete story that can be told about why each one of them represents a value added to the board." As testament to how the bank has advanced its diversity practices on its board, in 2018 it announced the election of Deborah Jackson as lead director, succeeding Knox and becoming the first woman and second person of color to serve in that position in Eastern two-hundred-year history. Jackson, who is African American, joined Eastern's board in 2002 and is the president of Cambridge College and former CEO of the American Red Cross of Massachusetts.

As a result of these various appointments, the atmosphere in the boardroom has become transformed. As Jackson notes, "When you walk into a governance meeting, you immediately notice a change visually. You can *see* the diversity in the room. There is now a diversified board with more women, African Americans, Asian Americans, and Latinos."[27]

Eastern's advocacy around the issue of inclusion was also quite pronounced and carried through into the community. In 2013, Eastern was the first bank to sign the amicus brief challenging the Defense of Marriage Act. Hundreds of companies nationwide followed suit.[28] The bank also affirmed its stance with a strong presence in the local LGBTQ pride parades, as well as with its naming of transgender board members.

Such moves and board diversification rankled some old-guard employees and board members. An employee in the finance department, a twenty-year company veteran, left because the bank's advocacy on behalf of the LGBTQ community clashed with her religious beliefs. At one annual meeting where Rivers spoke about LGBTQ advocacy, an older white man in attendance sat with his arms crossed and shook his head vigorously for all to see. When Eastern named its first

transgender board member, another board member called Rivers to complain bitterly and ultimately resigned from the board. In the face of such resistance, Rivers stuck to his commitment to not only appoint people of all backgrounds but also to affirm their inclusion and integration in the organization. "We, in the spirit of inclusion, follow a mandate," he says. "Your religious beliefs are your own, but the minute your actions and words disadvantage or hurt anyone, our commitment to equal opportunity for all is our guide. They should not impact how people are treated in their jobs, how their work is evaluated, and how we hire. There are some people for whom this is just a step too far, and [if so] this probably isn't the organization for them."[29]

The vast majority of company stakeholders applauded the appearance of new faces around the boardroom as well the bank's explicit commitment to equality for all. Existing board members approached Rivers to indicate their appreciation, recognizing the benefits of a more diverse and active board as supporting the organization's mission while also serving the bank's business interests. Employees loved it too. For ten years running, the bank has appeared in the *Boston Globe*'s ranking of the area's top employers.[30] "What's most important to us," Rivers notes, "is the level of employee participation in the survey, in addition to the scores. Over 90 percent of our 1,900 employees participate. That's off the charts and a solid indicator of our employee engagement."[31]

Among other sources of employee pride is the company's "Join us for Good" campaign, launched in March 2017 to celebrate those who are making a difference and rally others to ignite a movement. In a series of inspiring online and television commercials, as well as on billboards flanking the Commonwealth's major thoroughfares, Eastern presented powerful social justice images of "doing good" in the community, featuring pro-immigration themes or individuals draped in rainbow flags or at same-sex marriage ceremonies.[32] Paul Alexander, the bank's chief marketing and communications officer, who is African American and also vice chair of The Partnership board, summarizes Eastern's employee reactions to the campaign: "Many said, 'That's my company. That's why I'm proud to work at Eastern.'"[33]

DIVERSIFY AND THRIVE

As popular as it was, did board diversity really deliver better business results? Rivers and others believe so. And they're not alone. The case for board diversity has been compelling enough for some institutional investors to push for more of it. The California Public Employees' Retirement System (CalPERS), the California State Teachers' Retirement System (CalSTERS), TIAA-CREF, and UBS have all implemented policies geared toward more board diversity. To help organizations find suitable candidates from underrepresented groups, CalSTERS and CalPERS spearheaded the "diverse Director Datasource (3D)" database, which contains the names of qualified females and minorities who might make good board members.[34] Such "institutional investor activism" has made major headway in achieving board diversification, singling out boards who fail to consider diversity in their recruiting efforts.[35]

In arguing for board diversity, scholars and other experts have pointed to an especially important benefit: improved decision-making. In her study of Abraham Lincoln, historian Doris Kearns Goodwin emphasized the importance of spirited debate grounded in the presence of multiple viewpoints. She says that, "[b]y building dissent into his inner circle, a president is … more likely to question his own assumptions and to weigh various consequences, leading ultimately to more farsighted decisions."[36] Inspired by Lincoln, President Barack Obama aimed to create a cabinet of people who, as he put it, "are continually pushing me out of my comfort zone."[37] His actions and words on the subject have led to a greater appreciation of the connection between diversity, more productive debates, and stronger performance both inside and outside boardrooms.

Management experts have also emphasized diversity's positive cognitive benefits bearing on decision-making. Christopher Bennett, senior fellow at Human Capital, and Richard Crisp, professor of psychology at Aston Business School, have argued that diversity militates against the herd mentality that prevails among people with similarities. As Crisp explains in his book *The Social Brain: How Diversity Made the Modern Mind*, we activate similar skills when being creative as we do

when interacting with diverse people. Diversity uses the mind's "innovation muscle."[38] Likewise, Sheen Levine, professor of management at the University of Texas, and David Stark, professor of sociology at Columbia have argued that diversity sharpens peoples' analytical skills. As they've written, "Diversity improves the way people think. By disrupting conformity, racial and ethnic diversity prompts people to scrutinize facts, think more deeply and develop their own opinions. Our findings show that such diversity actually benefits everyone, minorities and majority alike."[39]

Levine and Stark based their conclusions on several experiments they conducted in classroom-like environments, where individuals assessed the price of stocks and then traded them with one another. "When participants were in diverse company," the two write, "their answers were 58 percent more accurate. The prices they chose were much closer to the true values of the stocks. As they spent time interacting in diverse groups, their performance improved."[40] Homogenous groups yielded the opposite. People unquestioningly copied the behavior and opinions of their racial and ethnic counterparts, while "diversity brought cognitive friction that enhanced deliberation." Particularly interesting was that people of difference didn't necessarily have to impart specific knowledge—their mere *presence* was the main benefit they provided. Diversity prompts critical inquiry and the detection of errors. Ethnic diversity is like fresh air: It benefits everybody who experiences it. By disrupting conformity it produces a public good. Of course, in many situations people of difference *do* impart specific knowledge that improves decision-making. I've seen this myself during my service on boards. In one instance, a board was voting on an important decision, and board members were addressing the issue through the lens of a financial analysis. As a person of color, who has constantly had to navigate different cultures, I was more attuned to the cultural factors that might impact the organization. I advocated that we at least take culture into account. Adding this perspective enabled the board to come to a more informed decision because it had considered multiple viewpoints. On another occasion involving a different board, a female Latino board member urged that marketing collateral for the organization be printed in English and Spanish. The board adopted

her plan, and as a result the company expanded its market share and increased sales. Without a Latino perspective on the board, and without another person of difference affirming the merit of her proposal, the company might have taken another year or two to come to the same decision. Board diversity enabled the company to respond more quickly to demographic trends and to help *lead* in the marketplace.

Reflecting on the impact of board diversity at Eastern, Rivers and others at the bank point to the deep and productive discussions that now routinely take place at board meetings. It isn't simply that more varied perspectives exist on an issue, leading to a wiser, more "balanced" decision. The board has come to welcome differing or challenging views, allowing for far freer, more wide-ranging, and more candid debate. As Deborah Jackson notes, board members since the diversification push are noticeably more willing to "share all sides" of an issue and to "listen to others' perspectives." Even during moments when the debates have been uncomfortable or challenging for those present, board members have learned to respect others' viewpoints and greet them empathetically. "Can you hear beyond the words to understand that person's experience and sensitivity? We've done that. There was a bumpy moment or two in there, but we've come through to a place where we feel good about where we are."

This atmosphere of true respect and acceptance is so important— and sadly, so rare. Reporting on their research in the *Harvard Business Review*, Boris Groysberg and Deborah Bell remarked that women sitting on boards frequently noticed the persistence of unconscious bias on the part of their largely male counterparts. "Women told us they were not treated as full members of the group, though the male directors were largely oblivious to their female colleagues' experience in this regard."[41] A full 87 percent of women in their study experienced gender-specific obstacles, with their male counterparts failing to listen to them or badgering them to justify their credentials. In one case, a woman with deep financial expertise and industry knowledge was asked by others to be "less vocal" and to "stop arguing her point" during meetings. During one debate, she was posing questions about a decision "when a male colleague interrupted her and exclaimed, 'You're behaving just like my daughter! You're arguing too much—just

stop!'"[42] Based on their findings, Groysberg and Bell suggest distinguishing between diversity and inclusiveness. "Diversity is counting the numbers; inclusiveness is making the numbers count. Boards need to improve on both dimensions."

As a woman of color who has served on many boards, I, too, have been impacted by unconscious bias. On occasion, other board members have ignored a point of view I've furthered simply because of my identity. I would make a point and receive no support. A white male would make the same point a few minutes later, and the idea would seem to possess legitimacy and merit. On other occasion, on a new board, I said something that an older white male board member perceived to be smart, and he expressed surprise, not expecting such a compelling idea coming from someone like me. In these cases, board members weren't trying to insult me, and they weren't even aware that they were doing so. In their view, they were equitable and fair-minded. But on some level, they felt more comfortable and more attuned to people who looked like they did. All of us have our unconscious biases, and in some personal contexts, it may be harmless. In professional or public contexts, it's damaging and counterproductive. As a woman of color, I carried an extra burden. Not only did I have to contribute valuable ideas. I also had to navigate these kinds of situations as diplomatically as possible, always working to break down boundaries and make my fellow board members feel more comfortable with me. My white, male counterparts carried no such burden.

Because I've experienced unconscious bias so often, I appreciate the tenor and quality of Eastern Bank board discussions that Deborah Jackson describes. The trustee and committee meetings that I've attended have evinced a unique environment of trust and respect, as well as a deeper feeling that other board members *appreciate* you for your difference. With trust and respect in place, we become aware of all that connects us—our common values of inclusion and public service. It's truly a special environment, a point of pride, and a vitally important ingredient in the bank's success. If all boards were more like Eastern, corporations would be better places in which to work and contribute. They would also be more successful.

BOARD DIVERSITY AND ITS BOUNTY

Besides better decisions grounded in more candid and inclusive discussions, diversity affords an array of other benefits, including an enhanced ability to acquire and leverage talent, increased innovation, and a heightened ability to reflect the marketplace and cement the organization's reputation.[43] For Eastern, talent acquisition was especially important. "Right off the bat," Wendell Knox observes, "our board diversity allowed us to identify talent from broader pools for the board and the staff, and that has been key to our success."[44] In a number of cases, the bank has hired individuals with impressive resumes who, on account of their untraditional backgrounds, might not have thought that a bank would welcome them in, or whom Eastern might not have been able to identify and recruit. Board diversity "has helped us tremendously in improving senior management diversity," Rivers says. "It's tough to attract diverse senior leaders because they don't necessarily want to be trailblazers. They say to themselves, 'I'm already in a safe place and I've got a good job. I don't know if I want to take that risk.' But when prospective senior hires could see diversity not merely among the rank and file but also on the board, they felt more comfortable taking a chance and bringing their experience and expertise to work at Eastern."[45]

Enhanced talent acquisition has directly resulted in more innovation at Eastern. In 2014, the bank established an innovation lab called "Eastern Labs," headed up by an experienced entrepreneur formerly affiliated with Capital One. As Rivers observes, the four initial leaders of the lab were all white men with Anglican names. "Yet they represented diversity for us. The reason was that they approached business challenges differently than we did." Within two years the lab had grown to 110 people, many of whom would never have considered working at an organization like Eastern were it not for the presence of the initial group in the lab. This group helped establish Eastern as a place for young, ambitious, entrepreneurial types, an organization where novelty, forward thinking, and risk-taking weren't just tolerated but encouraged and funded.

One of the first products developed by Eastern Labs was the Express Business Loan. Instead of waiting days or weeks for capital, this

loan platform can provide up to $100,000 to small-business owners within five minutes of starting the application process. Eastern has been the top Small Business Administration lender in New England for eight years running.[46] The research and consulting firm Celent acknowledged the innovation lab's efforts by naming Eastern its Model Bank of the Year, selecting it from more than one hundred other banks worldwide. Celent's senior vice president lauded Eastern for "building an entirely new loan origination system from scratch in 14 months, using internal resources" and for achieving results "on par with anything that the most disruptive fintech company has achieved in this space."[47] In May 2017, Numerated Growth Technologies launched as a spinoff from Eastern Labs, providing this platform to other banks.

Eastern has also redesigned its local retail bank branches and integrated cutting-edge voice-recognition technology to stay relevant among customers. We might consider board diversity as yet another "innovation" that complements these efforts. For years, Eastern has mobilized diversity to support its expansion into new markets in Boston and surrounding areas. Beyond the usual tactics of launching ad campaigns and sponsoring local events, Eastern has focused on networking inside the local business community and local interest groups. Diversity plays a key role, giving the bank far more credibility to gain a foothold with diverse individuals, who in many cases have historically regarded banking institutions skeptically. "If you've got a broader set of people in the decision-making and strategy bodies," Wendell Knox argues, "they are going to be able to bring you an incremental set of contacts from their networks and bring in new customers."[48]

More broadly, Eastern's leadership regards board diversity as a powerful way to stay relevant to communities with changing demographics. "We need to know how we're going to better serve different communities," Rivers says. "How do they want to be communicated with? What are their particular preferences? How do they use our products? What do they think about banks and insurance companies?"[49] Rivers notes that ethnic communities differ considerably from one another, in ways that far transcend language. Board diversity has allowed Eastern to get its messaging right and has prompted it to feature more people of color in its advertising. Rivers also points to

Eastern's annual reports. "You look at our reports from ten years ago as compared to now, and you can see an obvious difference. But it wouldn't be obvious to make a change like that if your lens is exclusively white and male."

Board diversity also connects Eastern to its mission going back more than two hundred years of providing underserved populations with fairly priced banking services. You can't serve communities well unless you also look like them. With changing demographics, *all* companies will need to look more like their customer base. And the faster pace at which markets are evolving will also require that companies become nimbler and sharper in their decision-making. Companies don't have the luxury of waiting an extra two years to ensure that their marketing reflects the needs of their constituencies, or to come out with a new product that a specific customer group may want or need. Companies need to move fast, and board diversity enables both speed and acuity of insight. Craig Weatherup, a board member at Macy's and former PepsiCo CEO, puts it well: "Boards that aren't looking for digitally savvy members, female, and ethnic board members are really going to fall behind. It's a key part of staying relevant in today's market."[50]

There really are no downsides to board diversity and inclusion. As Knox notes, even the advocacy that has accompanied board diversity at Eastern hasn't alienated large groups of customers. If it had, the institution wouldn't have continued to grow. Rivers goes further, identifying board diversity and advocacy as a strategically important means of differentiating the bank in customers' eyes. Many companies give their money and time to benefit the community. Very few take risks to advocate on behalf of inclusion and to promote diversity at the very top of the organization. Advocacy, he argues, is ultimately smart business. It "matters to people. Whenever we have the podium somewhere and we speak up someone invariably comes up and says, 'I love what you said. I'm going to move my accounts to Eastern.' It's amazing to me how many businesses have not caught on to this."

The challenge facing any company is to stick with board diversity and inclusion, even during the tough times, and even if it means taking considerable risks. "You have to be very intentional," Rivers says. "You have to get out there and develop relationships, and you have to

be willing to do things that are unique.[51] You can't allow yourself to fall back on excuses, like appointing white males after claiming an insufficient pipeline of diverse candidates." Deborah Jackson also counsels vigilance on the part of companies that have begun to diversify, particularly when it comes to the tenor of board conversations. "The moment you become comfortable, you will slip in areas that require sensitivity around diversity. Sometimes it's as simple as a look you give another person that says, 'I can't believe you just said that.' Of course, if you've built a culture of inclusion, a single look won't be fatal. Board members will quickly affirm their respect for differences and move on. You learn to give others the benefit of the doubt, but you can only do that if there's trust."[52]

Eastern isn't allowing itself to get too comfortable. The bank continues to push itself to become more accepting, and to recruit top talent into the organization. When Rivers was announced as Eastern's chair and CEO, he brought on a talented African American banking executive, Quincy Miller, to succeed him as president. Additionally, Rivers looks forward to taking stronger stances on behalf of underserved groups, with the support of a diverse board. "We strive to be a community bank with a conscience—one that is willing to advocate for solutions to social issues facing our neighbors and ourselves," he says. "As we begin the next two hundred years of this company, it's going to be in a way that our community has never seen before."[53] Let's hope so. And let's hope that leaders across industries take notice of Eastern and do more to diversify their own boards.

BOARD DIVERSITY AND BEYOND

On December 12, 2017, my organization, The Partnership, presented Bob Rivers with the Bennie Wiley CEO Diversity Award, bestowed annually to an outstanding Massachusetts CEO who has demonstrated exceptional leadership in diversity and inclusion.[54] Bob was an outstanding choice, for all the reasons I've explained in this chapter. But listening to Bennie Wiley welcome him to the stage, I was thrilled that our business community would learn about still other impressive ways that he has led on diversity.

Under Bob's leadership, in April 2017, Eastern launched the Business Equity Initiative (BEI) to address wealth disparities in our communities and help accelerate the growth of local enterprises of color, increasing job opportunities and wealth creation in our neighborhoods. Along with Nancy Stager, executive vice president of human resources and charitable giving at Eastern, Bob worked to understand why Boston has the greatest income and wealth gap of any major city in this country; the region's greatest inequalities and wealth gaps existed among Latino and black businesses. To help address these gaps, Eastern has allocated $10 million between 2017 and 2020 to BEI. The funding will provide diverse businesses with the opportunity to grow, build capacity, invest capital, and connect with larger anchor institutions to help sustain and power their future growth.

As Bob explained that evening, BEI was part of a larger vision he had to increase regional board diversity. Bob credited so much of the progress he has seen at Eastern to his diverse board, with people like Deborah Jackson guiding him, challenging him, and helping others make the best business decisions. The BEI program, he explained, was designed to increase the visibility and participation of many talented leaders of color from minority-owned businesses on the city's boards. "We're all on a lot of boards, and they all look like me," Bob noted bluntly, referring to his white male counterparts that dominate board membership rosters. Part of the problem, Bob explained, is that diverse businesses are often so small that the talented people powering them don't have time to serve on boards. BEI wants to change that dynamic by helping to grow these businesses into much larger enterprises. But what makes Bob such a visionary leader is that he wants to use BEI to help bridge the leadership gap in businesses plaguing our commonwealth and create an ecosystem of diverse talent that can be tapped across our business communities and bring more diversity and inclusion to the C-suite and boards of other private-sector companies.

We've been talking about diversity for a long time, but the needle has barely moved, especially when it comes to diversifying our companies' senior leadership. That's unfortunate, since board diversity is vital to preparing businesses for the inevitable shifts that will occur— indeed already *are* occurring. One of the many benefits that diverse

boards bring is a greater connection to the communities in which businesses operate. As I'll explore in the following chapter, the way companies engage with community stakeholders has come a long way in the twenty-first century. Instead of being siloed in corporate social responsibility (CSR) departments, community impact programming that encompasses and engages our diverse community stakeholders is becoming a focal point for organizations. The challenge is to channel that programming more directly toward diversity-related issues. Companies that manage to do so achieve a significant advantage over those that don't. Community relations constitutes another vital area that enables the most inclusive companies to win.

CONNECTING WITH COMMUNITY AT JOHN HANCOCK

IN 2000, MY HUSBAND, BERNIE, and I had the privilege of staying at the United States embassy in Dar es Salaam, Tanzania, as the guests of our friend and colleague, US ambassador Charles Stith. The country was still reeling from the 1998 bombings of the US embassies in Tanzania and Nairobi, Kenya, which left 224 dead, five thousand injured, and the two countries' economies in crisis.[1] We spent a good deal of time reflecting on the difficult tasks of healing, energizing, and rebuilding the Tanzanian and Kenyan economies. We also took the opportunity to go on safari in Kenya, exploring our heritage and focusing on Africa's impact on the United States. What caught my eye, as we traveled from village to village, was how many people I saw running. In Boston, I often spotted joggers running for exercise or sport along the Charles River and other popular pathways. However, in Kenya, everyone ran. Uniformed schoolchildren ran to school, smiling at one another. Adults ran together as well on their way to work, somehow managing to engage in conversation during their daily commutes.

One image of Kenyans running stood out above the rest. One afternoon, as the sun began to set, Bernie and I had just settled into our safari seats when we spotted a tribesman running across the desert

plain, the brilliant orange, red, and yellow of the sunset framing his silhouette. In that moment, I finally internalized why Kenyans tended to dominate international running competitions. I already knew about how Kenyans' starch-based diet, superior adaptability to altitude, unusual grit and determination, barefoot running style, and even slender ankles and calves had helped them set an astonishing number of world records.[2] Now, I came to realize that running for Kenyans wasn't simply a sport or athletic passion. It was a deeply meaningful, even spiritual activity—a mindset and way of life.[3]

I wasn't a runner myself, but I had connected with the sport in my role as senior vice president of corporate responsibility and brand marketing at John Hancock Financial Services. Part of my job was to oversee corporate social responsibility programs associated with our long-standing sponsorship of the Boston Marathon, the world's oldest annual marathon and one of the city's most popular and beloved traditions. Every year, John Hancock's marathon bib program helped raise millions of dollars for local nonprofits. Now, as I contemplated the extraordinary significance of running in Kenya, I had an idea. Wouldn't it be advantageous if Boston's public school students, many of whom were African American, could learn about Kenya in a unique way, discovering why Kenyans are the world's best long-distance runners and why they win the Boston Marathon year after year?

This insight would form the basis for a new philanthropic program at John Hancock, the Boston Marathon Kenya Project. This program built upon a creative initiative already in place, in which John Hancock brought in elite Kenyan runners to an elementary school in the suburban Massachusetts town of Hopkinton, where each year thirty thousand registered runners descend at the beginning of the marathon. Tom Payzant, then superintendent of Boston public schools, proposed this new program be geared toward third graders because third graders learned about world geography that year in school. The Boston Marathon Kenya Project would thus feature employee volunteers from John Hancock, who would teach third-grade students in the diverse Boston neighborhoods of Roxbury and Dorchester. These employee volunteers would introduce students to Kenya's geography, topography, tribal makeup, and long history of producing great

athletes. The employees would make learning engaging and interactive in the classroom, and in addition would travel with the children to the African Tropical Forest in Boston's Franklin Park Zoo, directing students on scavenger hunts where they could learn to correctly identify Kenya's indigenous flora and fauna. John Hancock employee volunteers would also personalize the lessons, dividing the classes into different Kenyan tribes, teaching them Swahili songs and commonplace greetings and expressions.

The program, which began in 2001, was repeated year after year. Employees loved it, as did the children. We even "upped the ante," so to speak, by arranging for Kenyan athletes to participate as well. Each year, the Kenyan winners of the previous year's marathon visited the schools to talk with the students about their tribes, the food they ate, and how the altitude in Kenya made their lungs so strong. "Why do you run?" the third graders would always ask, transfixed by the athletes.

"Well," one marathoner indicated, "I had to run to school to be on time. And I would run to get home at evening. And sometimes I would run home for lunch too."

Students were also fascinated to discover that most of these winners didn't keep their earnings for themselves but shared them with their local villages and communities. The students gleaned a powerful lesson, one that I tried to model through all of John Hancock's community-relations programming: when individuals succeed, the entire community should and even must succeed with them.

We at John Hancock might have contented ourselves with bringing employees and athletes together with students, but we saw an opportunity to take our engagement with the marathon further. The Boston Marathon falls on the third Monday in April each year, the day of the state's Patriots' Day holiday. In 2001 we began inviting the students into John Hancock's corporate offices for a special "Marathon Monday" visit. For some of these diverse children, the trip up the elevator in the John Hancock tower, Boston's tallest building, was likely as exotic as visiting Kenya itself. Our iconic building's sleek, shimmering facade was a sight they might glimpse on the distant skyline from the more modest streets in Roxbury or Dorchester. The building represented a world of power that was foreign to some students. Now,

however, on this momentous day for the city, the tower became a place they could access—a place that in some small sense now belonged to them. I'll never forget how one little girl, Lucy, looked up at me with her chubby cheeks and said, "When I grow up, can I come and work for John Hancock?"

After hosting the children, we guided them to the nearby marathon finish line, where they enjoyed VIP seating. On our walk to these seats the children proudly brandished their "credentials"—plastic passes needed to gain entry to the restricted areas—to police officers or anyone who asked. From their VIP stands, they waved Kenyan and American flags and watched as runners completed the grueling competition. In 2005, Catherine Ndereba, who had won the marathon the year before, visited with the children at the African Tropical Forest just days prior to Marathon Monday. That year, the children had a front-row seat as Ndereba crossed the finish line, clinching her fourth Boston Marathon victory (the first four-time women's winner in history).[4] The kids went wild!

Back in the early 2000s, many companies undertook philanthropic and community-relations activities, but seldom with John Hancock's depth and unique level of engagement. It was more common for companies to write a check to a cause or nonprofit organization. These days, fortunately, many companies do engage deeply with community and public service work, under the mantle of vibrant CSR or community impact programs. From the corporate perspective, such programs aren't simply good publicity. They also confer competitive advantage, increasing a company's reputation, energizing its workforce, and bolstering recruitment efforts. While some academics contend that CSR doesn't truly impact a company's bottom line, my career has taught me that such programs are vital and help forge invaluable relationships with customers, municipal governments, regional nonprofit organizations, local schools, lenders, potential employees, suppliers, and the community at large.[5] Such relationships aren't neatly reflected on corporate balance sheets but are nonetheless quite significant. Companies largely agree with this premise, which is why, as one CSR expert has noted, "We've witnessed a stunning transition as corporate social responsibility . . . evolved from a nice-to-have silo to a fundamental

strategic priority for businesses large and small."[6] In addition to help-ing businesses, such programs have also injected much-needed capital into local communities and have produced social and environmental breakthroughs throughout the world.

As important as CSR has become, companies can take these pro-grams further by following John Hancock's lead and tailoring them to more diverse stakeholders. As academics Katrin Hansen and Cathrine Seierstad note, though CSR and diversity management are two prom-inent areas of corporate engagement, there is "little intersection be-tween the fields, and their relationship is understudied."[7] That needs to change. Marrying CSR and diversity seems warranted on the basis of geography alone. Most American companies are headquartered or maintain facilities in large cities such as New York, Houston, Dallas, Chicago, and Atlanta. As with Boston, these cities tend to run ahead of the demographic curve, having already achieved majority-minority status, decades prior to 2042. By engaging with the community in these locales, companies are pursuing de facto diversity initiatives. It follows that most companies wishing to embrace diversity as a strate-gic and operational paradigm should engage to the fullest with CSR programs aimed at improving the lives of local residents.

When companies understand how their CSR programs can im-pact diverse communities, and when they tailor such programs to help empower these communities, they will find their CSR efforts can achieve durable, far-reaching impacts for both community and company. Take the Boston Marathon Kenya Project. The program made a difference in the lives of local children, the majority of whom were students of color. Instead of learning about Kenya from a text-book, they physically interfaced with Kenya's natural habitat at the zoo and engaged elite Kenyan runners in classroom conversations. These majority African American students had the opportunity to speak with Kenyan cultural ambassadors who served as examples of black leadership and excellence that they could admire and emulate. By venturing into the Hancock office tower, the students learned that the Boston business community valued and embraced them. They weren't outsiders anymore. And Lucy will probably soon work her way up the company pipeline!

The program also produced manifold benefits for John Hancock. As workforce surveys indicated, employees learned a great deal while volunteering and were proud to work for a company so committed to engaging youth and making a difference in the community. Employees felt more valued in the larger community as well. The program also engendered good will among municipal government officials, helping to distinguish the company as a positive force in the community.

The Boston Marathon Kenya Project was one of many CSR programs that connected the company with Boston's neighborhoods.[8] John Hancock employees now volunteer more than thirteen thousand hours a year to help improve the greater Boston area. The company also sponsors a series of corporate partnership programs such as InnerCity Weightlifting, which provides at-risk youth with careers in personal fitness, and Citizen Schools, which prepares eighth-grade students with skills they'll need to thrive in high school. Thanks to the company's community and sponsorship presence, Boston's nonprofit sector received $20 million in grants, matching gifts, and fundraising through the 2016 Boston Marathon. And those numbers are increasing. In 2017, the company provided more than one thousand invitational entries to 172 nonprofits. These nonprofits in turn gave these entries (called marathon bibs) to supporters of their cause, who competed in the marathon and raised money on behalf of the organizations. In 2017, more than one thousand John Hancock–sponsored runners raised $12.3 million. In the process of benefiting the community at large, these impact efforts also energize stakeholders, bolster recruitment pipelines, and strengthen John Hancock's corporate brand.

As we look ahead, more companies will need to create CSR programs that equal or even outshine those at John Hancock. Community stakeholders require more of today's corporations. Actively managed and diversity-oriented CSR is emerging as a vital and integral component of local and global businesses. Such community initiatives—when executed authentically and strategically—are quickly becoming an important means of recruiting the best talent, ensuring shareholder value, and generating brand loyalty. As you think about your business in the years ahead, consider what you might do to embody an

ideal similar to the one we taught to Boston schoolchildren: when *your* company does well, so does the entire community.

CORPORATION AND COMMUNITY: THE EVOLUTION OF A RELATIONSHIP

Modern CSR programs first took shape in the 1990s, largely emerging in reaction to socially engaged consumers and NGOs, or nongovernmental organizations, who demanded heightened ethical commitments on the part of companies.[9] At the time, AIDS was sweeping the world, and people around the world turned for help to pharmaceutical companies, who stood to benefit little from providing it. Around the same time, fast-food operators found themselves cast as culprits in the global obesity epidemic, and fossil-fuel giants discovered that if they extracted oil and natural gas with little regard for the earth, entire nations would boycott them and wreak havoc on stock prices (as happened in 1995, following oil giant Shell's decision to sink the Brent Spar oil platform and buoy into the sea).[10] In the late 1990s, global textile makers and retailers such as Nike were also attacked for using child labor and exploiting workers, suffering public relations turmoil and lower stock prices. "The Nike product has become synonymous with slave wages, forced overtime and arbitrary abuse," declared Nike CEO Phil Knight in 1998. "I truly believe that the American consumer does not want to buy products made in abusive conditions."[11]

Since the 1990s, the corporate world has undergone what CSR experts Jeffrey Hollender and Bill Breen have termed the "Responsibility Revolution."[12] Many companies no longer find it sufficient to abide by international ethical standards. Instead, leading corporations try to stand at the forefront of positive global change. John Hancock provided me with the opportunity to take part in this transformation. Right around the time the Boston Marathon Kenya Program began, I chose to rename the department "corporate responsibility" instead of "community relations." Here's why. When Hurricane Katrina devastated New Orleans in the summer of 2005, I organized Boston Women Build in the Bayou, a group of thirty-five Boston-based leaders, including the then first lady of Massachusetts, Diane Patrick, and then first

lady of Boston, Angela Menino, who both traveled to New Orleans to help that city rebuild. Along with a group of local John Hancock sales executives, we participated in the construction of the "Boston House," which one of Katrina's victims, a single mother, later occupied. For me, this wasn't a "community relations" action—it was part of my corporation's *responsibility* to support a distressed community. The rebranding of John Hancock's department away from community relations was a way to telegraph the message that as our company grows and benefits, so, too, do our local communities. And when our communities are in trouble, it is our responsibility to help.[13] When we returned home from New Orleans, we kept this community-oriented momentum alive, with a group of John Hancock volunteers helping to create housing for Boston's underserved communities under the auspices of the 500 Women Build Boston program.

In the wake of the responsibility revolution, global retailers such as Nike have chosen to respond to consumer interests by implementing living wages and working to end child labor. And Nike has promoted sports for kids and active lifestyles in general. Although much more remains to be done, large companies are addressing an array of social ills, assuming a role that government has traditionally filled—and making progress.[14] Of course, not all companies behave altruistically all the time. This past year, 2017, saw a number of scandals involving corporate malfeasance—Wells Fargo defrauding millions of customers, Volkswagen lying about emissions scandals, United Airlines brutally dragging off and injuring a physician passenger from one of its planes. In all too many organizations, CSR continues to sit in an uneasy tension with the drive for profits, while in some increasingly monopolistic and ruthless companies, executives are using any means necessary to drive results. Overall, though, corporate stakeholders are increasingly demanding that CSR mean something, not just serve as a convenient way of masking corporate misdeeds.

Whether involving their customer bases, investors, employee recruitment and retention initiatives, or supply-chain integrity, CSR is a twenty-first-century business imperative. A 2017 Cone Communications research study provides some arresting figures, illustrating the singular importance of contemporary CSR:

- 86 percent of Americans believe businesses should accomplish more than make money, and 79 percent want businesses to augment their CSR initiatives.
- More than 63 percent of Americans (and 71 percent of millennials) want companies to *lead environmental and social change.*
- 70 percent of Americans expect companies to assume such leadership even when it doesn't help the company financially.
- 87 percent of Americans would patronize a business if it was consistent with their values; 76 percent reported they would decline to support businesses that didn't embrace their values.
- 89 percent of Americans are willing to switch brands (for a similar product) if a different company more thoroughly embraced their values.
- 87 percent of Americans are more likely to trust companies that drive social and environmental change, and 88 percent are more loyal to such companies.
- 65 percent of respondents said they research whether a company's purported CSR program is legitimate.[15]

Most noteworthy for our purposes,

- 87 percent of Americans want companies to address racial equality, 84 percent want them to address women's rights, and 64 percent want them to address LGBTQ rights.

The rise of the purpose-driven corporation, simultaneously engaging local community needs as well as major global problems, has been an admirable development. But companies still have a long way to go to satisfy stakeholders and deliver to communities. One of the chief obstacles they face is structural. As Jeffrey Hollender and Bill Breen relate, CSR initiatives are often "deputized, then compartmentalized" within organizations.[16] Take Japanese automobile giant Toyota, which garnered international acclaim following the debut of its eco-conscious Prius line. In 2007, the company's commitment to the environment was nearly dismantled when it lobbied against heightened environmental standards in Detroit. "That's what happens when CSR

is decoupled from the organization's everyday workings," Hollender and Breen concluded. "Toyota took a hit to its reputation and lost a tremendous opportunity to do even better by the environment."[17]

Even in the absence of overt hypocrisy, consumers and stakeholders are understandably skeptical about a company's purported altruism. That's because it's often easy to discern that a business's laudable rhetoric thinly masks shrewd business strategy. As Aaron Chatterji, associate professor at Duke University's Fuqua School of Business, suggests, "When Walmart requires its suppliers to be more energy efficient, the company lowers its costs. When General Electric champions investments in clean energy, its wind-turbine business benefits."[18] In 2015, Facebook made international headlines when its founder, Mark Zuckerberg, announced he would allocate 99 percent of his $45 billion fortune to charitable causes. The *New York Times*, *Wall Street Journal*, *Bloomberg*, and other major media outlets lauded the gesture, declaring that the tech giant had set a new bar for corporate giving. When they examined the fine print, they quickly changed their minds. "Mark Zuckerberg did not donate $45 billion to charity," journalist Jesse Eisinger clarified. "Mr. Zuckerberg created an investment vehicle" that would garner him extraordinary tax advantages, while essentially enabling him to move his net worth "from one pocket to the other."[19] A 2009 McKinsey study referred to such actions not as CSR, but rather "propaganda," which is "potentially dangerous if it exposes a gap between the company's words and actions."[20] The same logic holds for diversity-oriented CSR. Your local community doesn't want you to simply espouse community support in your promotional materials or write checks. It wants you to develop a relationship and real partnership. Your customers, employees, investors, and community stakeholders look to you to embody a commitment to your increasingly diverse local community. And if you don't, they'll likely take their business elsewhere.

BUILDING AND BOLSTERING THE BRAND

As I've suggested, one way that well-executed, diversity-based CSR can be a boon to a company is by helping to build and enhance its brand.

During his visionary tenure at John Hancock, David D'Alessandro served in a variety of leadership roles—president, COO, then chairman and CEO—from 1984 to 2004. During that time, John Hancock transitioned from a mutual company to a publicly traded corporation and global industry power player. A big part of that transition involved a redefinition of the company's brand. Following D'Alessandro's leadership at John Hancock, the *New York Times* in 1999 ranked the company among "the 100 most powerful corporate, media and product brands of the 20th century."[21] Many factors accounted for the rise of the company's stature during D'Alessandro's tenure, but as I saw firsthand, community-impact programming played an important role.

His valuing of community led to the development of the company's Summer of Opportunity program and demonstrated the power of uniting CSR with diversity measures.[22] During the mid-1990s (before I joined John Hancock), when youth violence began to rise in Boston, D'Alessandro asked Mayor Thomas Menino and police commissioner Paul Evans how his company might assist. Rather than solicit funds, these city officials told him that urban teens needed summer jobs and skills training to steer them away from crime. In 1994, D'Alessandro acted, partnering with the Boston Police Department to create the Summer of Opportunity program.

That program employed forty students whom the Boston Police Department deemed at-risk, pairing them with John Hancock employee volunteers who introduced them to important job skills. The John Hancock–headquartered program also prepared and placed students in a yearlong after-school internship and summer program. By providing viable skills and confidence-building experiences, the program offered youth an alternative to a life of crime.

I learned so much from David D'Alessandro and am forever grateful. David taught me to think big and told me anything worth doing should have a huge impact. As a result, in 2008, I used the John Hancock Summer of Opportunity jobs program as a model to create the MLK Scholars program, the largest corporate summer jobs program of its kind in the country. Using a map of the city's neighborhoods I had secured from city hall, my colleagues and I identified various zip codes in which local youth most needed summer employment. As we

had suspected, the pushpins came to cluster in the most underserved and diverse communities of Boston—areas that happened to have substantial African American and Hispanic communities. In 2008, we awarded six hundred summer placements, many in underresourced nonprofits, to area youth residing in those zip codes. By providing jobs to young people clustered in the most underserved (and diverse) neighborhoods, we were fulfilling the company's longstanding commitment to serve Boston youth most in need.

Since then, John Hancock's reach has ballooned. In 2017, the company provided $1 million to support sixty-four nonprofit community groups. To date, the program has awarded some six thousand summer positions—and counting.[23] Under my talented successor, Tom Crohan, who oversees corporate responsibility at John Hancock, the program has become much more strategic and powerful. Nonprofits receive funding to hire young people for resourceful summer jobs that enable students to gain a variety of skills in coding, marketing, accounting, and other areas. In this way, as Crohan described to me in an interview, the program helps young people prepare for the contemporary job market. Crohan observes that today's job market requires specialization from the onset. In addition to helping them develop these skills at an early age, the MLK Scholars program provides young people with résumé workshops and financial literacy training to ensure they understand the basics of credit card interest rates, compounding interest, and money management. Instead of simply providing Boston youth with summer jobs, the MLK Scholars program empowers the next generation of leaders, ensuring they have the professional skills to thrive in a changing economy and the personal-finance skills to learn how to accumulate wealth.

I'll never forget one young African American woman, Stacy Botus, who in 2010 came to John Hancock for her summer placement. She was scheduled for a two o'clock interview but never showed up. After waiting for fifteen minutes, we called the reception area. "Nobody checked in," the receptionist reported, "but there's a young girl sitting over there on the couch." As it turns out, the young lady was there for her afternoon appointment but had never been in an office building before and had no idea how to check in. Following her interview, she

was placed in our CSR department that summer and became part of our vibrant employee culture. She even attended company luncheon seminars designed to inform all Hancock staff members of the various impacts of the divisions within the organization. After one such lunchtime gathering, she said, "I know what I'm going to be when I graduate from college." Looking at me, beaming, she said, "I'm going to be an investment manager at John Hancock." I was floored. She began the summer not knowing anything about office building protocol or how to check in for an interview. Two months later, she so strongly identified with the company that she wanted to make it a focal point of her future career and life. What a testament to how summer jobs programs and exposure to corporate opportunities can transform lives.

This experience also underscored the importance of actively managed programs. The MLK Scholars program didn't simply write a check for a community initiative. Just like the Boston Marathon Kenya Project, MLK Scholars ventured into the local community and invited residents inside the company. This reciprocal relationship demonstrated the depth of the organization's commitment to the community. In the eyes of participants, employees, and other stakeholders, John Hancock wasn't simply paying lip service to diversity. It was *living* it. The John Hancock brand gained a patina of authenticity, which in turn would allow the company to garner value, trust, and loyalty from stakeholders, including employees and customers.

John Hancock's sponsorship of the Best Buddies Challenge bicycle ride likewise illustrates how the company powerfully engages with its diverse community. In 2009, John Hancock added to its list of community sponsorships Best Buddies, a nonprofit organization that aids those with intellectual development disabilities (IDD).[24] Best Buddies' signature event is an annual hundred-mile cycling fund-raiser that starts in Boston and ends on Cape Cod. John Hancock has helped sponsor many riders each year. Best Buddies' founder, Anthony Shriver, praised John Hancock in 2015 for having raised $800,000 over the course of its long-term sponsorship, helping the nonprofit advance its mission of fostering inclusion, friendship, and employment opportunities for people with IDD.[25]

In addition to providing financial contributions and sponsoring employee cycling teams, Rob Friedman, John Hancock's assistant vice president of sponsorships and events management, brought Best Buddies inside the company by hiring participants served by the nonprofit. In this connection, Friedman had the opportunity to interview Dudley Williams III, an African American man with intellectual disabilities who had been involved with Best Buddies for several years.[26] Dudley had succeeded at a number of part-time jobs in Boston, but now he was interested in securing full-time employment, particularly as he had completed Best Buddies' leadership development programming. Rob hired Dudley to work in his sponsorships and event management department as a marketing coordinator. And Dudley has continued to excel in this role, taking on additional challenges. Every spring, for instance, he helps ensure the success of the Boston Marathon sponsorship by helping to support volunteers, athletes, and spectators. As Rob observes, "He's an integral part of our whole Boston Marathon planning project, which is a major undertaking for John Hancock."[27] And Dudley is a staple of the larger John Hancock community as well, making the rounds to ensure that staffers' marketing adminstration needs are met. His strong interpersonal skills, tenacity, and loyalty to the company make him a valued part of the team.

Dudley's competencies and self-confidence have steadily increased during his time at John Hancock. But he's given so much to everyone else. "I think a program like Best Buddies is a terrific asset to John Hancock," Friedman says. "It teaches our employees about diversity and working with different populations."[28] For Friedman, Dudley has "opened everyone's eyes to not look at what people aren't capable of, but to think about what they are capable of." Dudley's presence also bolsters John Hancock's image in the eyes of employees. After all, people like Dudley are routinely overlooked in the job market. As Laurel Rossi, CEO of the nonprofit Creative Spirit, detailed, "The employment rate among those with intellectual disabilities is around 15 percent. It's one of the worst diversity issues we're facing as a society, yet no one is talking about it."[29] It's easy to support others who look and think like you, but quite another thing to make underrepresented members of the community an integral part of your organization. By

employing a person like Dudley, and by engaging deeply with the Best Buddies program, John Hancock reaffirms its reputation as a meaningful place to work, a leader in the local community, and a company that values differences.

Beyond its importance for employee morale and engagement, diversity- and inclusion-oriented CSR is increasingly imperative when it comes to attracting a talented workforce. The millennial generation will soon dominate the workforce, accounting for three-quarters of all US employees by 2025, and half of those around the globe. Talented millennials increasingly consider a company's social impact in the world as crucial when deciding whether to accept a job offer. As the 2014 Millennial Impact report demonstrated, "Millennial employees most appreciated cause initiatives such as volunteering, service activities or making a donation that helped their surrounding community."[30] Millennials value how businesses impact the community and the character of business cultures. If human resources departments don't provide satisfactory answers, this talent will work elsewhere. By building diversity into its DNA via CSR, John Hancock makes itself a much more alluring brand in the eyes of prospective hires. Not only that: the company's MLK Scholars program has directly served to build a diverse pipeline of talent. The program helps train future workers, providing local talent with the skills they need to enter the workforce and succeed.

Micho Spring, who leads global corporate practice for the public relations firm Weber Shandwick, also understands how integral community impact programs are to recruitment efforts.[31] "Having deep roots in the community has gone from a wise choice to something that millennials now expect," she told me. That insight drives Weber Shandwick's approach to many parts of its business, including global mergers and acquisitions. Most of Weber Shandwick's competitors send their US workforces overseas to staff global accounts. Weber Shandwick, by contrast, expands its global reach by acquiring preexisting companies that are already rooted in the home community. Having a diverse group of people in their global offices who are attuned to the local community is enormously important for Weber Shandwick's clients. Such locally rooted diverse teams allow the firm

to understand relevant issues affecting the region and forecast risks for potential PR campaigns. "You've got to be community involved, community sensitive, and you've got to have core values that reflect diversity and inclusion," Micho said. One embodiment of this commitment is Weber Shandwick's annual social impact competition. Every office and department at the company develops and undertakes a community impact project and they compete to see which one has the most value for the local community.

Sarah Braswell, vice president of Weber Shandwick's Washington, DC, office, created a project that landed her a spot as a competition finalist. Braswell was appalled by the rates of childhood hunger afflicting the DC metro region and decided to do something about it. As her preliminary research revealed, a startling two hundred thousand children were at risk for hunger in the larger metropolitan area, with fifty-six thousand at-risk youth in the District of Columbia alone. That's one in two DC children. Her social impact initiative addressed this issue by partnering with Martha's Table, a local nonprofit agency that helps to raise awareness and fight hunger. Braswell used her communications expertise to help Martha's Table increase its nonprofit donations and bolster volunteerism efforts.

As at John Hancock, providing these capital resources was just the beginning. Braswell and her colleagues created and operated the "Joyful Foods Market," a pop-up farmers' market at an underserved DC-based elementary school. Braswell's colleagues served as market volunteers, guiding elementary students through cooking classes and professional culinary demonstrations, providing each child with up to twenty-three pounds of fresh fruits, vegetables, and healthy canned items. In the process, they got kids excited about cooking and healthy eating. Like the Boston Marathon Kenya Project, this program wasn't explicitly framed as a diversity initiative. But metropolitan DC joined Boston, New York, Las Vegas, San Diego, and Memphis as metro areas that became majority-minority in the early twenty-first century.[32] This social impact program is thus a diversity initiative by default, helping local families and children in the diverse region to succeed and thrive.

Such diversity-oriented CSR or community impact programs enhance a company's reputation in the wider community and among

potential business partners. Take suppliers. In recent years, Tom Crohan has noticed that John Hancock's supplier procurement questionnaires have become more thoughtful and more geared toward questions of equity and ethics. Suppliers increasingly prioritize social and environmental sustainability and want to know how John Hancock is positioning itself relative to these values. If the company can't provide adequate answers, they'll seek other business partners and investors. "If you take a broad view of CSR," Crohan says, "expectations have risen dramatically. If you're not doing it, and doing it well, you are falling behind." It matters to suppliers that you're working to further diversity. If you've engaged as strongly as John Hancock has been, you have an advantage.

In 2004, when John Hancock announced plans to merge with international financial giant Manulife, the company discovered that strong community engagement conferred regulatory benefits as well. This corporate transaction required government approval. I remember my colleague Tom Samoluk, then vice president of government relations, and I accompanying executive management to present our case before the Massachusetts Division of Insurance. At the hearing, we had the opportunity to detail our company's civic initiatives serving the diverse neighborhoods of Boston to officials on Beacon Hill. These government officials acknowledged John Hancock's strong civic participation in the community. "That's why we're concerned," they professed. "We don't want to lose that in our community." Tom Samoluk and I assured them that we would represent the US face of our international parent company Manulife. The merger would enable our business to grow, we told them, and as a result we would be able to provide even more community support. The officials felt comfortable that our responsibility and strong efforts in our community would continue. In this instance, our reputation and commitment to community served as important factors in regulators ultimately approving the merger.

Looking beyond branding, we find that diversity-based CSR programs can yield other important benefits for companies, such as helping to open new markets. By providing financial literacy courses, John Hancock helps ensure that its consumers in the region will be able to buy

its investment products and use its financial services. Traditionally, Crohan observes, John Hancock's advisers primarily sold insurance to high-net-worth individuals. Now, thanks to the rise of digital technologies, middle- and lower-income consumers have more access to the financial services market. The MLK Scholars program is a great way of accessing and gaining insight into these new consumer groups. "As the country is changing, the customer profile is changing," Crohan notes, "and we want to be sure we're well positioned to serve that new market."

Diversity-based CSR efforts also enhance marketing and innovation efforts by providing companies with a greater understanding of new markets. I'll detail how diversity outreach helps companies create the most effective marketing campaigns and innovative product lines a bit later. For now, it's worth pointing out that John Hancock has benefitted in these areas thanks to its CSR efforts. In recent years, the company's involvement with area youths has clued it into trends affecting young people—trends that many of John Hancock's competitors can't directly access. In particular, the company learned quite early on that young people were increasingly interested in socially responsible investment. That insight led John Hancock in 2017 to launch COIN, a socially conscious investment startup designed to "build tools for people to improve their financial lives while getting conscious about their investments."[33] If an investor is worried about climate change, for example, this product allows her to simultaneously avoid environmentally irresponsible companies while allocating funds into renewable technologies. As Crohan argues, it would have been challenging for the company to create this pathbreaking product had it not been engaging so deeply with diverse local communities. "I think our social partnerships play a big role in forging products like COIN," Crohan notes. The products in turn help reinforce John Hancock's empathetic, customer-centric brand identity. By creating COIN, the company telegraphs to consumers that it cares about what they themselves care about.

BE THE BRAND

Companies interested in developing diversity-oriented CSR programming might look to leaders such as John Hancock. But how can they

begin to implement such programming in their own organizations? Consider these best practices. First, stick close to who and what you already are. For your company's diversity-oriented CSR programs to create shared value for both your business and society, it's important that these programs remain focused on and reflective of your core brand identity.

When deciding how best to engage with the community, John Hancock first had to determine what the company stood for and what its values were. During his tenure, David D'Alessandro remained keenly aware of John Hancock's stature as a life insurance company named for one of the nation's founding fathers and most celebrated patriots. John Hancock's oversize signature on the Declaration of Independence led to his name being synonymous with "signature"—a personal marker of truth and integrity. You only put your "John Hancock" on something that is moral and true—something on which you are willing to stake your reputation. But when it came to the corporate brand, D'Alessandro had to grapple with the reality that the company's core product, life insurance, was a cold business, something he likened to "bookmaking and loan-sharking."[34] During his stewardship, D'Alessandro decided to turn this apparent liability into an advantage, building a brand rooted entirely around old-world integrity and individual-oriented empathy.

With this corporate identity in mind, the leadership group at the company looked to the community and asked what challenges the mayor and city faced at the time. While brainstorming different ways to help redress these municipal problems, we filtered every major initiative through the prism of our empathy/integrity identity. It was determined that the best way to create shared value was to focus on empowering youth of difference. Through the Summer of Opportunity program and the MLK Scholars program, awareness of empathy and integrity was raised. Boston mayor Martin J. Walsh has lauded the MLK Scholars program as "a model for the country in providing meaningful summer employment for young people," while Robert Scannell Jr., president and CEO of the Boys and Girls Clubs of Dorchester (a neighborhood of Boston), suggested that "being a[n] MLK Summer Scholar is a badge of honor among our young people,"

whose increased capacities and confidence propel them to become future leaders at nonprofits like his.[35]

As you think of optimal programming for your company, engage in some introspection and reflect on what your business's core brand identity and values are. You can then tailor a set of community impact initiatives that help reinforce those values.

When creating and implementing such programming, it's also essential that your company start small. Here, the Hershey Corporation provides an instructive example. In 1894, chocolatier and confectioner magnate Milton Hershey founded his company "with a promise to help children thrive."[36] In 1909, Milton and his wife, Catherine Hershey, pursued that promise via philanthropy, opening a school to provide educational opportunities to orphan boys. Upon his death, Hersey bequeathed his entire $60 million fortune to the school so that it could continue to help this underserved demographic.[37] The school has helped youth of difference ever since.

As Hershey has increased its corporate footprint and geographical reach, it has scaled its impact programs accordingly. Its "Feeding America" initiative provides children with healthy food during the weekends, when they don't receive publicly funded school lunches, while "Project Peanut Butter" has helped alleviate hunger for malnourished children abroad.[38] The "Nourishing Minds" program has helped expand the company's youth outreach mandate throughout the globe, dispensing Vivi, a "highly fortified groundnut based supplement," to schoolchildren in need.[39] "From neighborhoods across the United States to the streets of Shanghai and Mumbai and villages of West Africa," the company notes, "our goal is to nourish one million minds by 2020."[40] And they are well on the way to accomplishing that. But as Hershey has increased the depth and breadth of its CSR and philanthropy programming, it is still firmly rooted in its Pennsylvania community. Today, the Milton Hershey School spends approximately $75,000 a year in room and board, dental care, housing, and other educational expenses for each of its students. The Hershey Company began locally, wove youth outreach into its corporate fabric, and has since expanded on that mandate as the company has grown, while never losing site of serving disadvantaged communities near its headquarters.[41]

To create shared value and galvanize community stakeholders, your company should also look beyond short-term profits and quarterly reports. I believe in the truism that we "do well by doing right," but that comes with an important qualification: not every community-relations initiative is going to fuel profits every quarter or fiscal year. As I discovered at John Hancock, diversity-oriented corporate engagement that stays true to the brand and is focused on social impact instead of quarterly earnings reports produces many long-term benefits. You can't easily measure how much the Boston Marathon Kenya Project or the MLK Scholars program benefited the bottom line. But as we saw, these community initiatives energized employees and stakeholders, created future labor markets and customer bases, and made a positive difference in the community.

John Hancock's diversity-based CSR initiatives also enabled it to develop innovative new products that will help ensure its future success. But this connection between diversity and innovation is by no means incidental. Research has shown that diversity acts as a kind of jet fuel for innovation and creativity in teams and organizations. To reap success, companies cannot content themselves with the "spillover effect" on innovation that comes from well-conceived and well-executed CSR programs. Rather, they should seek to mobilize diversity directly to enhance innovation. Let's take a look at a few companies that are breaking from the pack and doing precisely that.

MARKETING
OUTSIDE THE BOX

IF YOU'RE A LARGE, established business in a competitive industry, what can you do to expand most aggressively into promising new markets? Patrick Smith, who is African American, faced this question in 2007, when he was leading a digital marketing team at Bank of America's (BOA) global wealth investment management division.[1] BOA had long excelled in retail banking services and had built a well-established reputation in middle America. In 2006, however, the company acquired the wealth management giant US Trust, known for serving American economic royalty such as the Rockefellers and Vanderbilts.[2] BOA now needed to continue providing its traditional banking and credit-card services to middle-class clients, appeal to its new affluent US Trust customer base, and expand into other untapped and emerging consumer markets.

In pursuing these strategic objectives, BOA found itself at a significant disadvantage next to competitors such as Merrill Lynch and Charles Schwab, who dwarfed BOA in the size of their cumulative assets and, as a result, were able to maintain much larger marketing budgets. BOA was determined to hold its own, and in 2007, it launched an eye-catching new advertising campaign called "the new face of wealth," created by the advertising firm Hill Holliday (whose chairman and CEO, Karen Kaplan, is my good friend).[3] The campaign

dramatized social and economic shifts that had created not just a class of multimillionaire or even billionaire investors, but also a rapidly expanding class of racially, ethnically, and generationally diverse millionaires. Building on this strategy, Patrick's team needed to develop and deploy a digital marketing campaign compelling enough to win new clients without the benefit of direct conversations between prospects and company employees.

Like "the new face of wealth" campaign, Patrick's marketing team courted the industry's "emerging wealthy" demographic, defined as individuals with substantial assets who hadn't yet reached "elite wealthy" status. Instead of inheriting wealth, members of this group usually built it themselves, and they were more racially, ethnically, culturally, and geographically diverse than traditional wealth management clients. Forging an emotional connection with this group would mean deviating from typical digital advertising, with its images of yachts, vacation homes, and other staples of traditional wealth.[4] And instead of relying only on teaser rates and monetary incentives, as firms sometimes did, Patrick's group would have to develop new promotions and offerings that resonated with the needs and mindsets of this specific customer group.

To attack these challenges, Patrick turned to his team's key differentiator: diversity. He had assembled an inclusive team whose members included an African American male, a Hispanic woman, and a few white men and women. His team members brought a wide range of relevant knowledge and experience to bear, resulting in more and better ideas that drove this project forward from the very first meeting. The Hispanic woman on the team, Mariana, made an especially important contribution. Latinos at the time were fast becoming a formidable US demographic, representing more than half of the country's population growth.[5] A 2006 University of Georgia study projected that Hispanic buying power would soon eclipse that of African Americans for the first time in the country's history.[6] In many pockets of diverse emerging wealth, especially in coastal cities such as Miami, Boston, and Los Angeles, Hispanics were a large part of the population and accumulating more wealth.

As Mariana advised, the team could appeal to this group, but not by creating a standard Spanish-language website. Her colleagues

were surprised: market research suggested that consumers generally wanted to be served in their native language. Mariana explained that when it came to financial services, a subset of Hispanics disliked Spanish-language websites because they feared companies offered Spanish speakers rates and products that were inferior to those on English-language sites. Given such suspicion, merely offering a Spanish-language website might cause more problems than it solved. But how, Mariana's colleagues wondered, would BOA overcome the language barrier with Hispanic consumers? Mariana explained that this would not be a problem. Many Latinos spoke English, and those who didn't often had access to English speakers who could help navigate English-language materials.

In Mariana's view, BOA would also stand a better chance of capturing the emerging wealthy if it concentrated on relationships. On the face of it, that insight was fairly obvious: everyone on the team knew that relationship-building drove business in the financial services sector. But having personally experienced the centrality of relationships in Hispanic culture, Mariana brought an authentic perspective that helped illuminate what the Hispanic emerging wealthy demographic really valued. As a result, the team was able to learn that this demographic longed for more interactive and personalized financial advice from their banks, *without* the expense of a full-time brokerage firm. "Let's figure out a way to get people financial advice earlier in the relationship," she said. Following her lead, the team brainstormed strategies to establish relationships with these new customers while simultaneously offering them the financial relationships they desired.

The team wound up creating an innovative product solution, offering customers checking and savings accounts coupled with a brokerage account. Instead of banking at one institution and managing investments at another, customers could buy a joint product at BOA built around a single relationship. This relationship, moreover, would be reciprocal, offering customers a value-added service. As customers reached certain financial thresholds in overall assets, they would enjoy a series of incentives, including lower rates and greater access to financial advisers and investment advice.

Bank of America executives liked the idea and invested $20 million in the digital strategy. The result was a highly successful wealth management campaign. BOA's assets under management increased for both new and existing customers, and the company made inroads in coastal markets, increasing market share among people of color. Patrick's team was able to bypass generic commercial research reports about Latinos and go right to the source, gaining deeper, more nuanced insights that made all the difference. "Research is fantastic," says Patrick, reflecting on the campaign, "but there's nothing like having the lived experience that [Mariana] brought."

I've already described how valuable it is to inject diversity into human resources, board deliberations, and corporate social responsibility programming. But diversity is especially important when it comes to marketing. As America's demographic makeup changes, companies need access to as many diverse market segments as possible. Employees of difference provide such access, keeping our companies compelling and relevant and thus better able to withstand the pressures of digital disruption. Some companies, like BOA, understand this and are reaping the financial and reputational benefits that diverse marketing teams confer. But despite considerable talk about diversity, too many companies haven't yet made it a central feature of their marketing function. These companies must change, lest they risk losing the opportunity to offer compelling products and services to a country that is quickly becoming majority-minority.

NEW VOICES IN MARKETING

It's hardly earth-shattering to suggest that diversity might bear some relevance to how companies market their goods and services. During the 1950s and 1960s, large corporations such as Unilever, Tide, General Foods, Lipton, Chevrolet, and Pan Am were already focusing on creating reliable and compelling brand identities (or "brand propositions").[7] Branding, which marketed corporate identities and reputations more than discrete products, required targeted knowledge of specific consumer markets. Large advertising firms, famously centered on New York's Madison Avenue, as depicted in the popular

show *Mad Men*, shifted from undifferentiated marketing campaigns to consumer segmentation approaches, gradually tailoring their messaging to specific groups of consumers, such as African Americans or women. Advertising became visibly more integrated,[8] with companies like McDonald's, Coca-Cola, and Hanes increasing the number of diverse people in their marketing campaigns and hiring African American spokespeople to serve as brand representatives.[9]

Today, this first generation of multicultural marketing strikes audiences as biased and stereotypical. McDonald's ads of the 1970s, for instance, featured middle-class African American families consuming their products, but made widespread use of "g-dropping," with taglines such as "Do Your Dinnertimin' at McDonald's." The company also released a series of advertisements suggesting that African Americans "get down" with their food and beverage offerings, while Burger King gratuitously placed stereotyped slogans such as "Have mercy!!" in its ads. For Charlton McIlwain, an associate professor and a race and media specialist at New York University, these companies were trying to do the right thing, but they didn't have the requisite tools. Mainstream advertisement agencies had no firsthand experience of racial and ethnic minorities, and this caused them, McIlwain says, "to design ads that were racially naive and necessarily relied on stereotypes for lack of any other information."[10]

Advertising has come a long way since the 1970s. With the advent of the internet, digital marketing and e-commerce services began offering increasingly personalized and targeted products and advertisements.[11] And with the rise of social media, consumers began actively seeking out and promoting their own product selections, rather than just serving as the targets of advertising.[12] Along the way, marketing departments and agencies came to understand the value of knowing diverse markets, and they've spearheaded diverse marketing initiatives to penetrate them. While many companies used to presume a largely "general" white audience and then create smaller niche marketing campaigns geared toward diverse communities, this is often no longer the case.[13] Instead, marketing teams have increasingly moved the periphery into the center, using people of difference to fuel and energize all marketing campaigns and advertising initiatives.

My friend Donna Gittens, a veteran African American marketing executive, has witnessed the transformation of the advertising space over the course of her successful career.[14] In a 2017 conversation with me, she recalled the *Mad Men* era of advertising, which she observed while working in the sales department of television station WBZ in Boston. She also recalled the changes brought to the media space by the civil rights era. As large companies pushed advertising firms to pay more attention to the diverse audiences they served, more people of difference migrated into creative roles. In 1997, Donna followed suit, leaving an influential position as vice president of community programming at WCVB to found Cause Media, an advertising agency focused on important social issues and causes. Over the next decade, she grew her company from two to thirteen employees and began expanding its activities from small, niche projects to broader campaigns. In 2008, she rebranded her company as MORE Advertising, a name that reflected its increased scale and heightened ambitions.

As Donna's company has grown over the years, her focus on diversity and inclusion has remained constant. To this day, hers is one of a very few ad agencies in New England owned by an African American woman, and a third of her staff are people of color. "That feeds the kinds of clients that we can go after," she explains, referring to organizations including the Massachusetts Department of Public Health, which needed creative help for its anti-tobacco programs (and more recently, for its opioid prevention campaigns). Previously, a much larger firm, Arnold Worldwide, controlled this multimillion-dollar government account. In 2011, Arnold partitioned the contract, seeking to partner with smaller firms on targeted prevention campaigns focused on Latino and African American communities. MORE Advertising won the bid for the African American campaign. Since then, Donna and her colleagues have collaborated with Arnold, developing addiction-prevention campaigns aimed at women and girls of difference called, for example, "Keep It Fresh" and "Stop Addiction in Its Tracks." Donna's television, digital, and social media campaigns, dramatizing the pain of addiction, have been extremely powerful and effective, and she's gone on to produce anti-tobacco work for the government. For the past fifteen years, MORE Advertising has also

had the Boston Red Sox Foundation as a client, helping to increase awareness of the team's community efforts. As acknowledgement of her efforts, the team has given her two World Series rings and invited her to throw out the game's ceremonial first pitch on MORE Night at Fenway Park.

Large corporations have followed the lead of boutique firms like MORE Advertising, leveraging the power of difference to increase their revenues. Beginning in the 1990s, Neil Golden, who later became McDonald's US chief marketing officer, launched the "Fiesta menu," which featured spicy, Mexican-food-style offerings such as *tortas* and guacamole.[15] These offerings fared decently with the marketing team's intended audience of West Coast Hispanics but did very well among non-Hispanic groups. Spotting an opportunity, Golden went on to launch the "Leading with Ethnic Insights" campaign, which increased the number of diverse people on the company's advertisement committee. McDonald's focus groups similarly featured a significant percentage of underrepresented groups and most of its advertisements featured members of these groups. By allowing nonmainstream tastes to dictate and inform marketing considerations (instead of the other way around), McDonald's has seen improved results. In 2010, McDonald's enjoyed a 1.5 percent increase in sales, which Golden credits "to the success of new menu items" and to "an improved perception of the brand among all ethnic groups."[16]

Large companies likewise understand that Latinos are not only fueling US population growth but will also account for more consumer spending going forward. In 2015, Target launched its innovative "#SinTraducción" (Without Translation) marketing campaign, which focused on "cultural concepts."[17] One advertisement depicted a multigenerational home celebrating *sobremesa*, the Latino custom of socializing after meals. No English word or expression exists to convey this cultural tradition. "What we want to do is celebrate the fact that our bicultural guests live in two different worlds," said Rick Gomez, Target's senior vice president of brand and category marketing. "One is this Hispanic culture and the other is the American lifestyle." #SinTraducción, according to Gomez and Jeff Jones, the company's executive vice president, was, of course, intended to court Latinos, but

it was also intended to stimulate discussion about joint identities and those parts of our difference that aren't readily translatable. Target's outreach to Latinos has proven successful, especially among millennial Hispanics. According to Jones, 54 percent of this demographic cite Target as their favorite brand.

McDonalds, Target, and MORE Advertising are a few examples of companies that have launched increasingly sophisticated and inclusive marketing campaigns. But such initiatives still remain the exception in corporate America. One reason: the lack of diversity in our country's marketing teams. As of 2014, the Bureau of Labor Statistics reported that "of the 582,000 people employed in advertising and communications in the U.S., less than half were women, 10.5% Hispanic, 6.6% were black, and 5.7% Asian."[18] These statistics don't tell the full story either. While women held half of creative positions, for example, only 11 percent occupied creative leadership roles.[19] In 2016, multiple scandals featuring high-ranking ad executives cast light on endemic racism and sexism in the industry. When the chief communications officer at J. Walter Thompson, one of the country's oldest and most respected advertising agencies, accused chief executive Gustavo Martinez of "an unending stream of racist and sexist comments as well as unwanted touching and other unlawful conduct," the entire industry took note, and began to question the lack of meaningful diversity within its ranks.[20] "The white-male-dominated culture of advertising agencies, as depicted in the TV show 'Mad Men,'" noted a *New York Times* article, "is still a reality, and some brands are looking for change."[21]

In fact, some brands were *demanding* change. In the wake of these scandals, General Mills, HP Inc., and Verizon wrote to their ad agencies, telling them to diversify immediately or they'd fulfill their marketing needs elsewhere.[22] "You don't need to be a mom to make some Cheerios ads, but if we have more moms on the team making Cheerios ads, maybe we increase the probability we do work that connects with moms in a richer, deeper, more powerful, meaningful way," remarked Michael Fanuele, the chief creative officer of General Mills. Fanuele, who expressed a desire for genuinely inclusive marketing atmospheres, referred to the country's current creative leaders as "a bunch

of middle-aged white guys with baseball caps and funny beer jokes up their sleeves." Diego Scotti, an Argentine native and Verizon's CMO, agreed. "We're still in a very male-dominated and nondiverse industry," he said. "In order for us to create work that's more connected with the consumer, it needs to come from a deeper connection to what's going on in society and what's going on in culture." These executives are correct. Without more diversity, Madison Avenue's homogenous creative industry will remain troublingly out of touch with America's diverse consumers.[23]

Absent authentic and more inclusive marketing campaigns, companies like General Mills and Verizon know they'll risk returning to the mistakes made in the 1970s during early attempts at multicultural advertising. Remember the story of the culturally insensitive 2016 Pepsi advertisement? Sadly, this wasn't an isolated incident. Advertisements beset by stereotypes have been fairly easy to find. In 2013, Ford Motor Company uploaded a series of advertisements promoting its Ford Figo hatchback. One of these depicted three women with ample cleavage gagged and bound in the back of the car. Meanwhile, controversial Italian media mogul and former prime minister Silvio Berlusconi sits up front, smiling and holding his fingers up in a peace sign. Most observers, including me, were shocked and outraged. The advertisement's objective appeared not only wildly inappropriate but unclear. Was this supposed to make men want to buy this car? WPP, Ford's advertising agency, blamed the offensive ad on a lack of oversight.[24] Having learned nothing from its competitors' grave mistakes, General Motors issued a spot called "Fu Manchu" later that year to promote its Chevrolet SUV. "The lyrics," observes a *Huffington Post* write-up, "reference the racially-cast Asian villain Fu Manchu, Chinese females who say 'ching ching, chop suey!' and Japanese females who call Americans 'Amelicans.'"[25] Racial stereotypes like these have no place in our businesses. Companies that perpetrate them will pay the price as their reputations decline and customers flee.

In the summer of 2017, the real estate company Bedrock, established by Quicken Loans founder Dan Gilbert, unfurled a "See Detroit like we do" advertisement along one of its high-rise buildings downtown.[26] The ad depicted an energetic sea of mostly white faces

with a saxophone player rising above the crowd, heralding the future march of progress in one of America's most historically depressed urban centers. Angry residents and outsiders took to social media in protest. According to US Census Bureau data from 2010, Detroit is 82 percent African American, leading city inhabitants to wonder who exactly "sees Detroit" in such a whitewashed way. "Detroit is home to the largest African-American population in the country, and the city is home to concentrated neighborhoods of indigenous African American communities that are not only being pushed out of the city, but seemingly intentionally left out of the new vision for Detroit," said Khaled Beydoun, an associate professor at the University of Detroit's Mercy School of Law. "The Bedrock ad vividly and brutally illustrates what has been taking place on the ground in the city for years, particularly in downtown, Cass Corridor and other sections of the city that have been rapidly remade without tending to the needs, interests and humanity of black families."[27] Making matters worse, the art installation marked the fiftieth-anniversary commemoration of the Detroit race riots.[28] Gilbert abruptly canceled the ad and apologized profusely for the "dumb" campaign, emphasizing how important diversity and inclusion were for his company's and the city's future.[29] But how much can the company truly prize diversity if it apparently didn't have any in its creative department?

Despite clamor for diversity and inclusion, examples like these regrettably persist across corporate America. We like to think that marketing has come a long way since the 1970s, but in truth it hasn't come nearly as far as it needs to.

MODELS IN DIVERSITY MARKETING

Amid these gaffes, customers in the United States and elsewhere have become increasingly interested in inclusive marketing. Millennials are applauding large companies such as Verizon and General Mills, saying they'll reward diverse marketing with their pocketbooks. A 2016 marketing research study found that 80 percent of parents like diverse advertisements and 66 percent would consider such diversity when it came to product purchases.[30] The media firm YouGov documented

that from November 2016 to February 2017, Americans gave 31 percent more to causes they believed in. The three top categories of support included immigration (51 percent), women's rights (43 percent), and diversity and inclusion (41 percent). These categories, all bearing on questions of difference, overwhelmingly eclipsed spending on other worthy causes such as the environment, education, health care, and the protection of children and animals.[31] The increasingly active and socially conscious generation of younger Americans provides an amazing business opportunity. If companies create more diverse marketing teams, they can deepen relationships with existing customers while simultaneously growing market share by appealing to different demographic groups.

Despite its recent missteps, PepsiCo was one of the first American companies to leverage the power of diverse marketing teams to penetrate new customer markets.[32] In 1940, the company's visionary leader, Walter S. Mack Jr. (president from 1938 to 1950), created an African American sales/marketing team to reach the untapped and long-ignored African American community.[33] Eventually growing to a dozen people, the "Negro-market team," as it was known in the 1940s, was a marketing first. "On their way to nudging their country to a better place," relates Stephanie Capparell, a *Wall Street Journal* editor who wrote a book on the topic, "the sales team helped define niche marketing some thirty years before it became a widespread business strategy."[34] The strategy also helped establish the company's popularity and brand loyalty among African Americans.

Like many large American businesses in 1940, Pepsi was reeling from the Great Depression, and Mack needed to venture into new markets. The company faced enormous competition, especially from Coke, which dwarfed Pepsi in brand recognition, market share, and popularity. In 1939, Coke allocated $20 million to advertising, compared with Pepsi's meager $600,000.[35] Pepsi's new marketing strategy took an innovative and bold direction, elevating African Americans to positions of leadership and harnessing that power to connect with customers. Mack's marketing team traveled extensively throughout the country, speaking about the company and circulating sample products at churches, convention halls, local businesses, and colleges. Though

team members had little training and modest budgets, they inspired audiences and made an enduring impact. "The audience found the Pepsi special-markets representatives infinitely more interesting than the free samples of the product they were handing out," Capparell writes.[36]

The popularity of the marketing team had a clear business impact. "Sales of the cola surged wherever the team members went," Capparell recounts. "At one point, they helped Pepsi outsell all its rivals in some Northern cities."[37] The team disbanded in the early 1950s, and without a durable infrastructure in place, this remarkable foray into diversity marketing ended, its members going on to enjoy promising careers in different industries. But PepsiCo reclaimed the mantle of diversity trailblazer in 1999, when Steve Reinemund became CEO.[38] Like his immediate predecessor, Reinemund understood the business imperative behind diversity. My longtime friend, diversity icon Bennie Wiley, who as CEO of The Partnership brought the organization to prominence, told me that Reinemund "really tried to integrate diversity into the DNA of the organization."[39] Reinemund diversified the company's product portfolio, making the organization less reliant on sugary drinks and more oriented to a wider stable of products that would appeal to an increasingly health-oriented consumer market.[40] He also spearheaded the removal of trans fats in his Frito-Lay products and acquired Quaker Oats, giving the company access to sports drinks such as Gatorade.[41]

But Reinemund especially prized demographic diversity throughout PepsiCo. In a startling move, he linked executive bonus compensation to ambitious diversity targets.[42] In 2002, he reduced executive compensation because diversity projections hadn't been met, prompting an uproar from board members and executives.[43] The company enjoyed increased revenue, they argued, and this was the metric that counted. Reinemund disagreed, insisting that diversity was more important. Even when the board wanted to give Reinemund a significant bonus following high-revenue years, he declined the extra pay if the company hadn't met all of its diversity goals.[44] "That sent a very clear signal throughout the organization about his seriousness and the accountability that he was putting on himself as well as on his

executive-level team," recalls national diversity expert David Thomas, president of Morehouse College.[45]

A significant part of Reinemund's diversity efforts centered on marketing. As he realized, the company was underperforming in multiethnic urban areas.[46] To better reach these demographics, Reinemund helped revamp his company's marketing plans, creating the Latino/Hispanic Advisory Board (2000), and tailoring products, such as Mountain Dew Code Red, to multicultural urban communities.[47] As Earl Graves Sr., then the chairman of Pepsi's African American Advisory Board as well as of the country's largest minority-controlled Pepsi franchise, said, "All of a sudden, PepsiCo's market share became much more significant in many places. . . . They understand that if they don't go after diverse markets, somebody else will."[48] In addition to the African American board, which Reinemund and Graves had asked Bennie Wiley to chair, Reinemund created new advisory boards dedicated to other demographic groups and *personally attended every single one of their meetings*.[49] "He treated them very much like he treated his fiduciary board," said Thomas, holding them accountable for diversity objectives.[50] Since 2000, PepsiCo's multicultural marketing efforts have powered revenue increases across all of its major divisions.[51] During Reinemund's tenure, moreover, the company experienced a $9 billion increase in revenues.[52] As the *New York Times* reported, "Earnings per share rose 80 percent, and the stock price increased 44 percent."[53]

In 2006, Indian national Indra K. Nooyi succeeded Reinemund as CEO, becoming one of the first female and foreign-born chief executives of a Fortune 100 company, and among the world's most powerful women.[54] Nooyi was just one of many talented people of color whom Reinemund mentored in his quest to diversify PepsiCo's leadership ranks and strengthen the company. During his tenure, for example, Reinemund also appointed African American David Andrews as senior vice president and general counsel. Andrews in turn was succeeded by African American Larry Thompson, who in turn was succeeded by African American Tony West.[55]

Nooyi's landmark appointment, which elevated Pepsi to one of the largest woman-led corporations in the United States, also coincided

with another Pepsi milestone.[56] Just prior to her being named CEO, PepsiCo emerged victorious over its historical foe, beating Coke in market capitalization for the first time in more than a century.[57] That result owed in part to the company's impressive knowledge of changing consumer markets, which were moving away from carbonated drinks and into water, sports beverages, and snack foods.[58] "Throughout the past five years under CEO Steve Reinemund," notes a 2006 *CNN Money* profile, "the company has deftly moved with every shift in consumer tastes."[59] Intending to continue Reinemund's legacy of financial performance and ethical leadership, Nooyi has spearheaded the company's Performance with Purpose campaign, which focuses on helping diverse communities, creating healthier products, and supporting environmental stewardship.[60] To date, Nooyi's investments in diverse communities, nutrition, and the planet haven't hurt corporate revenues and organizational growth, both of which have substantially increased during her tenure.[61] That's the power of diverse marketing and principle-driven leadership.

Toy giant Mattel is another example of a company that catapulted its business forward by appealing to a diverse marketplace. For decades since its debut in 1959, the Barbie doll—flawlessly thin, high-heeled, and white-skinned—was a cultural sensation and one of the world's best-selling toys. But she was also a wellspring of controversy, attracting the ire of activist groups such as the Barbie Liberation Organization and Feminist Hacker Barbie. To expose the unrealistic body standards and sexism they believed the doll promoted, and ultimately to undermine Barbie's sales, these groups hatched publicity stunts and crowdsourced internet campaigns.[62] Over the years, Mattel responded by modestly diversifying the toy's occupations and ethnicities, creating a Barbie businesswoman (1963), a Barbie astronaut (1965), an African American Barbie (1967), and a Barbie surgeon (1973).[63] Despite successive waves of "Barbie backlash," Mattel's efforts mollified consumers, and the doll maintained about a 90 percent market share in girl-oriented toys for most of the twentieth century.[64]

By the mid-2000s, Barbie's dominance and brand appeal began to lag. After four straight quarters of plummeting sales (all told, Barbie sales decreased by 3 percent in 2012, 6 percent in 2013, and 16 percent

in 2014), the blue-eyed and blond-haired Elsa doll, from Disney's movie *Frozen*, overtook Barbie as the world's most popular doll in 2014.[65] That same year, the Danish company Lego overtook Mattel as the world's biggest toymaker.[66] "The brand was losing relevance," said Lisa McKnight, a senior vice president at Mattel. "We knew we had to change the conversation."[67]

A creative team within Mattel, working for two years under the secretive code name "Project Dawn," began Barbie's modern makeover, designing a more inclusive set of dolls that more accurately reflected the size and complexion of America's children as well as the values of parents.[68] To overcome its increasing lack of brand relevance, Mattel directed a series of YouTube advertisements in 2015 called "Imagine the Possibilities," portraying the doll as a budding career woman occupying the esteemed roles of veterinarian and scientist.[69] But the reflection of occupational differences was only a modest start, as Barbie consumers increasingly clamored for increased diversity across many fronts. As a *Time* article noted, "Though young moms might be the most vocal on social media when it comes to Barbie's body, Mattel's extensive surveys show that moms across the country care about diversity in terms of color and body, regardless of [their] age, race or socioeconomic position."[70]

In 2015, Mattel unleashed the fruits of Project Dawn, launching a new generation of dolls, complete with curvy body sizes, twenty-three hair colors, twenty-two hairdos, eighteen eye colors, and an array of different skin tones.[71] This product launch, Mattel's most significant rebranding effort to date, has proven revitalizing and lucrative. Parents and children alike flocked to the ethnically, racially, and bodily diverse product lines. Barbie became the most diverse doll product line, and at the Toy Industry Association's annual Toy of the Year awards gala in 2017, the company won the coveted "Doll of the Year" award.[72]

This new generation of Barbies wouldn't have been possible without a diverse workforce inside Mattel. To help design a culturally sensitive and compelling black Barbie, for example, the company's marketing teams consulted the Mattel African American Forum (MAAF), the toymaker's African American employee resource group. MAAF members helped get the dolls' names, skin tone, and hair just

right. "They asked us very candid questions about the look of the doll. Did they get the skin tone right? What about the nose and the hair?" said David Simmons, associate manager of account planning and an MAAF member.[73] This was important because consumers roundly criticized the 1967 African American Barbie ("Colored Francie") for her inauthenticity—besides having a darker skin tone, she lacked any bodily features or hair styles typical of African Americans.[74] As African American Tom Burrell, a diversity advertising trailblazer and founder of the Burrell Communications group, famously quipped, "Black people are not dark-skinned white people."[75] A lack of authenticity plagued previous Barbie diversity efforts as well, with the wheelchair-bound "Share a Smile Becky" doll (1997) lacking the correct proportions to fit into her own dream-house elevator, and the Computer Engineer Barbie product line (2014) requiring help from boys to actually code.[76]

For its 2016 line of gamer Barbies, Mattel drew on female engineering leaders such as Molly Proffitt, CEO of Ker-Chunk Games; Julie Ann Crommett, entertainment industry educator in chief at Google; and Kimberly Bryant, founder and executive director of Black Girls Code, to help it design a compelling doll that resembled a real tech geek.[77] These women advised Mattel during the design process, ensuring that the new Careers Game Developer Barbie was authentic, compelling, and would help inspire a new generation of budding female computer scientists and STEM leaders (instead of fashionistas). "The computer has [JavaScript] on it and you can see various instances of game engines on her laptop," said one of the leaders, commenting on the new line. "I really know that girls need an icon that shows that they can be a part of the [tech] space and Barbie does that. She has power to tell girls they can be makers and builders."[78] Even Barbie's companion, Ken, received a total diversity makeover in 2017. "Prior to the new iteration of Ken dolls, Barbie's plastic beau typically sported blond hair, blue eyes and a chiseled figure. Revamped Ken comes, in one case, with a man bun, while another sports a dad bod," a *Fortune* article observed.[79]

All of this increased diversity has led to more prosperity for the company. Mattel's brunette Latina Barbie, with curves and brown

eyes, became the company's 2016 bestseller in the Fashionista line (a feat that *Huffington Post* senior reporter Emily Peck calls "a clear victory for the toymaking giant").[80] Following four years of declines, sales of the dolls increased 7 percent in 2016, earning nearly $1 billion for the company.[81]

Because diversity has such potential to supercharge marketing, the demand for people of difference in this area has increased in recent years. My friend and Partnership board member Yvonne Garcia, senior vice president of investment management services at State Street Financial, can attest to that.[82] At the beginning of her career, in 2002, she joined the Association of Latino Professionals in Finance and Accounting, the nation's first and largest Latino professional organization. Back then, this organization, which helped supply a diverse pipeline of highly skilled Latino CPAs and bankers to organizations across the country, boasted five thousand members, thirty professional chapters, and sixty university chapters. Ultimately, its corporate board began to realize that the demand for Latino talent extended far beyond the finance and accounting sectors. Each market sector, whether it was banking, insurance, human resources, health care, technology, or law, greatly needed emerging Latino talent. The organization therefore diversified, rebranding itself the Association of Latino Professionals for America (ALPFA) in 2010. Since 2012, Yvonne has served as national chairwoman of the organization, which, as of 2017, had expanded to more than 83,000 members, 155 university student chapters, and 41 professional chapters. One of the striking differences Yvonne has noticed during her tenure is the increased accountability for diversity among corporate leadership ranks. Whereas ALPFA used to work chiefly with middle management and junior members, now the group meets with top executives. "The conversation has been elevated to integrate the C-suite as well," Yvonne said.

As a marketing expert, Yvonne knows why ALPFA has swelled in scope and relevance. "When I embark on a new client relationship," she says, "and all individuals are from the same background, it's a little bit discouraging, because I feel that I'm not going to get the best results from that client relationship, versus walking into a room and seeing either a woman sitting there or a Latino, Asian, or African

American. You feel that the thought process is going to expand and be just a bit more innovative." With the right blend of diverse talent, she has found, innovative marketing solutions become more likely. In 2010, for example, when she served as director of segment marketing at Liberty Mutual Group, she created the most diverse team she could to design and execute a Hispanic marketing campaign. She needed diversity of ethnicity, race, skill sets, and background. And she needed generational diversity. She knew that the millennial generation behaves and communicates differently from its predecessors, and that absent their input, the campaign would be hopelessly out of date. But she also needed individuals with long tenures at the firm to bring historical knowledge and organizational experience. "When you have these mature and young members together, it's a powerful combination," Yvonne observed.

With the help of her diverse team, Yvonne put the insurance firm's Hispanic-focused marketing strategy into operation through television and radio spots, community events, and magazine ads. The strategy proved a resounding success, increasing awareness of Liberty Mutual among a whole new population segment (especially young, Latino biculturals) and developing them as a significant revenue source. The millennials on the team proved vital, creating a public service announcement that featured a driving-while-texting accident. The younger members of the team executed every part of that ad, which, as Yvonne noted, "served as a vivid showcase of what it looked like to crash while texting." Yvonne needed the creative ideas from a generation that grew up amid the "texting while driving" epidemic to lend the message credibility. And while the PSA wasn't specifically focused on Hispanic millennials, these consumers strongly connected with it. Two years into the campaign, in 2012, Liberty Mutual enjoyed a significant uptick in "consideration" and "awareness of brand" in the national Hispanic demographic.

UPGRADING YOUR MARKETING FUNCTION

Judging from success stories like those of Pepsi, Mattel, and Liberty Mutual, it's easy to see why diversifying America's marketing and

advertising teams is increasingly on the corporate agenda, with white papers, international conferences, and industry studies all offering ideas and solutions.[83] So what is my advice? To increase creative diversity in your marketing department and teams, nurture employee resource groups and other networking and sponsorship programs. As I've said before, leadership is vital, setting the tone for the entire organization. But as the global marketing, advertising, and design company 72andSunny has found, "Leadership too often waits for perfection before they reveal a plan. The sooner you can share the intent [to diversify], the sooner the broader organization can help with the plan."[84] Employee resource groups (ERGs) have played a great role in advancing diversity, providing networking opportunities and other resources to employees of difference. Not only do such groups help foster camaraderie and reduce employee turnover, but they also serve as extraordinary repositories of knowledge about diverse consumer markets. Pepsi needed African Americans on its marketing team to help penetrate new markets in the twentieth century, as well as to avoid mistakes (such as its ill-conceived "protest" ad) in the twenty-first, while Mattel relied on its African American ERG to help effectively design and market its new Barbie dolls.

If the ERG model isn't ideal for your organization, try embracing different types of diversity-related programming. 72andSunny created a "Monthly High Fives" program, which partners senior creative directors with midlevel employees for sponsorship and inspiration. "Given [that] our industry has a huge drop-off in female creatives before the director level, this program ensures that leadership knows the mid-level female creatives and that these women know they have access to the leadership team," the company reasoned.[85] It also created a "Moms Who Lunch" program, designed to help parents network, and an "Adulting" group, which taught younger employees valuable adult life skills such as handling finances, nutrition, and childcare.[86]

When seeking to recruit and retain the best emerging marketing talent, your company should consider nontraditional approaches to hiring and creative partnering. I've already discussed how peer-to-peer recruitment methods under way in Silicon Valley help perpetuate a homogenous "mirrortocracy" in American technology. The larger

marketing and creative industry suffers from something similar, hiring people based on college degrees or similar credentials (such as participation on a team that created a famous advertising campaign)— requirements that help perpetuate homogenous workforces and stifle creative expression.[87] "Agencies have to be very intentional about reaching out to kids of color who are interested in the field," Donna Gittens observes. Diverse ad agencies are rare. For instance, only about four agencies of color serve the New England area as of this writing.

Consider seeking emerging talent in creative internships, mentorship programs, multicultural career fairs, and boot camps. Club Bootcamp is an organization that pairs a young minority creative with an ad agency to help work on a real campaign, while 72 U unites a diverse slate of candidates around a problem and offers need-based assistance so everyone can join.[88] Seek out such organizations in your region before you embark on your next round of hiring. If you work in a large company that contracts with advertisement agencies, partner with creative organizations such as Adcolor and the One Club, which include diversity and inclusion as part of their mission statements.[89]

The stakes are high when it comes to diversity and marketing. Imagine what would have happened if Bedrock, the Detroit company mentioned earlier, had possessed an inclusive creative team. I suspect that its advertising campaign would have featured a representative sample of the city's multiethnic population. Imagine if Patrick Smith's marketing team at Bank of America had lacked Latino representation. It might not have helped BOA penetrate the new "emerging wealthy" sector. And consider PepsiCo. While this company remains on the vanguard of diversity efforts, would it have produced an ad that portrayed a serious social protest movement so flippantly if it had had a more diverse marketing team? As brand expert David D'Alessandro, my former John Hancock CEO, noted, "It can take one hundred years to build a good brand and thirty days of bad publicity to destroy it."[90]

Marketing, of course, won't ensure a company's survival if it doesn't have innovative products and services to offer customers. As important as diverse creative teams are to allowing companies access to consumer markets, they are just as important to powering innovation. Whether it's in technology, health care, venture capital, or even our

government's civil service, innovation is born of diverse team members who have the freedom to ideate and generate novel products, services, and solutions. As I'll explore in the next chapter, a wealth of research suggests that diverse teams are more innovative than their nondiverse counterparts. That's because they power divergent thinking, one of the most important ingredients in creativity and innovation. In our age of technological disruption and demographic upheaval, diversity is the best strategy for becoming more competitive and future-proofing your company.

INNOVATING A MORE COLORFUL COMPANY

ON CHRISTMAS EVE 2015, Jean Paul Kambazza immigrated to Boston from Uganda, hoping to find a job in America's bustling technology sector.[1] It seemed a reasonable ambition: for twenty years he had worked in the IT departments of East African banks and telecom companies. And yet, the more Jean Paul learned about the ultracompetitive, fast-moving world of American IT, the more he realized he didn't quite have the skills or cultural knowledge he needed to break in. To bridge this gap, he postponed his job search and enrolled in a master's program in computer science at the University of Massachusetts, Boston.

In October 2016, as he neared graduation, Jean Paul received an email about Hack.Diversity, a public-private partnership dedicated to helping talented graduates from underserved backgrounds navigate the tech industry's job market. Jean Paul applied to the program and was accepted into its first cohort of eighteen interns. For six to eight weekends during his final semester at school, he attended workshops where he participated in mock interviews, polished his résumé, and learned practical skills. The internship culminated in a series of placement interviews, during which regional tech companies considered interns for positions in their companies. Wayfair, the Boston-based

e-commerce giant specializing in home furnishings, selected Jean Paul for an internship.

In a conversation with me, Jean Paul spoke glowingly about the three months he spent at Wayfair. This brief stint was just as valuable, he felt, as the full year and a half he spent at school. "When you're in school," he said, "your universe is theoretical, and you approach things in theoretical ways. My internship at Wayfair, thanks to Hack .Diversity, opened my eyes to how it is in the real world." At Wayfair, he gained a better sense of how his coding decisions actually impacted the company's bottom line, and he found himself embraced by the organization's culture. "At Wayfair, minorities were few," he recalled, but he nonetheless immediately felt at home, "part of the brotherhood." That's partly because Hack.Diversity not only mentored students but also focused on retaining diverse talent, helping companies to cultivate inclusive management policies.

Jean Paul now had the skills and the experience to compete in the job market. "I'll be a better employee for the next job I get, thanks to the industry preparation provided by Wayfair," he noted. He needed Hack.Diversity to help provide him an entree into a market where people of his racial and ethnic background have traditionally gone underrepresented. Hack.Diversity, he said, "gives [members of underrepresented groups] a shot to prove that we're just as smart or we're competent, which is all we can ask for."

Hack.Diversity cofounder Jody Rose recognizes the importance of connecting talented graduates like Jean Paul with tech startups and industry heavyweights.[2] Having spent most of her career helping tech startups scale, she knows that innovative talent is imperative for any company's success. Since 2015, she has focused on talent acquisition, becoming executive director of the New England Venture Capital Association (NEVCA). Instead of thinking about talent and innovation on the company level, her role had her exploring ways to leverage the venture capital platform to champion regional entrepreneurship and drive innovation and growth. "Every single thing we do is mission focused," she noted of NEVCA. "We want to address all the gaps that the region has to make it the most competitive in the world and the most attractive for companies who want to come here, scale,

and grow—companies like General Electric," she noted, referring to the corporate giant's 2016 decision to relocate its world headquarters from Connecticut to Boston's Seaport District, the innovation hub.[3]

Jody was therefore chagrined when, in January 2016, shortly after assuming her post, she read a *Bloomberg* article headlined "Why Doesn't Silicon Valley Hire Black Coders?"[4] Many players in the innovation economy blamed an insufficient pipeline: "There simply aren't enough diverse candidates to fill these jobs," they said. But Jody knew that wasn't true. A huge pool of untapped diverse talent existed that didn't make it into standard recruitment channels. "There's an economic imperative for us to tap into this huge and capable workforce," she realized after reading the *Bloomberg* piece, "because if we don't, our ability to be globally competitive won't exist." That's when she conceived Hack.Diversity.

At first, Jody hesitated to embark on the project. As the first black woman to lead NEVCA, she was already a novelty in the larger venture-capital community, which consisted predominantly of white men, who in turn provided capital infusions to companies run predominantly by white men.[5] In 2015, women received 5 percent of all US venture funding, while African Americans and Latinos received 1 percent each.[6] Jody was understandably concerned about featuring a diversity initiative as her inaugural venture. "It almost felt like that would be expected. And I wasn't sure that it would be well received." But in November 2016, she cofounded the venture anyway. As she detailed, "Hack.Diversity addresses one of the region's most glaring workforce inefficiencies, the enduring gap between the increasing demand for computer science and IT professionals and the underrepresentation of highly skilled black and Latino professionals in those fields."[7] Jody felt it would have been economically irresponsible not to leverage the venture platform to address such a widespread problem plaguing her region.

As of this writing, Hack.Diversity has recruited black and Latino computer science and information technology majors coming from coding boot camps (such as Year Up and Resilient Coders), community colleges, and urban four-year colleges. "We do that because of intersectional issues," Jody said. "We know that [diverse] coders coming out

of MIT and Harvard aren't the ones having a hard time landing a job." Hack.Diversity then trains these students, developing them into the type of talent attractive to Boston's most selective companies. After all, Carbonite, Wayfair, and other participating firms must offer more than internships. To qualify for participation, these companies must have full-time employment positions they hope to fill. The Hack.Diversity internships thus function as a "try before you buy" model—at the end of their time together, the company decides whether to extend an offer to an intern.

Creating a robust pipeline and accessing talent was just the first step. All of these efforts would be in vain, Jody felt, if companies didn't attend to retention. The program thus paired host companies with diversity and inclusion experts who identified any diversity gaps or potential growth areas at each business. In some cases, companies found that they needed to broaden their applicant pool by recruiting from public academic institutions in addition to the elite private colleges they had been targeting.

Since its launch, Hack.Diversity has generated a groundswell of support in the Boston area. CEOs, CPOs, and other tech executives have approached Jody asking to partner with her. As Jeff Leiden, chairman, president, and CEO of Boston-based Vertex Pharmaceuticals, explained, "If we don't develop our talent pool, we won't win the innovation race." Niraj Shah, cofounder and CEO of Wayfair, echoed those remarks: "These students are thanking us," he said, "but really we should be thanking them."[8] A 2016 New England Partnership study, discussed at Hack.Diversity's inaugural community event, predicted that "by 2018, Massachusetts' economic growth rate would drop by half, from 3% to 1.5%, precisely because the state will not produce enough college-educated workers to fill jobs in high-demand industries."[9] As Tom Hopcroft, president and CEO of the Massachusetts Technology Leadership Council (MassTLC), remarked, "We just can't afford to leave people on the sidelines if we want to compete as a region in the global battle for technology talent."[10] Mohamad Ali, president and CEO at the Boston-based information technology firm Carbonite, noted that Boston faced "an impending economic disaster" if it didn't get serious about diversifying its ranks.[11]

In its second year, with nearly forty interns entering the program as of this writing, Hack.Diversity is poised to scale nationally, with pilots soon to roll out in cities across the country. Given the importance of innovation for every company and sector, I believe that this regional and national expansion will succeed. And more generally, I also believe companies must pay far more attention to the link between diversity and innovation than most currently do. As research shows, diversity isn't just incidental to a team's or organization's capacity to innovate. It's vital—a fact that largely goes underappreciated.

INNOVATE OR DIE

Skeptics might contend that American companies long have been sufficiently innovative without special concern for diversity. Given all the "disruptive" technology we've pioneered, why should we even bother to focus on diversity? The answer is that appearances notwithstanding, we're currently struggling to innovate. We need to deploy *all* the tools at our disposal to make our organizations more creative and dynamic.

As scholars have argued, innovation in the United States has actually stalled in recent years. We're in the midst of a long-term "Great Stagnation," according to Tyler Cowen, the Holbert C. Harris chair of economics at George Mason University.[12] The twentieth-century technological revolutions, premised on internal combustion, petrochemicals, electricity, the telephone, and modern plumbing, are over.[13] As Tyler notes, our planes fly the same speed as they did in the 1960s, while our homes, consumer durables, and automobiles haven't changed drastically in appearance or function. Yes, the iPhone you hold in your hand might have some impressive new features, but in the broader context, this innovation is incremental and not radical. As venture capitalist Peter Thiel famously quipped, "We wanted flying cars; instead we got 140 characters."[14]

American entrepreneurialism, which fueled US innovation during the twentieth century, is partly responsible for this decline. As a 2015 National Bureau of Economic Research study found, "During the 1980s and 1990s, when entrepreneurial activity was high, new companies played an outsize role in boosting innovation, productivity and

job creation."[15] They no longer do. A 2015 Brookings Institution report discerned a "precipitous drop" in startups since 2006, noting that "this decline has been documented across a broad range of sectors in the U.S. economy, even in high-tech."[16] Many more studies similarly demonstrate, according to one innovation expert, that "American entrepreneurship, the social force that made this country the envy of the world, is dying."[17] Innovation certainly remains central to America's brand, with former political leaders such as Barack Obama and Hillary Clinton; US senators Elizabeth Warren, Chris Coons, and Pat Roberts; and tech enthusiasts from Silicon Valley all proclaiming the United States to be the world's most innovative country. Economists who track the numbers, however, "have been sounding the alarm that the U.S. is facing an 'innovation crisis' that threatens America's future economic prosperity."[18] US companies are getting older, more sluggish, and less competitive, while fewer Americans are taking the risk to start leaner and nimbler startups.

Take health care, an industry that appears at first glance to be hyperinnovative. As we've increased our knowledge of the human genome, physicians have provided personalized care, targeted gene therapies, and other interventions to isolate tumors and correct mutations in our genetic code. A new generation of geneticists and biotechnology experts is poised to mobilize quantum computing, artificial intelligence, nanorobots, and 3D printing to help us usher in the next generation of medical breakthroughs.[19] But while some believe these imminent innovations will herald longer, healthier lives, others discern the same innovation slump plaguing other sectors of the US economy. During the twentieth century, biomedical innovation helped us conquer smallpox, yellow fever, polio, and other scourges that had plagued the species for millennia. As an *Economist* report notes, nothing in the twenty-first century has come close, and our life expectancies have plateaued: "Life expectancy at birth in America soared from 49 years at the turn of the 20th century to 74 years in 1980. Enormous technical advances have occurred since that time. Yet as of 2011 life expectancy rested at just 78.7 years."[20] The scientific and biomedical industries continue to confront the complex diseases of cancer and neurodegeneration, searching for major medical breakthroughs, while

health care costs continue to skyrocket. "Such problems beg for innovative solutions involving every aspect of health care—its delivery to consumers, its technology, and its business models," according to Regina E. Herzlinger, the Nancy R. McPherson professor of business administration at Harvard Business School.[21]

Education is another industry that could benefit from systemic innovation. Everyone has heard of the massive open online courses (MOOCs) that threaten to disrupt standard colleges and universities. For innovation expert Michael Horn, "Online learning is the first disruptive innovation [in education] since the advent of the printing press."[22] Such online content delivery often emphasizes practical learning, in which students progress according to the extent of their skills acquisition instead of following a traditional two- or four-year curriculum. Coding boot camps, which Jody Rose partners with at Hack.Diversity, are great examples of skills-acquisition learning.

But how can these breakthroughs disrupt primary education as we know it? Grade school, Horn notes, hasn't changed significantly since the Industrial Revolution: "Patterned after the dominant factory model of the era in which public schooling scaled, our education system functions as though all students learn at the same pace and have the same learning needs, which we know is not true."[23] And despite online skills-based programming, employers today largely insist on college degrees for jobs, even though these degrees often leave young people bereft of the skills they actually need in the marketplace. According to Bill Coplin, professor of public policy at Syracuse University, "Our education system is producing too many thinkers and not enough doers" who are able to provide products and services to consumers.[24] Stigmas against vocational training and a "college for all" mindset stubbornly persist. In today's knowledge economy, existing educational models would seem to cry out for more disruptive innovation.

Many people might acknowledge an innovation lag plaguing key sectors of our country's economy, but most would probably be willing to make an exception for Silicon Valley, America's technology capital. After all, within that fifty square miles of Northern California real estate, innovators and technologists have generated more wealth than in any other region or during any other period of time in

world history.[25] Venture capitalists, elite universities, and freewheeling, blue-jeans-wearing tech enthusiasts have helped create a fertile startup ecosystem, which has designed and marketed creative software and other digital products to consumers. Past concentrations of wealth required oil, gold, or gems. American technology seems to require only an entrepreneurial spirit, creativity, and innovation. "Silicon Valley," according to one businessman "is the story of overthrowing entrenched interests through innovation."[26]

That's why I was stunned when, in the fall of 2011, I heard Peter Thiel declare that, in America, innovation is "somewhere between dire straits and dead."[27] At the time, Silicon Valley seemed brimming with entrepreneurial energy—new startups peddling the latest smartphone applications, staggeringly high rents, and lavish vacation homes for the tech elite cropping up in surrounding resort regions such as Lake Tahoe.[28] Thiel's comment also seemed odd in light of newspaper articles that constantly heralded imminent breakthroughs in technologies such as artificial intelligence, drone delivery systems, and self-driving automobiles. But Thiel isn't alone. Tech engineers and industry analysts increasingly agree that the twenty-first century has inaugurated an innovation plateau in information technology, following the first flurry of internet-based breakthroughs in the American tech space. As one software engineer put it, "The sort of information revolution that the Internet spawned in the 1990s has leveled off. We may have moved to mobile and we may be on social networks, but these aren't the same kinds of revolutionary shifts that occurred when the population first became networked in the 1990s."[29] An *Economist* feature, appraising the history of twentieth-century innovation, has spun a similar narrative: "The various motors of 20th-century growth—some technological, some not—had played themselves out, and new technologies were not going to have the same invigorating effect on the economies of the future. For all its flat-screen dazzle and high-bandwidth pizzazz, it seemed the world had run out of ideas."[30]

I'll let the tech experts deal with prognostications of the next big thing, whether Silicon Valley is gearing up for another innovation explosion, or whether we can expect standard cyclical growth and decline in American technology. One point remains certain: having endured

disruption after disruption in the marketplace, twenty-first-century companies recognize the need for more innovation inside their organizations. It's essential to their very survival. According to a 2016 *Deloitte Business Confidence Report*, which polled six hundred of the country's most successful business leaders, "innovation and its relationship with technology" and "the increasing pressure to find, develop, and keep the right talent" were among the top three concerns leaders cited as determining their future success (the third involved "bold leadership").[31] The financial consulting firm KPMG's US CEO Outlook poll (2016) also revealed innovation to be the top CEO concern: "Seventy-seven percent of the CEOs surveyed say it's important to include innovation in their business strategies, yet 36 percent say their companies' approach to innovation is still siloed, outsourced or unpredictable."[32] As Lynne Doughtie, chairman and CEO of KPMG, concluded, "Leaders recognize that they are operating in a new world, where boundaries are no longer defined and where innovation is vital for growth." Soren Kaplan, affiliated professor at the University of Southern California's Marshall School of Business, agrees, remarking, "More and more companies are realizing they must reinvent their cultures by infusing innovation into their DNA."[33]

DIVERSITY: THE INNOVATION SUPER TOOL

Companies are, of course, responding to the need for more innovation, with some continuing to create innovation labs in the tradition of Xerox Park and Bell Labs. Examples include Google X and Waymo (pioneering self-driving cars, augmented reality, and high-altitude Wi-Fi balloons), Microsoft Research (creating artificial intelligence "smart chips"), and GE's FirstBuild (responsible for manufacturing innovations such as the Opal line of ice and ice-cream makers, the Monogram pizza oven, and ChillHub, a smart refrigerator).[34] Other companies have taken a more organizational approach, weaving innovation into their business models and core operations. CSAA Insurance Group, for example, trained workers in incremental, evolutionary, and disruptive innovation, integrating innovation into the company's core mission and values and creating mechanisms whereby no employee's

ideas would be ignored.[35] Whether they involve creating experimental innovation labs or taking an integrative approach to innovation, these initiatives have been successful and promise future growth.

Whatever your company is doing to enhance innovation, you can mobilize diversity as a means of supercharging your efforts. I've understood the close relationship between diversity and innovation since I was a child. At the age of twelve, I had the rare opportunity to attend an international summer camp in Switzerland. This wasn't because I came from money. Rather, I had a strong, enterprising, and determined mother. As the first African American female manager at Swiss Air Lines, she took advantage of employee discounts on airline fares, getting my brother and me $22 round-trip tickets to Europe for four summers of camp. During these four years in the Swiss Alps, I met campers from Saudi Arabia, Egypt, Europe, India, South America, and the United States—virtually everywhere in the world. To my surprise, my fellow campers weren't familiar with African Americans. Believing that my family was Hispanic, they would speak to us in Spanish. "I'm Negro," I would quickly respond. And I remember them saying, "Oh, Martin Luther King." Dr. King was their only reference point for Negros in America.

These children opened my eyes to their cultures and backgrounds, just as I introduced them to what it was like being Negro in America. And through this process of cross-cultural contact, I came to understand how exposure to diverse environments enhanced and broadened *everyone's* perspective. This is where I first learned to understand through listening, and where I gained respect for the many different religions, customs, beliefs, values, and traditions that exist around the world. I learned that no one perspective was better than another, and that good ideas could come from anywhere. My fellow campers learned from me what it was like to be perceived as a second-class American citizen and how we were struggling for equality. Overall, I think my summer camp experience is what enabled me to create diverse programs and to think creatively as an adult, pushing the boundaries of social impact and CSR programming. I've always believed that to be truly innovative, our companies must be places where as much human difference as possible is represented and where these differences are

given free rein, so that everyone can contribute confidently and so that the widest possible array of ideas can be expressed. For me, no matter what other tactics we might deploy to stay ahead of the innovation curve, our companies now have the opportunity to reflect the international summer camp of my childhood.

What I've intuited about innovation since childhood has received increasing confirmation in the scholarly literature. As researchers are demonstrating, diversity represents an especially promising way to enhance creative thinking—and one that remains underutilized in business settings. The scholarship is conclusive: the more diverse your company, the more innovative and successful it will be.

A wealth of scholarship, for example, links innovation to diverse organizations and company teams. A Deloitte study, which polled employees across the health care, manufacturing, and retail sectors, found a "tangible uplift in business performance when employees think that their workplace is highly committed to, and supportive of, diversity *and* they feel highly included."[36] "If innovation is needed, or higher levels of productivity," notes the study, "this research suggests that some of the answers lie within easy reach. They are locked up in the individual or group potential of diverse employees, and can only be unleashed by creating an inclusive working environment."[37] A *Forbes* Insights study forcefully echoed these findings: "The business case for diversity and inclusion is intrinsically linked to a company's innovation strategy," because diverse minds are needed to help a company "power its innovation strategy."[38] Global managers are taking note. "We have a vast amount of diversity [within the company ranks]," notes Rosalind Hudnell, director of global diversity and inclusion at Intel, who collaborates at work to ideate and innovate. "You can't be successful on a global stage without it," she concludes.

Companies such as Intel that have managed to harness diversity's innovative power also activate another important finding emphasized in the research: to achieve positive impacts, you must cultivate diverse and inclusive workplaces. One way to stimulate inclusive cultures is to create an atmosphere of psychological safety. Amy Edmondson, the Novartis Professor of Leadership and Management at Harvard Business School, is an expert on teams. As her research has demonstrated,

psychological safety is integral to team performance, and it is especially important when teams are diverse, according to her Harvard Kennedy School colleague Dr. Robert Livingston.[39] There has to be a baseline of safety and trust for people to engage in information sharing. "Information sharing," notes Dr. Livingston, a trusted friend and Partnership faculty member, "is a mediator of creativity and innovation."

People will feel reluctant to share ideas if they are ridiculed or dismissed. But in an atmosphere of psychological safety, people are more likely to share, which, per Livingston, "increases the likelihood that people will come up with really novel perspectives and points of view that could stimulate creativity and innovation." Carla Harris, vice chairman of wealth management at Morgan Stanley, agrees, noting, "Having an environment where everybody gets a chance to contribute, gets a chance to be heard, and is rewarded contributes to the firm's overall leadership. Because when people feel like they can't play, they just don't play. You won't get the best ideas; you won't get the most innovative ideas."[40]

In addition to powering creative thinking, diverse teams perform the vital task of keeping companies in touch with consumer markets, ensuring that innovative products and services are culturally sensitive and appeal to diverse consumer bases. The French cosmetics multinational L'Oréal emerged from the Great Recession as the global leader in makeup and skin products, but trailed industry giant Procter & Gamble for dominance in hair care.[41] To keep ahead of competitors such as Revlon, Estee Lauder, and Unilever, L'Oréal has had to constantly expand and create new product lines (approximately 20 percent of its offerings each year are new).[42] Unlike many multinationals, which adopt structural adaptations to expand (such as acquiring subsidiaries or establishing regional units), L'Oréal instead focused on assembling diverse team leaders to keep product lines fresh and appeal to diverse consumer markets.[43]

Consider, for example, how the company updated its line of moisturizers. While most moisturizers in Asia tended to tint a person's skin and help reduce wrinkles, European equivalents tended to either lift or tint (but not do both). Observing this disparity, a French-

Irish-Cambodian manager struck an innovative solution. As Hae-Jung Hong, professor at NEOMA Business School, and Yves L. Doz, Solvay Chaired Professor of Technological Innovation at the business school INSEAD, reported, "Drawing on his knowledge of Asian beauty trends and their increasing popularity in Europe, he and his team developed a tinted cream with lifting effects for the French market, which proved to be a success."[44]

Scholarly data suggest, furthermore, that another of inclusion's major benefits is the ability to stimulate a profusion of ideas. Research has demonstrated, for instance, that the *mere presence of visible people of difference* sparks creative and divergent thinking. Katherine W. Phillips, of the Kellogg School of Management at Northwestern University, and Denise Lewin Loyd, of MIT, conducted two studies that distinguished "surface-level" diversity (race, gender, accent, and other diversity markers that are immediately apparent) from "deep-level" diversity (which includes nonapparent factors such as background, experiences, and expertise). Research had already demonstrated that diverse teams are stronger than homogenous ones, but in order to advance to the next phase of inclusive diversity in our organizations, these scholars believed that we must understand the ways in which these two types of diversity interact and collide at the team level.[45] Among their major findings was that in situations where people with surface-level similarities espoused divergent perspectives, having a visibly diverse individual on a team facilitates the sharing of information. That's because nondiverse people are more willing to disagree with each other in the presence of a diverse person.[46] "In contrast to the conventional wisdom about the benefits of diversity," concludes the study, "we have shown that surface-level diversity may be beneficial for groups, not only because people who are different can bring divergent perspectives to the table, but also because the mere presence of surface-level diversity reduces expectations of similarity, thereby improving individuals' likelihood of expressing dissenting perspectives."[47] If you want the most vigorous, frank, and creative discussions inside your company, you need a person of difference at the table— and in my experience, more than one.

POWERING THE FUTURE THROUGH DIVERSITY

Despite the overriding innovation lag, a few leaders have chosen to operate their companies like L'Oréal, harnessing the power of inclusive diversity to spur innovation. Ken Chenault, former chairman and CEO of American Express, is one of them.[48] When Ken began at the company in 1981, American Express competed with just a few other industry heavyweights, enjoying record profits. Over the next few decades, the picture changed. The proliferation of financial technology ("fintech") startups increased competitive pressure, while the 2008 economic crisis led to greater governmental oversight of the industry. "Since the onset of the 2008 financial crisis," notes a *Fortune* profile on the company, "[American Express] has found itself in a highly competitive, highly regulated, ever-changing business in which profit margins are being squeezed at every turn despite the considerable belt-tightening that the company has undergone."[49]

So how would American Express continue to compete and win in a tougher business environment? Speaking at The Partnership's twenty-fifth annual Partnership Conference, on Martha's Vineyard in 2013, Ken told of how he had once met with his corporate board to lay out a vison of the company's future. "Right now," he told the board members as he held up a slim plastic credit card, "all our services are delivered through this card. In the future, it's going to be totally different." He then described how digital technology would mediate all future interactions, rendering plastic credit cards obsolete. Continuing with the story, he played an audio tape to his board members of American Express employees talking about how much they valued the company, how innovative and creative it was, and how the company was poised to make meaningful changes in the digital landscape. Board members could only hear the male and female voices expressing excitement about the company and the innovative projects they were working on. "Now," Ken said, "I'm going to show you who these critical American Express employees are." He played the audio file for the board members again, this time accompanying it with video of the individuals speaking. The speakers were young individuals with visible body art, earrings in their noses, and edgy hairstyles and clothing. They also represented a panoply of racial and ethnic backgrounds.

As Ken recounted, the board members were surprised, so differ-ent was the profile of these employees from what they expected. By contrast, these diverse young people in every sense of the word rep-resented the new era of team-based, collaborative innovation. "These are the people," Ken said to the board, "who will take us to the fu-ture." And my guess is that Ken's words, dramatized as they had been through sound and image, made quite an impression.

As one of only five African American CEOs on the Fortune 500 list in 2016, Ken understood how powerful divergent thinking is when it comes to innovating our companies.[50] The next generation of lead-ers of color also understands the importance of diversity and innova-tion. Other people of difference in leadership positions have displayed similar understanding.[51] Take Javier Barrientos, whom I introduced earlier. When Javier served as senior director of global diversity and inclusion at the biotechnology company Biogen from 2012 to 2017, he took an integrative and balanced approach to helping the company harness the power of diversity. When he arrived at the company in 2012, people of difference occupied 18 percent of the workforce. By 2016, they accounted for 31 percent. During that same period, women nearly achieved gender parity in the senior vice president leadership roles, after having initially occupied only 11 percent of those positions. But such changes represented just the first step along the company's diversity journey. Under Javier's leadership, Biogen took a proactive role in progressive policy debates, ensuring that health care benefits extended to same-sex couples and taking a firm stance on equal pay and female representation on the corporate board. Biogen executives partnered with socially responsible investors, who would do business only with inclusive companies, and began moving toward supplier in-clusion (a topic I'll discuss later). During Javier's tenure, Biogen went from being a fairly nondiverse biotech company to an industry leader in diversity. Over that same period, the company's stock price rose from $100 to over $300.

Biogen has leveraged deep diversity to position itself on the cutting edge of innovations in multiple sclerosis (MS), where it is a global leader. To better reach consumers and ensure its products were well suited for diverse markets, Biogen created the Diversity Innovation

Lab, a 125-member group that convened diverse minds to think through specific solutions and business needs. Representing different genders, races, ethnicities, ages, and sexual orientations, group members sequestered themselves in a London hotel conference room, thinking through new ways to position the company. "So many great things came out of that Diversity Innovation Lab," Javier notes. One idea was to create an MS diagnostics video on YouTube so that patients wouldn't need to wait to go to the doctor to receive a diagnosis. Instead, the clinic would come to them in the form of the video. This innovative idea came from people located in diverse markets who joined forces to address gaps in patient care. The idea was implemented, and it is currently driving the increase in early diagnosis for patients with MS. As doctors will tell you, the earlier you diagnose the disease, the more effective Biogen's therapies are at halting its progression. This innovation lab leveraged the power of diversity to break through traditional ideas about customer service and deliver what patients really needed. "In the midst of that kind of tension and working together, they were able to energize the region," Javier says. Biogen is a more successful and innovative company thanks to its comprehensive, integrative approach to diversity.

We can also spot leaders promoting innovation through diversity in the public sector. When diplomat Farah Pandith first arrived at the US State Department, in 2007, she found a fairly segregated landscape.[52] Many civil servants and contractors were dark-skinned, but the people wielding power were almost always white. There was also a remarkable lack of ethnic and class-based diversity. "This really affected me," she said. "It didn't make any sense to me that an organization that promoted the three principles of diversity, freedom, and equality across the globe" wouldn't embody such a mandate. As Farah also observed, the State Department, like other government agencies, regularly issued official statements and created videos and programming around diversity. These materials recognized individual countries' national days, such as Bastille Day, religious holidays such as Eid for Muslims and Hanukkah for Jews, and Black History month commemorations in America. Farah couldn't help but feel that many of these statements were bland, formulaic, or even downright stereotypical. Like many of

our businesses, the US government extolled the benefits of diversity instead of embodying that commitment.

Appointed the State Department's Special Representative to Muslim Communities in 2009, Farah was tasked with representing the United States to all Muslim communities around the world. As the first occupant of this special envoy post, she enjoyed a great deal of latitude in shaping her activities. She decided to embody the agency's principles of diversity, inclusion, and human dignity, leveraging the power of inclusive diversity to innovate.

Here's how she did it. Like many large bureaucracies, the State Department follows prescribed protocol. Every department connected to a particular issue has to review proposals and clear them before they can make their way up the leadership hierarchy for consideration. On all Muslim ideas and programs, Farah noticed, the final clearance was always the Middle East and North Africa regional bureau, known as the Near East. But to Farah that sent the wrong message. "Every single regional bureau needs to be on any clearances that have to do with Muslims," Farah told her colleagues, "because Muslims aren't simply located in the Middle East. They are all over the world." She eventually convinced her colleagues that all regional bureaus in the world had to be on the Muslim clearances. At the State Department, this procedural change was extremely innovative. It enriched the agency's conception of global issues related to Muslims. Years later, when Farah helped coordinate President Barack Obama's 2015 summit on entrepreneurship, she ensured that all Muslim communities were included, and not simply those from the Near East. This led to a more inclusive and productive summit that truly welcomed in Muslim entrepreneurs the world over.

BUILDING YOUR COMPANY'S INNOVATION MUSCLE

Your company can leverage the power of diversity, as Ken Chenault, Javier Barrientos, and Farah Pandith did. Begin by creating and nurturing a pipeline of diverse talent, keeping a keen eye specifically on innovation. Your company might need to contact an organization such as The Partnership or Hack.Diversity to help build your pipeline. Or

your company might follow Morgan Stanley's and Google's lead, extending your recruitment channels into historically black colleges and universities.[53] Either way, your recruitment pipelines must be well stocked if you want your organization to remain ahead of the innovation curve.

You must also consciously develop diverse talent once it is onboard. "The most successful companies today," Dr. Livingston observes, "are those that invest resources, time, energy, and commitment into creating the next generation of leaders." In 2009, for example, Credit Suisse's Asia Pacific branch created a women's leadership development program called the Edge. It helps budding executives navigate the company's corporate culture, network, learn about brand development, and advance professionally. "For women in the Asia Pacific region, they sometimes need more help developing their confidence, working on their communication skills, and figuring out how to weather their way through the ranks," said Niki Kesoglou, Credit Suisse director and regional head of diversity and inclusion in the Asia Pacific region. The program was so successful among female executives that the company expanded it to other regions, including the Americas.[54]

Another tactic for developing diverse leaders and unleashing their innovative capacities is to establish incubators and accelerators. By trading startup capital and infrastructure for equity in startup businesses, accelerators give large companies a stake in the growth and success of these fledgling concerns. Carla Harris recently told me of an accelerator she spearheaded at Morgan Stanley that focused on entrepreneurs of color. "If you talk to any accelerators like Y Combinator, TechStars, Village Capital, or Newer Venture Partners," Carla says, "and ask them why they don't have more entrepreneurs of color, the first answer you're going to get is 'We can't find any.'"[55] Like Jody Rose, Carla knew the "insufficient pipeline" mantra was wrong. After announcing her diversity-oriented accelerator on social media, she received an astounding one hundred submissions in two weeks. That was absent any external marketing or postings. As she told me, the first five companies she selected for the pilot program were stellar. In supporting diverse talent, Carla was creating more innovative clients

and future partners for Morgan Stanley. By focusing on recruitment and development, your company can do the same.

Even if your organization has been slow to cultivate inclusive diversity, you can make a profound difference working on an individual basis. Consider Farah Pandith. Her insistence that the State Department adopt a global perspective when thinking about Muslim communities didn't always win her friends among her colleagues. Some officials dismissed the adoption of a global perspective as just another administrative burden. But Farah was unwavering in her advocacy, and as a result, some in the State Department can now engage with Muslims in more nuanced ways. Her experience shows how one person can take charge and forge cultural change within a large bureaucratic organization that otherwise resists it.

Patrick Smith of Bank of America, who has led marketing teams in the banking and insurance sectors, is another example. Patrick understands that when companies promote diversity and inclusion on their websites or in their vision statements, they often achieve little. What matters is whom you hire and promote. Early in his career, Patrick instituted his own, informal version of the Rooney Rule, considering women and people of color for every hire on his teams. "I think the biggest mistake that people who care about diversity make is that they actually think that the world needs to change in order for them to do something different," Patrick said. "Actually, the world doesn't need to change."[56] You can take ownership of your hiring process and create the change you wish to see.

When she began work at Morgan Stanley, Carla Harris didn't wait for the culture to change. As a second-year associate at the firm in 1988, she volunteered for her new company's recruitment events at Harvard Business School, seizing the opportunity to influence hiring decisions. In 1992, when the company was trying to be more aggressive around diversity, Carla collaborated on a scholarship program that expanded the recruitment net to include five historically black colleges, a novelty among Wall Street firms at the time. She later founded an employee resource group (ERG) to help develop black talent, which she now chairs. Such proactive individual attention to

diversity makes a difference, especially when it continues over decades, as in Carla's case.

Lastly, your company must exercise vigilance around diversity. As Dr. Livingston explains, whether it comes to our social circles or businesses, "the default is homophily."[57] If you're not familiar with the term, "homophily" is just a fancy word meaning that, all else being equal, people tend to feel more comfortable and associate with people who resemble them. Such a tendency hurts our companies, producing over time organizations that are largely homogenous. These companies in turn lack the divergent thinking so essential for powering innovation.

Often the "homophily default" occurs on a completely unconscious basis. Dr. Livingston consulted for an international bank that had an informal policy of leadership selection. Managers would tap an employee on the shoulder, grooming him or her (usually him) to become part of the organization's next generation of senior leadership. Leaders at the company approached Dr. Livingston, saying that they wanted more female executives in the organization, but that almost everyone was male. Dr. Livingston appreciated the very thing that Jody Rose did—the problem wasn't with the talent pipeline. Instead of using the shoulder-tap method, which enabled default homophily, Dr. Livingston encouraged the company to generate an objective set of criteria determining who was qualified for leadership positions. Perhaps it was the person who brought in $10 million in revenue per year, who had a certain amount of assets under management, or who simply possessed the right degrees or certifications. The criteria had to be strictly quantifiable and related to the job, with no subjective personality or "cultural-fit" assessments.

The company immediately discovered that when it generated viable candidates in this way, more women emerged for consideration. As an additional measure, Livingston advised that the company adopt a speed-dating-type event at which executives would meet with every person on the list, rotating after a brief conversation. The company did so and, in Livingston's telling, "something magical happened." People looked beyond superficial similarities and discovered common interests and developed relationships with individuals who didn't look like them. "This intervention alone," Livingston noted, "dramatically

increased the number of women that were represented in that organization's leadership ranks." Whether or not you deploy speed dating at your organization, exercise vigilance and guard against the ever-present trap of homophily.

Progressive and smart managers such as Darren Donovan, managing principal at KPMG's Boston office and a white male, make focused, personal efforts to guard against homophily.[58] Since joining the Boston branch of this auditing giant in 2001, Darren has seen the company evolve from a traditional accounting firm to a diversified professional services company, harnessing robotics, artificial intelligence, and other technologies to market and deliver innovative solutions for a global clientele base. To pull off such a transformation, the firm has had to become more sophisticated in recruiting and retaining diverse employees. Darren plays an important role through proactive mentorship and sponsorship of diverse talent.

Take Darren's colleague Corie Fletcher, who is African American and also head of KPMG Boston's African American Network (AAN) employee resource group. During a national meeting of managing partners across the country, Corie was asked to present to the group about the impact of the AAN. When Corie got up to leave the room after the presentation, Darren discretely stopped him, insisting he remain. "Corie," he said, "here's a piece of advice: participation is vital. When you're in the room with all the leaders and they're not kicking you out, stay. Stay at the table unless they ask you to leave." Darren's intervention affirmed Corie's value at the company and exemplified for him how to advocate for himself in the future. On another occasion, Darren struck up a conversation with his colleagues at a reception. The group was predominantly male and the conversation turned to sports. Darren noted that one woman in the group, who was from France, would likely be lost in a conversation about American baseball and would have to disengage. Darren wondered: was this really an inclusive conversation? In short order, he seized on an opportunity to shift the conversation to something more inclusive, a subject the French woman could identify with, and she lit up and immediately engaged. Trust me: small gestures like this count. I admire Darren's efforts at KPMG, and as a person of color and a woman, I can tell you

how meaningful they are in creating an inclusive culture and retaining diverse talent.

Even if you take deliberate steps like Darren did to help your diverse talent feel included, you might still discover that your organization is unconsciously falling back on its old ways. In the 1980s, I was asked to join the board of the Advertising Club of Boston, the trade association for the New England ad industry. At one board meeting, with some of the most creative leaders in the city present, a board member brought in his creative manager, who shared a mock-up of the organization's annual Christmas card. Proud of his card, this gentleman circulated it around the table to solicit feedback. The card featured a standard Christmas scene with Santa, elves, reindeer, and other traditional images and themes. Everyone seemed to love it. But when it reached me, I said, "But it's not diverse."

The creative looked at me and said, "But it's Santa!"

"But in my neighborhood," I responded, "Santa is black. Christmas is not the only holiday celebrated during December, either. There's Hanukkah and Kwanzaa." The creative manager fell silent, his jaw clenched. He had interpreted my suggestion as a threat rather than merely an effort to enlighten us as a creative community. I wasn't trying to take anything away from the Christmas celebration. I simply wanted to make the card richer and better able to resonate with the diverse New England region, to have it reflect the many holiday traditions its residents observe. Today, the Ad Club circulates holiday cards instead of Christmas cards—just one small reflection of our organization's greater efforts at inclusion. And in fact, the Ad Club is well known as a leader in diversity and inclusion. For the past twenty years, its Rosoff Awards have honored visionary leaders who are willing to shake things up and embrace diversity not as a mandate, but as a movement. "Gone are the days of diversity being a mandate," the club declared at its awards ceremony. "Today's diversity is cognitive. Smart, creative companies and their leaders see inclusion as an innovation tool. It's a way to spark ideas, imagination, and collaboration."[59]

I believe that inclusion provides the bedrock of creativity and innovation in our companies, especially as we approach 2042. Whether it's R&D departments, innovation teams, or startup incubators, and

whether its finance, technology, pharmaceuticals, or government bu-reaucracies, diversity is imperative. We must have divergent perspec-tives to generate new ideas. We must also have people of difference on our teams and throughout our organizations to help us reach increas-ingly diverse consumer markets. I'd like to next look at another im-portant mechanism for keeping our companies competitive long into the future: ensuring that our suppliers and supply chains are diverse and inclusive. In addition to enhancing local communities, working with diverse vendors and companies buttresses the bottom line, grants our companies access to diverse consumer markets, and helps us to procure the most innovative products and services available. Increas-ingly, companies that win won't simply be diverse. They'll *buy* diverse.

CHAPTER 7

SUPPLYING FOR SUCCESS

EVERY DAY OVER THE PAST FEW YEARS, I've gazed out my office window overlooking Boston's Seaport District and watched towers of glass rise up from the ground, one after the next. As companies such as General Electric, Reebok, and Vertex have relocated their head-quarters to the city, and as hundreds of startups have also made Boston home, this former warehouse district has been transformed into a mecca of glittering office buildings, exclusive condos, and high-end restaurants. And the building continues. In May 2018, I attended a ribbon-cutting ceremony for one of the most innovative development projects yet: a new Omni hotel.[1] Boston has long lacked sufficient hotel space, a deficit that in turn limited its ability to attract business to its convention centers and tourists to its cultural and historical treasures. With more than one thousand rooms, this Omni property, slated to become the city's fourth-largest hotel, will help redress the room shortage. But what makes this eight-hundred-thousand-square-foot, $550 million showpiece property exciting isn't its deluxe fitness center, large ballroom, or elevated pool spaces. It's the project's revolutionary approach to diversity in hiring.[2]

When evaluating proposals for this development project, the quasipublic entity that owns the land, the Massachusetts Port Authority (Massport), insisted that businesses owned by women and people of difference have a chance to participate. In fact, supplier diversity repre-

sented one of Massport's four primary selection criteria during the project's competitive-bid process.[3] According to Kenn Turner, Massport's director of diversity and inclusion/compliance, this approach makes it one of the most comprehensive and rigorous supplier-inclusion initiatives in the United States to date. "Across the country, no one has done this," Kenn said. "If you truly wanted to be competitive [in this request for proposals], you had to have a comprehensive diversity program, soup to nuts, across all aspects of the program."[4] Omni Hotels & Resorts prevailed over other proposed developers because it presented the most competitive and inclusive plan.

Massport's supplier-inclusion requirement is the brainchild of my longtime friend L. Duane Jackson, an architect by training and an African American. Now a managing member of Alinea Capital Partners, he initially cofounded the award-winning firm Migliassi/Jackson & Associates. Here Duane cultivated a workforce that resembled the United Nations, employing twelve people from twelve countries and leading the firm in tandem with a Chilean business partner. In April 2012, then governor Deval Patrick appointed Duane to Massport's board of trustees, a powerful post given Massport's $22 billion in real estate holdings, including massive swaths of the burgeoning Seaport District. And in 2018, Governor Charlie Baker reappointed him to the board. As chair of Massport's real estate and strategic initiatives committee, Duane was eager to encourage long-term capital investments that both generated business and benefited the entire city. When evaluating proposals for the new Seaport hotel, he worked with Tom Glynn, Massport's CEO, and Jim Rooney, then the executive director of the Massachusetts Convention Center Authority, as well as with David Gibbons, who became the new executive director when Rooney moved on to become president and CEO of the Greater Boston Chamber of Commerce. The group proposed requiring diverse participation at each level of the project's development. Recognizing the merits of the policy, Massport's board embraced it.

Typically, diversity initiatives in the development and real estate sectors extend only to construction jobs. This is especially true in Boston. "Almost no blacks hold leadership roles in Boston's construction unions," notes the *Boston Globe*, "or at the general contractors that have

built the Seaport."[5] In the case of the new Omni hotel, though, diversity requirements extended far beyond construction to include ownership, development, and operations.[6] In evaluating bids for all phases of the project, from the hiring of engineers to the selection of Omni as the hotel operator, Massport based 25 percent of its decision on diversity, weighting it equally alongside a business's ability to perform the work, its financial capability, and the quality it could deliver. This was highly unusual. As the *Boston Globe* observed: "Public agencies often make it clear they want to see diversity when considering bids, but rarely give it a 25 percent weight for scoring purposes."[7] Here such weighting was necessary because Massport sought to include businesses owned by people of color and women at all levels. It wanted to hire architects, lawyers, surveyors, and other professionals who were diverse, and it wanted to ensure that the hotel's eventual workforce reflected Boston's rich tapestry of social and ethnic diversity.[8]

Massport's diversity strategy has paid off. Instead of one large institutional investor or private equity firm investing in the project, the Omni project has more than twenty-five local investors who are people of difference. The supplier diversity program has facilitated business opportunities and knowledge transfer between traditional firms and firms owned by people of difference. Companies with diverse ownership often are invisible to larger, more powerful businesses, who wouldn't think to involve them in projects. For example, my longtime colleague Richard Taylor, a real estate developer and former Massachusetts transportation secretary who is African American, had long sought to break into the city's hospitality sector. "There is no way to get in without [an opportunity like a Seaport hotel]," Taylor said. "You qualify if you have hotel experience. But if you never have a chance to get hotel experience, how can you qualify?"[9] African American real estate developer and restaurateur Darryl Settles puts things more pointedly: "I don't know one person of color that has made any money from the development of the Seaport [prior to the Omni project]. Not one."[10]

The Omni deal has helped change this status quo by encouraging novel business alliances and extending opportunities to diverse firms to deliver quality goods and services. In one stroke, diverse firms became more competitive, gaining access to larger jobs and contracts.

That in turn has meant increased revenue and profits, more money for the local tax base, more community impact programming empowering local residents, and more-extensive hiring opportunities within a broad spectrum of Boston's communities. Ultimately, it means wealth redistribution, which in Boston is sorely needed.

In 2016, a Brookings Institution study revealed that of America's ninety-seven largest cities, Boston suffered from the greatest wealth disparity, a gap almost double the American average.[11] The numbers are startling. A 2015 Duke University and Federal Reserve Bank of Boston study found that the median net worth of Boston's white families was $247,500; African American family net worth was a scant $8.[12] Such inequities are especially glaring in the Seaport, where public transportation is scarce, the median family income is $133,000, and two-bedroom apartments routinely rent for more than $5,000 a month (and sell for several million dollars). It's no wonder African Americans are a rare site in the neighborhood's restaurants, fitness studios, and technology companies. As the *Boston Globe* characterized it, "The Seaport has become like an exclusive club created, frequented, and populated almost exclusively by the white and the wealthy."[13] African Americans received only three of the 660 residential mortgage loans issued there between 2007 and 2017, and represent a mere 3 percent of the innovation hub's population.[14]

Such inequities can damage Boston's brand. In a 2017 *Boston Globe* survey, African Americans rated Boston as the least welcoming of eight large American cities, and more than half deemed it "unwelcoming" in general.[15] Our country's celebrities and comedians routinely single out Boston as a racist place, with *Saturday Night Live's* Michael Che declaring it, in 2017, "the most racist city I've ever been to."[16] And the Seaport helps reinforce this national reputation. In 2011, Vertex Pharmaceuticals relocated to the Seaport, embarking on one of the country's largest private-sector construction projects. But amid the fanfare and excitement, many were discouraged to discover that "none of the 21 companies on the development team—engineers, curtain wall consultants, architects, elevator specialists—had black ownership or black executives in leadership," according to the *Boston Globe*.[17] This lack of nonwhite participation was routine across the Seaport, helping

to cement Boston's long-standing reputation as a place inhospitable to diverse businesses.[18]

Massport is changing this perception. "To attain significant diversity on the project," recalls journalist Jule Pattison-Gordon, "Massport had to fight against a prevailing perception that Boston is unfriendly to minorities and women, which dampens diverse businesses' interest in the city."[19] Massport combatted this stereotype and demonstrated the city's seriousness about supplier diversity by hiring as a consultant Ernest Green, one of the most respected African American power brokers on Wall Street. Green, in turn, reached out to his national network of diverse leaders, informing them about the new program.[20] Little by little, Boston's brand among African Americans is changing, as Duane has observed as he travels around the country. A better Boston brand could boost municipal revenues because promising young companies might give the city and its Seaport District a chance instead of taking their innovative business models (and jobs) to Houston, Chicago, New York, or Los Angeles—all places that have traditionally embraced and actively promoted diverse entrepreneurship.[21]

When Massport's diversity requirement was proposed, skeptics predicted it would diminish the project by dampening competition. The opposite has happened, and as a result, Massport has adopted the 25 percent performance requirement for all of its real estate development projects. "This is not a one-off," Kenn Turner said. "This is how we're now going to operate as an entity."[22] Other agencies have taken notice and now seek to emulate Massport. The CEO of Dormitory Authority, which provides construction and financial services to public projects throughout New York State, has met with Duane in order to learn more about the requirement's language and process. The Port Authority of New York and New Jersey has reached out to Duane as well.

Massport serves as a model for public sector supplier diversity initiatives, but what about the private sector? Here as well, opportunity beckons. Although corporate supplier diversity programs have blossomed in the late twentieth and early twenty-first centuries, too many organizations still view them through a compliance lens—something the organization *has to do* rather than an initiative it should fully

embrace. These companies do the minimum, and thus fail either to reap significant economic benefit or to change the broader business environment. As one study of "global 1,000" companies has demonstrated, many firms don't effectively measure the financial impact of diverse suppliers on their overall revenues.[23] This makes these programs window dressing or public relations initiatives, designed to garner the support of clients and customers instead of driving meaningful, long-term change. "What we see here is serious misalignment," observes Kurt Albertson, North American procurement advisory program lead for the Hackett Group, a leading digital consultancy. "Many companies are taking the easy way out, and as a result aren't driving real supplier diversity benefits. They are focused on making the numbers they need to meet government requirements or getting recognition from their customers or industry. But they aren't showing the attention to detail required to create programs that have real impact."[24]

The news here is not all bad. Many forward-thinking companies are mobilizing diverse supply-chain management to power increased revenues and position themselves for increased market share and future growth. As the National Minority Supplier Development Council (NMSDC) has observed, the business potential of supply-chain diversity is enormous: "Corporations . . . benefit from minority supplier development programs through expansion of their markets, a larger pool of qualified suppliers/contractors, cost savings and higher quality products and services due to increased competition."[25] These benefits will only increase over time. We've seen that businesses are seeking to maximize their innovative and marketing capacities and to stay ahead of digital disruption while remaining profitable and securing strategic market advantages. Contracting with diverse and inclusive suppliers offers a prime means of accomplishing these objectives.[26] As the demographic profile of the country shifts, diverse businesses (defined as firms with at least 51 percent diverse ownership) represent one of the fastest-growing slices of the American economy.[27] In the years ahead, large corporations will secure partnerships with these firms to stay ahead of market trends and please the country's increasingly inclusive stakeholders. If you have tended to underplay supplier diversity, do what Massport did, and embrace it.

THE ORIGINS OF SUPPLIER DIVERSITY

Although they may reside on the periphery of corporate strategy, supplier diversity initiatives actually have a long history, dating from civil rights–era legislation and policies. Beginning in the 1960s, the federal government sought to redress past injustices by promoting certain historically disadvantaged individuals (in the case of affirmative action) or businesses owned by ethnically or racially diverse individuals (in the case of supplier diversity).[28] Following rioting and unrest in Cleveland, Detroit, Los Angeles, and other cities during the late 1960s, national attention turned to promoting African American businesses in particular. President Richard Nixon sought to ameliorate urban unrest partly by championing so-called "black capitalism."[29] By the 1970s, private companies began responding to these federal procurement initiatives, creating supplier diversity programs of their own in order to make themselves more competitive for public contracts.

Today's supplier inclusion has likewise built on the "responsibility revolution" that swept the world in the 1990s. Beginning in the late twentieth century, government agencies, customers, and concerned citizens began demanding more ethical corporate behavior. In this context, modern corporate social responsibility (CSR) arose, including socially responsible supply-chain orientation. In the 1990s, for example, the footwear and apparel industries came under scrutiny for routinely violating international labor practices.[30] To restore public confidence, companies enacted governance and oversight of all areas of the supply chain, which up to that point had been fragmented and disorganized.[31] Responsible supply-chain management now encompasses a variety of issues, notably environmental stewardship. In a rapidly diversifying country such as the United States, such management should extend to include diversity as well.

Like their affirmative action counterparts, the first generation of supplier-diversity initiatives focused on quotas and were largely compliance driven. Public Law 95–907, enacted in 1978, mandated that all federal contracts exceeding a half-million dollars required the express articulation of minority contracting targets, as well as accompanying documentation for how companies would include historically

underserved business vendors and suppliers.[32] These initiatives spurred supplier diversity in the short term but faced court challenges. In *City of Richmond v. Croson* (1998), the US Supreme Court overturned a Richmond law requiring that 30 percent of all construction contracts be given to diverse firms.[33] This decision led to the dismantling of similar supplier programs across the country and discouraged the creation of new public and private supplier-diversity programs.[34] Public sentiment against affirmative action policies, including the banning of public affirmative action programs in California (with Proposition 209 in 1996), Washington State (with Initiative 200 in 1998), and Michigan (with Proposal 2 in 2006), also put a damper on corporate supplier diversity nationwide.[35]

Supplier-diversity initiatives have since made a comeback, spurred less by legislation than by America's changing business and demographic landscape.[36] During the 2010s, the business case for diverse contracting has become more apparent. Many large purchasing organizations (LPOs) observed the exponential increase in the number of diverse firms and took note of their increased profitability. Between 2007 and 2012, the number of diverse firms increased by 38 percent (skyrocketing to eight million). The gross receipts of non-majority-owned firms increased 35 percent within the same period.[37] Since the turn of the twenty-first century, such diverse organizations have represented one of the major engines powering the US economy.[38] In this context, LPOs voluntarily created diversity supplier programs and proactively cultivated relationships with diverse firms.

In particular, LPOs have steadily flocked to the NMSDC, a nonprofit public-private intermediary association that has promoted diverse supplier and procurement efforts since its establishment in 1972. The NMSDC encourages all major US LPOs to become members, facilitates job fairs and other networking opportunities for businesses of difference, and provides accreditation for diverse businesses. As scholar Ian Worthington, a reader in corporate social responsibility at the UK's Leicester Business School, and his colleagues detail, the NMSDC "has played a pivotal role in bringing together some of the largest private and public sector organizations and minority

enterprises."[39] NMSDC members have exponentially increased their purchases from businesses of difference—from $86 million (1972) to approximately $100 billion today.[40] These diverse companies employ nearly six million workers and generate an annual $1 trillion for the US economy.[41] The NMSDC therefore doesn't make its case for supplier inclusion based on fairness or social justice (though this is certainly on its mind). Instead, the organization asserts that diverse procurement efforts are financially beneficial to both diverse businesses and LPOs.[42] To ensure business success, smart companies will increasingly flock to the NMSDC and study its supplier diversity best practices to remain competitive.

PERFECTING THE SCIENCE
OF SUPPLIER DIVERSITY

One firm that already has done this is the Ford Motor Company, a global leader in supplier diversity and a member of the Billion Dollar Roundtable, a select group of twenty-two firms that purchase $1 billion or more from diverse and female-owned vendors each year.[43] A leader even within this elite group, Ford as of 2016 had purchased a combined $100 billion from diverse companies.[44]

The automotive giant's diversity-procurement efforts began in 1978, making it one of the country's inaugural diverse supplier programs.[45] Early on, Ford acknowledged the market rationale for engaging with diverse suppliers: it promised not only to create local wealth and, in turn, demand for company products, but also to power the company's penetration of new markets and increase its revenues.[46] As a Ford representative related, however, nurturing supplier diversity would require some coaching and mentorship on the company's part. According to an anonymous Ford purchasing employee, the company knew that "if we are going to have minorities in our value chain then it has to be more than providing them with opportunity—we actually had to start working with them and understand what it would take to build a long term relationship."[47] After all, the automotive industry has strict and demanding requirements. As business scholars Mayank Shah and Monder Ram note, "Ford seeks volume suppliers with high

technical capabilities."[48] Instead of bemoaning an insufficient pipeline, Ford proactively cultivated diverse corporate talent that could meet and exceed its demanding standards.

Ford was an early and active participant at NMSDC trade shows and opportunity fairs, trying to attract firms of difference.[49] It then cultivated this talent, developing in-house mentorship programs, such as Supplier Skills for Life, to help enhance the companies and entrepreneurs. This program engages industry experts and diverse firms on timely business topics to overcome obstacles in maintaining and scaling their companies. For instance, Ford partnered with the Michigan Minority Supplier Development Council to sponsor a seminar on succession planning with estate planning and probate attorney Michael Witzke.[50] As Witzke advised, succession planning is important for every business because it helps avoid negative tax consequences, interpersonal problems, or hurt feelings in families. But when it comes to firms of difference, succession is especially important because, as Witzke recounted to Ford's suppliers, minority certification does not transfer automatically to subsequent owners. Witzke therefore advised current owners about the importance of planning for their lenders, suppliers, and customers. He offered additional advice about family limited-liability companies, corporate redemptions (in which families buy back stock), buy-sell arrangements, and third-party sales.

In 1993, Ford extended its leadership in supplier diversity to the entire automotive industry by founding its 2nd Tier Program. This program was designed to help small, diverse firms develop and grow as Ford partners with large suppliers in the industry, helping them to implement supplier diversity development initiatives similar to Ford's.[51] These efforts in turn help increase the opportunities for smaller diverse suppliers seeking to increase their size, scale, and technical proficiency so that they might one day directly contract with giants like Ford.[52] As of this writing, the program generates $2 billion in diverse procurement efforts annually and has expanded to include female entrepreneurs and service veterans.[53] Prior to 2012, Ford didn't include veteran-owned businesses in its own diverse supplier scorecard. Four years later, it was spending more than $1.1 billion with such suppliers.[54]

What also makes Ford's 2nd Tier Program so robust is that it articulates strong diversity requirements and actively monitors program participants. To become a Tier 1 purchaser (or a direct supply-chain vendor) in good standing, you must work with Ford's supplier diversity department to set aggressive goals for diversity procurement and submit minority purchasing reports every six months.[55] While these companies don't have to meet Ford's ambitious goal of procuring 10 percent of all US products and services from diverse enterprises, they must still maintain high diversity standards. Per company policy, "We encourage our 1st Tier suppliers to establish a goal of purchasing at least 6% of all goods and services from certified minority business enterprises, 2% from certified women-owned business enterprises and 3% from certified veteran business."[56] As Ford's guidelines make clear, companies that fail to meet these standards and don't demonstrate a proven record of diverse engagement aren't welcome to conduct business with the automaker. "Ford believes that everyone benefits when all businesses are afforded an opportunity to compete in the marketplace," and the company therefore "wishes to partner with suppliers who share this philosophy."[57]

This program has greatly benefitted small, diverse suppliers. After Detroit Pistons star Vinnie Johnson retired from professional basketball, he opened Piston Automotive in 1995, hoping to stimulate Detroit's local economy.[58] His company, which supplies chassis, powertrain, and suspension parts, began contracting with major automotive companies in Detroit.[59] After the Great Recession in 2008, Ford needed to trim its budgets and began outsourcing certain in-house services. It had a preexisting relationship with NetApp, an American multinational and Fortune 500 giant. Ford notified the California conglomerate that, to maintain this business relationship, NetApp needed to contract with Ford's diverse suppliers. NetApp contacted Piston, which became a NetApp reseller, and both companies have thrived as a result. The Piston contract enabled NetApp to expand its regional footprint in Detroit, while the collaboration increased Piston's sales to more than $4 million in 2011 (a significant increase, as the company was still recovering from revenue declines stemming from the economic downturn). In the summer of 2011, NetApp and

Piston jointly advertised on billboards flanking Detroit's major free-ways and planned a joint international expansion. "We both had to do some internal selling to get this business going," Darrin Hands, au-tomotive global enterprise manager at NetApp, concedes. "But we're better together than we are separate."

Ford's leadership in supplier diversity and development has paid dividends for its own company as well, powering its growth and helping it to become more environmentally sustainable. Speaking of Ford's diverse suppliers, Carla Preston, the company's supplier diversity development director, has remarked: "As innovators, these business leaders are creating new sustainable products that help us meet our goal to reduce our environmental footprint while at the same time accelerate development of advanced, fuel-efficient ve-hicle technologies around the world. They have made substantial contributions to Ford's profitable growth. And we expect continued growth with our minority, women, and veteran business owners for years to come."[60]

Ford is hardly the only large company with a strong and innova-tive supplier diversity program. Another corporate initiative worthy of note is Google's Small Business Supplier Diversity program, launched in 2014.[61] As late as 2012, Google wasn't focused on vendors at all. As Adrianna Samaniego, senior global program manager of this Google diversity program, recounts, "Initially, we were looking at the diver-sity of our customer base and the diversity of our workforce but not the diversity of our supply chain."[62] The company realized that in try-ing to attract diverse customers and clients, it also needed to diversify its procurement strategies. Yet Google had no formalized registration and application process to catch a small, diverse company's attention. "Googliness is the core of our culture," Samaniego says. "Many of our successes as a company have been the result of innovation teams that had the autonomy to go out and find suppliers rather than work from a list. That matches our culture, and not quotas and certification pro-cesses."[63] Small and diverse vendor recruitment thus initially occurred thanks to word of mouth, prompting some diverse suppliers to go to comical lengths to catch the attention of Google. "One small business spent two and a half years asking around at our bus stop areas for the

right person to talk to about their company before they found a contact," Samaniego recalls.[64]

A few Google employees observed this shortcoming and began addressing it. Given Google's focus on data analytics, this team first had to present a quantitative business case for how and why a diverse supplier program would economically benefit the company. The team members critically assessed the profitability of their own vendors and then examined how other companies and governmental agencies approached the topic. They also garnered critical information from small businesses throughout the country.[65] They discovered, not surprisingly, that diverse vendors wanted clear, simple, and straightforward application procedures and that they also sought coaching from the company so they could better compete in the digital space. By July of 2013, Google's team had created a program that included a straightforward application process; provided timely feedback following a vendor's application; offered incentives for participants, such as discounts on Google's advertising platforms; and even initiated a supplier development program.[66] The company advertised on social media, notifying national supplier inclusion organizations such as the NMSDC of their new platform.[67]

In line with its method of "launch and iterate," Google progressively modified its early-stage diversity initiative to improve its scope, reach, and effectiveness. The company realized, for instance, that small businesses might excel in developing a product, service, or solution, but not necessarily in integrating themselves within a supply chain. Absent these skills, the small business wouldn't get ahead, and Google would also expose itself to supply-chain problems. To solve the problem, Google collaborated with Dartmouth College's Tuck School of Business in 2015, providing coaching around search engine optimization, data analytics, web design, and other skills that would enable small businesses to achieve "digital excellence."[68] Since 2015, the program has mentored two hundred participants, and both Dartmouth and Google have deemed it a success.[69]

Google also tweaked the program's marketing. The company had created a series of webinars to advertise the new initiative, but the supplier diversity team discovered that small, diverse vendors needed

more direct forms of outreach. "It was critical to meet diverse businesses where they do business," Samaniego says. "That's where we heard feedback and that's where we demystified the process. A lot of small businesses think that because they're not a technology business they don't have anything to offer to Google or they may not be ready to do business with Google."[70] The project also required internal modification, as the team discovered that Google employees used the standard Google search platform when in need of suppliers. That may not have included small, diverse vendors who lacked a digital presence and therefore escaped the search algorithm. In response, the company in 2015 launched Pivot, an internal search tool that its employees could use to connect with a wider array of small, diverse businesses.[71] This platform increased small, diverse business exposure and helped improve Google's efficiency and selection of talented partners.

Without Pivot, Matthew Moses's brand licensing and apparel design company, Shalimar Media Group, might not have scaled. The partnership began when Moses sought Google's assistance to design a garment honoring Black History Month. Moses subsequently became more involved with the company and enrolled in Google's Tuck Business School mentorship program. "My main takeaway from the three-day course was that even as a small business, I can compete with the biggest companies if I have a solid digital strategy," Moses confirms.[72] Shalimar is now firmly integrated into Google's supply chain, designing garment collections.[73]

As different as Ford and Google are, these two companies have both harnessed the power of diverse suppliers to fuel their future growth. Ford has drawn on its diverse suppliers to help it produce the next generation of clean-energy automobiles, while Google is poised to expand its supply-chain diversity program globally, as it prepares to innovate around customized health care solutions, retail, and autonomous vehicles. "Google and our parent company Alphabet are now expanding into almost every industry you can think of," Samaniego declares. "In order to continue to be innovative," she adds, "our supply chain needs to be inclusive."[74]

How innovative is your supply chain? If you have a program in place, have you made it easy for small, local suppliers to find you?

Have you built it out to include coaching and other offerings to help sustain suppliers and build relationships with them? And if you don't have a formal program, what kinds of opportunities are you leaving untapped? Now is the time to take action around supply-chain diversity and to lead your industry before your competitors do.

SECURING YOUR DIVERSE SUPPLIERS

Your company can devise a customized supply-chain initiative by following a few simple steps. First, *establish clear goals*, without necessarily mandating specific quotas. Massport eschewed quotas, opting instead to broaden its evaluation criteria for public-works projects to incorporate diverse firms. Google has also effectively articulated its supplier diversity goals in nonnumeric terms. Significantly, its Small Business Supplier Diversity program doesn't target diverse firms but rather small businesses, aiming to empower members of groups that are currently underrepresented in the digital space.[75] To be eligible for participation, companies need only be based in America, generate less than $15 million in annual revenues, and employ fewer than fifty individuals.[76] Since firms of difference are underrepresented at Google, and online in general, Google's small business program works to ensure it is a diversity and inclusion initiative. Aerica Banks, a patent analyst at Google, establishes this linkage as follows: "In closing the digital divide, we also close the divides on race, on social inequity, on injustice, that we face in our communities and the wider world. It's very important that Google, which is a company and a tool that is universally familiar to everyone, truly makes itself universally accessible."[77]

A second step your company should take is to *proactively find, mentor, and sponsor diverse firms*. Duane speaks with great enthusiasm about the partnerships and collaborations that Massport's policy has created in Boston's Seaport District. Majority construction firms have reached out to diverse companies, engaging in smaller projects to prepare for their joint Omni hotel project. Google learned that it couldn't simply create marketing materials and online programs but had to actively engage with small businesses throughout the country, asking about their specific needs and communicating the company's interest in working

with them. Throughout its history, the NMSDC has facilitated net-working events and fairs, helping to forge longstanding partnerships between large purchasing organizations and diverse companies. Seek out these events, as well as opportunities furnished by other industry leaders, such as the National Hispanic Business Group, the National Association of Women Business Owners, the Center for Veterans Enterprise, and the myriad regional, state, and local chapters of these organizations.

Once you find diverse firms, your company should follow the lead of Ford and Google and *provide these firms with the tools they need to become optimal supply partners.* Here, midsize businesses can make a difference—you don't need the resources of a Fortune 100 firm. As I described earlier, Eastern Bank's board of trustees in 2017 launched its Business Equality Initiative, a program that provides professional and monetary assistance to help black and Latino businesses scale in the Boston area. In facilitating their growth, Eastern Bank seeks to strengthen its stable of successful and dependable suppliers and vendors, all the while helping to grow the greater business ecosystem and to fight against regional wealth disparities.[78] This program fits the larger vision and brand purpose of Eastern Bank, which is to proactively invest in the diverse communities it serves.[79] Your business, too, can design and launch mentorship and sponsorship programs that fit its value proposition and needs.

My friend Jim Rooney, president and CEO of the Greater Boston Chamber of Commerce, has mobilized and exceeded these best practices in his pursuit of diverse procurement.[80] As mentioned earlier, prior to assuming his role at the chamber in 2015, Jim served as executive director of the Massachusetts Convention Center Authority, on whose board I also served. I can tell you that Jim's efforts were very much supported by the board as he strategized to include more local and diverse businesses in the convention's food-service suppliers. Still, well-meaning procurement directors registered objections, seeking to protect their companies. "Well, we buy all of our eggs from a national supplier and the farms in Massachusetts can't fill our orders," was one example. Jim countered by getting granular: "Well, you don't need to buy *every* egg from this national supplier." As Jim would explain,

diversifying your suppliers, even just a little, makes solid business sense. "Your workforce and customers are more diverse than ever before, and they are looking for this kind of behavior," he advised.

In 2016, Jim convened the Greater Boston Chamber of Commerce's board to discuss the persistent problems of wealth inequality in the Boston area. As Jim said to his colleagues, "You're the policy-making body. You set the direction. You set the priorities for the chamber of commerce. And I have a question. What is the role of the business community and the chamber on issues of race, wealth, and income inequality in this region?" A stimulating and thoughtful discussion ensued, and the chamber decided that as representatives of the major corporations and businesses in Boston, they could make a concrete impact by contracting with diverse purveyors of goods and services. They began by looking to national best practices for contracting with and mentoring small, diverse, and female-owned businesses. Such programs provided a useful framework for the chamber but were also lacking in certain areas. "What these programs tend to do," Jim reflected, "is provide [diverse businesses] with all this nurturing, training, and support and then say, 'Okay, go out into the world and succeed.'" And that's where the chamber decided to innovate. In addition to establishing a robust supplier diversity program, setting clear goals for diverse supply buys against national benchmarks, and providing marketing and training to diverse businesses, the chamber put buyers and suppliers in a room together to make business deals! The Greater Boston Chamber of Commerce Pacesetters Initiative partners companies to create opportunities to scale local enterprises of color.

In providing this missing link, the Greater Boston Chamber of Commerce fulfilled the mission of all chambers—to come together around a common purpose to achieve a collective good. Chambers have persisted for centuries because they've successfully been able to embrace what defines commerce at a particular time, such as shipping and port control in the nineteenth century or online commerce today. By addressing these fundamental needs, chambers have helped all businesses to participate in commerce and succeed. As Jim reflected in an interview with me, the chamber's fundamental proposition has

changed over the past quarter-century and now centers on diversity. "The demographics of Boston and its work force are both younger and more diverse," he said, and must be represented, included, and mentored for this larger business community to succeed. The Greater Boston Chamber of Commerce and Massport have taken this value proposition seriously, instituting comprehensive supplier diversity programming to elevate the entire business ecosystem.

THE RIGHT THING TO DO

On September, 23, 2017, my husband, Bernie, and I had the privilege of attending the seventy-ninth annual meeting of the NAACP New England Area Conference, in which Duane Jackson was awarded the NAACP's illustrious Chaney, Goodman, and Schwerner Advocacy Award. The award is named for three civil rights champions: James Chaney, Andrew Goodman, and Michael Schwerner, who, in the summer of 1964, traveled to Neshoba County, Mississippi, to participate in a historic voter-registration effort known as the Freedom Summer. These men, all in their early twenties, were staunchly committed to fairness, equality, and social justice. They became acquainted with one another in New York at the Congress of Racial Equality, which prepared them for the registration campaign and coached them on how to deal with the resistance and harassment their efforts were likely to face in the Deep South.[81] Goodman and Schwerner, both from New York City, were white; Chaney, from Mississippi, was black. They drove together to Neshoba County to volunteer. Shortly after arriving that summer, they were brutally slain by Ku Klux Klansmen.[82]

Chaney, Goodman, and Schwerner have long been an inspiration to me. I was just twelve years old at the time of their murders, but ever since, when I have faced racist taunts or discrimination of any kind, I have looked to their example and found the strength to endure. It was thus with extreme pride that Bernie and I watched Duane Jackson receive this award for his contribution to promoting fairness and equality in Boston. Over the course of his career in real estate, Duane has championed people of difference, spearheading the construction of more than $800 million in affordable and specialized housing projects.

But on this fall evening, we all gathered together to honor his latest, greatest achievement—the supplier-diversity program he created for Massport.[83] Our country has come a long way since the 1960s, but we still have significant progress to make. In Boston, Duane's initiative at Massport has helped create positive change. I hope his example inspires you as you consider supplier inclusion programs in your company. It's the economically prudent course. It's also the right thing to do.

Of course, even the most robust diverse-supplier programs can't succeed without the unqualified support of a company's senior executives. Neither can diversity and inclusion initiatives generally. But given the changing expectations of customers and other stakeholders, senior leaders must no longer simply support such initiatives. They must act decisively to defend them, joining in public debates about diversity and inclusion even when doing so might risk their companies' immediate economic interests. I want to now explore the increased importance of executive leadership in powering diversity and inclusion throughout our country and the wider world. Your organization will certainly need the programs and policies I've already described to remain successful, but, ultimately, being successful will also require bold, courageous, and inspiring leadership around diversity issues. If you serve on a board or an executive team, or if you're poised to do so one day, now is the time to make your mark. Stand up for what is both right and good for business. Stand up for diversity.

A NEW AGE OF BUSINESS ETHICS

IN AUGUST 2017, neo-Nazis, Ku Klux Klansmen, and other "alt-right" activists descended on Charlottesville, Virginia, setting off a chain of events that left three people dead and dozens injured. As America looked on in shock, the vast majority of the country's politicians publicly registered their indignation and anger. Then Virginia governor Terry McAuliffe told the white nationalists that their behavior was unacceptable, while then Charlottesville mayor Michael Signer echoed these sentiments, saying, "I am heartbroken that a life has been lost here."[1]

One of the few exceptions to this chorus of indignation came from our country's president. In a press conference following the violent clashes, Donald Trump blamed "both sides" engaged in the protest.[2] Hearing the president utter these words, which placed peaceful protestors and those espousing Nazism and white supremacy on the same moral plane, I, like so many others, was shocked and dismayed. I anticipated that condemnations of Trump's statement would issue from many quarters, and I was not disappointed. But I did wonder how American business would react. Would individual leaders perceive it to be in their interests to stand up and challenge the president and white nationalism?

They did. Nearly two dozen CEOs from our country's most powerful and influential companies vocally registered their disgust, circulating

memos and taking to social media.[3] Merck CEO Kenneth C. Frazier, the grandson of a slave, resigned from Trump's manufacturing council, inspiring the chief executives at Intel, Under Armour, and other major corporations and nonprofits to follow suit.[4] The corporate exodus from these advisory panels was so swift that the president was forced to dissolve his manufacturing council and his economic strategy and policy forum.[5]

CEOs didn't simply register their outrage against racial hatred but also publicly reaffirmed their commitment to diversity and inclusion. Frazier voiced his concerns "as a matter of personal conscience," decrying the violence and Trump's response, while proclaiming, "Our country's strength stems from its diversity and the contributions made by men and women of different faiths, races, sexual orientations, and political beliefs."[6] Satya Nadella, Microsoft's CEO, declared in an email that the "bias, bigotry and senseless violence" on display in Charlottesville had no place in this country or in his company: "At Microsoft, we strive to seek out differences, celebrate them and invite them in. As a leader, a key part of your role is creating a culture where every person can do their best work, which requires more than tolerance for diverse perspectives."[7] Jamie Dimon, CEO of JPMorgan Chase, released a memo criticizing Trump and affirming his company's ethos. "Racism, intolerance and violence are always wrong," Dimon wrote. "The equal treatment of all people is one of our nation's bedrock principles. There is no room for equivocation here: the evil on display by these perpetrators of hate should be condemned and has no place in a country that draws strength from our diversity and humanity."[8] Lynne Doughtie, CEO of KPMG, wrote: "This weekend, in my home state of Virginia, a violent protest took place that has rippled throughout our country. . . . Make no mistake: The KPMG community rejects any and all expressions of hatred, bigotry and group supremacy. . . . As we move forward, we will continue to embrace our differences and respect all individuals as we believe that diversity makes KPMG better and stronger."[9]

I found this outpouring of CEO sentiment reassuring. For much of my long career, companies have tended to remain silent about social and political events, especially if they bore some relation to diversity

and inclusion-related issues. "Silence used to be the default posture," acknowledges Aaron Chatterji, a professor at Duke University's Fuqua School of Business, who specializes in CEO activism.[10] During the 2000s and 2010s, companies began flexing their muscles around issues such as global warming and the environment, hoping to appeal to a large, socially conscious generation of millennials. Still, they continued to steer away from taking stands around diversity and inclusion.

Some CEOs thought speaking out on controversial issues around race and ethnicity (not to mention gender and sexual orientation) would have alienated shareholders, stakeholders, and customer bases who held other views. With Charlottesville, however, it was clear that we'd entered a new era of corporate ethical engagement in relation to race. As Darren Walker, president of the Ford Foundation and a PepsiCo board member, observed, Charlottesville represented "a seminal moment in the history of business in America. In this maelstrom, the most clarifying voice has been the voice of business."[11] Business leaders weren't simply registering their opinions about diversity and inclusion. They were leading and guiding the national conversation.

Such engagement is the wave of the future—and it makes sound business sense. Since June 2017, more than four hundred CEOs have signed the CEO Action for Diversity & Inclusion initiative, the most extensive "CEO-driven business commitment to advance diversity and inclusion within the workplace" to date.[12] All signatories commit to exercising leadership in their companies and the nation, sharing best (and worst) inclusion practices with their colleagues, and creating climates of trust by working against unconscious bias. Such executive leadership on the topic is inspiring, but as a *Washington Post* article pointed out, even the most well-meaning declarations aren't enough: "Companies have been funneling millions of dollars into diversity and inclusion programs as research underscores the business case for having more diverse teams, which improve decision-making and better represent a company's customers. If companies ignore political actions that hurt certain groups, they undermine the credibility of those programs, making them ring hollow."[13] As the nation continues to diversify, the calculus regarding CEO activism has changed, and will continue to change, with the price of silence on diversity- and inclusion-related

issues becoming too high. Going forward, CEOs and other leaders will have to articulate bold, ethical positions on diversity and inclusion, like they did in response to Charlottesville, or they'll face stakeholder backlash, diminished reputations, and decreases in their revenues and market share. Welcome to a new age of business ethics.

THE RISE OF THE ETHICAL CORPORATION

Traditionally, companies have intervened in national politics only if the issue at stake bore on fiscal policy, trade, or other topics directly affecting an organization's bottom line.[14] With few exceptions, firms avoided public interventions in matters of social justice. Consider how surprised Woolworth's was in February 1960 when four African American men went to the company's Greensboro, North Carolina, lunch counter, requesting meal service.[15] The company's official policy was to "abide by local custom" and uphold race-based segregation in the dining establishment. The manager therefore denied these men service. But Americans would no longer accept the status quo, and in subsequent weeks, the numbers of nonwhites demanding lunch at this counter multiplied, with sit-ins eventually engulfing the entire country.[16] The Greensboro establishment lost business for its refusal to support equality, and four months after this momentous incident in civil rights history, this lunch counter welcomed in people of all races.[17] It was the right decision—and the right *business* decision.

For most of the twentieth-century, companies behaved like Woolworth's, sluggishly changing their policies when consumer dissatisfaction hurt their business but generally declining to exhibit principled ethical behavior on their own. During World War II, the Swiss company Nestlé had no qualms furnishing food and coffee supplies to both German and American military units, while the German textile company Hugo Boss outfitted SS units, SA storm troopers, and Hitler Youth in their trademark uniforms (and even forced Polish and French prisoners to assist to help keep pace with war demand).[18] In 1990, Harvey Gantt challenged Jesse Helms, described as "the last prominent unabashed white racist politician in this country," for a US Senate seat from North Carolina.[19] When asked to support Helms's

ousting from Congress, legendary basketball star Michael Jordan, a North Carolina native, demurred, remarking, "Republicans buy sneakers, too."[20] Though Jordan was a celebrity and not a company, he served as the public face of Nike's brand, which was hardly at the forefront of political change.[21] Since then, as is well known, Jordan and Nike have reversed course, becoming more ethically conscious. (Many multinationals, including Hugo Boss, have also expressed regret for collaborating with the Nazi regime.)[22] With few exceptions, however, most companies and celebrities of the twentieth century have studiously avoided controversy when it comes to social justice.

What businesses feared was consumer backlash and decreased profits—and rightly so. On January 1, 1996, the Walt Disney Company extended health-insurance benefits to the long-term, nonmarried life partners of their LGBTQ employees. For the company, it was a matter of ethics. "We made this decision because it brings our health benefits in line with our corporate nondiscrimination policy," said Disney spokesman John Dreyer.[23] When LGBTQ people began gathering at Disney parks in the early 1990s for informal "gay day" celebrations, others took offense, alleging that the gatherings conflicted with the company's "family values" brand.[24] In 1996, the Southern Baptist Convention spearheaded an eight-year boycott of the company.[25]

This particular boycott didn't ultimately damage Disney's financial fortunes.[26] But as James Surowiecki, author of *The Wisdom of Crowds*, noted, "Boycotts are not just futile griping; they often work."[27] Professor Brayden King, of Northwestern University's Kellogg School of Management, has documented the efficacy of boycotts in changing corporate behavior. Studying boycotts between 1990 and 2005, he found that each day a boycott appeared in the news, the target company's stock price fell.[28] Skittish shareholders and negative publicity were enough to change corporate policy or direction in about one-third of all cases he examined.[29] In the 1990s, conservative watchdog groups such as the American Family Association (AFA) spearheaded a series of boycotts against television programs and networks they perceived to endorse "the homosexual lifestyle."[30] In 1991, NBC decided to cancel an episode of the science fiction series *Quantum Leap* that dramatized a gay youth considering suicide. NBC rightfully feared

advertiser pullout, which would have cost the network $1 million in lost advertising.[31] "NBC's action proves that our boycotts are having a positive effect," said the AFA's outspoken president, Donald E. Wildmon.[32] And *Quantum Leap* wasn't an isolated case. Just two years prior, in 1989, the show *thirtysomething* featured same-sex story lines, and that cost ABC an estimated $1 million.[33] Perhaps due to the success of such boycotts, late-twentieth-century companies tended to avoid taking progressive stances, perceiving themselves as operating within a largely traditional social context and fearful of turning off "mainstream" American consumers.[34]

Today's corporations couldn't be more different, reflecting changing expectations about the role of business in society. As a 2016 Weber Shandwick study observed, one-third of all Americans believed CEOs should speak out on social-political issues, but *almost half* of the diverse, socially liberal, and self-expressive millennials believed this to be the case.[35] "Not only are millennials the generation most likely to see CEO activism as a duty," affirmed the study, "they also think this responsibility is increasing. Nearly six in 10 millennials (56%) believe CEOs have a greater obligation for speaking out on issues than they used to."[36] Such CEO engagement, furthermore, has emerged as a great predictor of millennial spending decisions, with more than half of millennials claiming that they would be more inclined to purchase from a company whose CEO had articulated a viewpoint with which they agreed.[37]

As studies have shown, principled executive action now directly correlates with improved financial performance. As the leadership consultancy KRW International has demonstrated, companies led by ethical CEOs saw nearly 10 percent (9.35 percent) more return on assets than their nonethical counterparts.[38] To arrive at these results, KRW researchers analyzed cross-cultural anthropological data, distilling four nearly universal personality qualities (integrity, forgiveness, compassion, and responsibility) that most societies associate with character. The company then interviewed leadership teams and CEOs, analyzed corporate financial results, and surveyed employees at eighty-four organizations, asking them to rate their company's leaders. From this data, the researchers developed an ethical leadership

spectrum, with highly ethical "virtuoso CEOs," such as Sally Jewell, former CEO of the outdoor retailer REI, occupying one end, and unprincipled, "self-focused CEOs" occupying the other. The researchers anticipated a modest correlation between virtuoso CEOs and strong financial performance but were shocked by the results. As Fred Kiel, KRW's cofounder and author of a 2015 book on the topic, *Return on Character*, conceded, "I was unprepared to discover how robust the connection really is."[39] And the return on character (ROC) wasn't simply financial: "In addition to outperforming the self-focused CEOs on financial metrics," notes a *Harvard Business Review* article, "the virtuosos received higher employee ratings for vision and strategy, focus, accountability, and executive team character."[40]

As striking as Kiel's research is, we're years away from a scenario in which shareholders widely measure a company's ROC instead of its ROI (return on investment), the traditional measure. Or are we? It's tricky. CEOs now find themselves in a precarious situation. On the one hand, politics have become so inflamed that consumer backlash seems to occur no matter what stand a company takes on an issue. When Matt LeBretton, the vice president for communications at New Balance, told the *Wall Street Journal* that "we feel things are going to move in the right direction" after Donald Trump's election in 2016, he was referring specifically to the incoming president's opposition to the Trans-Pacific Partnership, which threatened to undermine the athletic-apparel company's profits, not Trump's policies in general.[41] Progressive activists nevertheless took to social media in outrage, trashing or burning New Balance shoes, while the antigay and white nationalist website Daily Stormer endorsed the Boston-based company as purveyors of "the official shoes of white people."[42] A year later, after conservative commentator Sean Hannity backed Republican senatorial hopeful Roy S. Moore, the coffee company Keurig publicly declared that it would stop advertising on Hannity's Fox TV program. While in his thirties, Moore had allegedly made inappropriate sexual advances toward teenagers. Hannity fans, believing such accusations to be fabrications or financially motivated, showed their displeasure by setting their Keurig machines on fire, tossing them into swimming pools, or otherwise destroying them.[43]

Corporate executives observing such episodes likely wince, seeing themselves doomed to suffer a consumer backlash no matter which course they take—including neutrality. "In an age where everything can be politicized," says Norm Johnston, global chief digital officer for the marketing and advertising firm Mindshare, "it may be impossible for brands to not take a position on core values."[44] But don't allow fear to paralyze you. Instead, behave in an ethically consistent fashion, articulating your values and then standing up for them. Yes, you might antagonize some customers, but over the long term, you will establish a strong reputation, and with that, a loyal and committed customer base.

Some of your ethical positions will likely be industry-specific. If you operate using fossil fuels, you might consider following Royal Dutch Shell's lead. In the fall of 2017, the company pledged to invest $2 billion per year in green technologies and otherwise significantly reduce its carbon footprint.[45] If you are in technology, you might follow the example of Salesforce CEO Marc Benioff, who has dedicated millions to help alleviate the income disparities and homelessness that plague the Silicon Valley region.[46] But no matter your industry, don't neglect diversity and inclusion. It's no longer enough to hire and develop diverse talent, institute a supplier inclusion program, or even create positive community impact programming. In order to improve your business results and please your increasingly inclusive stakeholders, you must go beyond the confines of your day-to-day operations and take principled, ethical stands in favor of diversity and inclusion. This might sound overwhelming, but it actually involves two simple steps: articulating your company's values in an ethical code and taking concrete action to reinforce those principles.

CREATING YOUR COMPANY CODE

Creating a corporate code of ethics is nothing new. Such codes have been mandatory since the early twenty-first century for public companies doing business in the United States.[47] Following the corporate malfeasance of the late twentieth-century, in which WorldCom, Enron, Adelphia Communications, Tyco International, and others deceived

the public and defrauded investors of billions, the public clamored for increased corporate ethics. In response, in 2002, Congress passed the Sarbanes-Oxley Act, requiring heightened monitoring and ethical disclosure requirements from companies. In turn, beginning in 2004, the New York Stock Exchange and Nasdaq required that all publicly listed companies draft and publish codes of ethics.[48]

Even if they are not legally bound to draft a code of ethics, many companies have voluntarily undertaken this exercise, understanding how advantageous it can be for their organizations. Company codes of ethics help employees and suppliers of all backgrounds and cultures interact with one another in predictable and appropriate ways. These codes also help attract the next generation of leaders seeking to work at mission-driven, ethical companies. They allow firms to react more nimbly and with a united front during times of upheaval. As foundational charters, such codes give companies' ethical commitments longevity and a sense of permanence. After all, a company CEO or executive can espouse the most high-minded ethical principles imaginable, but how much real action will those principles generate, and how sustainable will such action prove, in an era of digital disruption and endless mergers and acquisitions? Formalizing ethical principles in a company code can give them a power that transcends management changes, shifts in strategy, and corporate transformations. As a *Harvard Business School* article on the topic argues, "Given all the legal, organizational, reputational, and strategic considerations, few companies will want to be without a code."[49]

I encourage your company to draft or update its code of ethics, drawing on your organization's diverse workforce and viewpoints to best articulate your company's values, ideals, and larger sense of purpose relating to diversity and inclusion. The ultimate shape and character such codes takes will vary. Some company codes contain a mission and/or vision statement, supplier requirements, as well as philosophies, standards, policy statements, credos, declarations, business principles, and even something called a "deontological code" (which articulates duties or norms).[50] Within the vast umbrella of corporate codes, moreover, we find many kinds of specific provisions and statements. Some codes focus on issues of compliance, while others

are stakeholder oriented (ensuring the commitment to protecting and honoring customers and employees, and meeting the ethical expectations of suppliers and vendors). Though your particular code of ethics and mission statement will necessarily reflect the nature of your business, it is increasingly important that all such codes somehow feature diversity and inclusion.

To understand the key role a code of conduct can play, consider the example of Starbucks. During his tenure as the company's CEO, Howard Schultz, now executive chair, delivered on its mission "to inspire and nurture the human spirit" with unflinching moral courage and conviction.[51] Growing up in subsidized housing in Brooklyn, Schultz recalled how frightened his family was when his father, who didn't have health insurance, was injured on the job.[52] As CEO, Schultz was alarmed at the health-care system in America (prior to the passage of the Affordable Care Act) and took the unprecedented step back in 1988 of providing health-insurance benefits to his full- and part-time employees.[53] "I wanted to build the company my father never got to work for," he said.[54] In 2013, he aroused the ire of many Second Amendment activists by declaring that guns weren't welcome in his stores, and in 2015, he embarked on his most controversial social initiative, the "Race Together" campaign, which I described earlier. This campaign, launched to help spark a national discussion on race relations, was met with widespread criticism. Believing his intentions to be noble and the issue of paramount importance, Schultz was unfazed: it "was not a failure," he insisted, and "I'd do it again."[55]

The Steve Jobs of coffee wasn't a lone CEO activist undertaking personal social-impact projects. He knew his social initiatives required the participation and conviction of all his employees. This is one of the reasons why, in 2011, Schultz decided to revamp his company's ethical code under the title "Business Ethics and Compliance Standards." This refurbished code strongly reflects the company's emphasis on the values of diversity, inclusion, and human dignity in driving its global purpose of togetherness and community. "Each of us is personally responsible for supporting our core values," notes Schultz in the code. The values include "a commitment to integrity, acting honestly and ethically, and complying with the letter and intent of the

law."[56] Diversity looms large in the document, guiding all of the company's strong sense of ethics and underlying its financial performance:

> Starbucks actively creates and promotes an environment that is inclusive of all people and their unique abilities, strengths and differences, and promotes diversity as a strategic and competitive business advantage for the company. As we continue to grow, embracing diversity in every aspect of our business—from the way we work together to the way we procure goods and services—is vital to our long-term success. We respect diversity in each other, our customers and suppliers and all others with whom we interact. Our goal is to be one of the most inclusive companies globally, working toward full equity, inclusion and accessibility for those whose lives we touch.[57]

The code details how fair treatment and ethics are put into practice each day, and what employees (whom the company terms "partners") should do if they feel they are being bullied, taunted, or intimidated. After reading the code, every partner was armed with practical knowledge and company resources to ensure that he or she was respected and valued. Certainly that code was put to the test in April 2018 at a Philadelphia Starbucks, when a store manager, a white woman, called the police when two African American men who did not order and asked to use the restroom while waiting for a business partner to arrive. The police arrested the two men. Starbucks' response was swift and helped refocus the company on its code of ethics. All eight thousand US stores would shut down at the same time several weeks later while every employee attending diversity training specifically designed for the company. That day $4.4 million in revenue was lost.[58] However, customers valued the company for taking decisive action. We also must consider the strong influence that Starbucks board member Mellody Hobson and group president and COO Roz Brewer exercised. Clearly, these exceptional African American women leaders brought powerful perspective to the issue. This certainly reinforces the importance of having diverse leadership in key roles given our diverse marketplace. Similarly, in another racial incident, it was an African American woman, Channing Dungey, president of ABC

Entertainment, who in May 2018 issued the statement that Roseanne Barr's new show was being cancelled after the comedian posted a racist tweet. As we witnessed, company codes that include diversity are critical. And companies that ensure their culture embody these codes be seeing that diverse leaders are at the helm will bring their organizations through challenging times. This is particularly true when the company is faced with a diversity crisis.

In April 2017, when Schultz stepped down as CEO, markets and consumers were understandably skittish, having so long associated the company's financial performance and moral leadership with the person of Schultz. After all, the tripling of his company's profits (from $315 million at the onset of the Great Recession in 2008 to $945 million in 2010) and his bolstering of the coffee chain's market value (from $15 billion to $84 billion) represent a textbook story of corporate recovery and leadership.[59] But thanks in part to this 2011 code, his social legacy of philanthropy and diversity-premised ethical commitments will continue into the future. Instead of reflecting Shultz's identity alone, this code of ethics has allowed his philosophy to become part of the company's very identity and DNA.

The history of another large American company, Goldman Sachs, also illustrates the importance of writing diversity into an ethical code. Although Goldman Sachs long ago grew into the world's most powerful investment bank, its reputation as an ethical operator has been mixed.[60] A *New York Times* profile of the company described the "button-down partners of Goldman lore" as "plutocrats who wore their power on their sleeves and turned the bank into the most vaunted, feared and secretive company on Wall Street."[61] *Rolling Stone* magazine echoed these remarks in more colorful language, describing the financial services behemoth as "a great vampire squid wrapped around the face of humanity, relentlessly jamming its blood funnel into anything that smells like money."[62]

Such criticism was popular following the 2008 Great Recession, after Goldman Sachs was proven to have engaged in securities fraud and other misconduct that led to the near collapse of the global financial system. Perhaps no one felt these pressures more than Lloyd C. Blankfein, who became CEO in 2006, at the height of the country's

housing boom. The company had begun moving in a socially progressive direction, offering gender reassignment surgery options in
its health care plan in 2002.[63] Blankfein continued these policies,
granting his employees remuneration for any extra tax penalties they
incurred in paying for their domestic partner benefits.[64] Around 2011,
Blankfein became vocal on other social issues, lobbying New York
politicians and his financial services colleagues to support marriage
equality.[65] In recognition of his surprising leadership on the topic,
the Human Rights Campaign, the preeminent organization promoting equality among the LGBTQ community, appointed Blankfein
its inaugural corporate spokesman for same-sex marriage in 2012.
"America's corporations learned long ago that equality is just good
business and is the right thing to do," Blankfein said at the bank's
downtown Manhattan headquarters after receiving the honor.[66] As
part of its commitment to increased transparency and inclusiveness,
the company also decided to publish its racial and gender diversity
data beginning in 2012.[67]

Like Starbucks, Goldman Sachs's progressive stances reflected a
revamped ethical code. Prior to 2009, Goldman's code of ethics had
focused on shareholder protections and extolled the values of confi-
dentiality and fairness in financial transactions. Ethical behavior on
the part of the company didn't figure prominently in the document.
"A significant proportion of the Code," investment bankers John N.
Reynolds and Edmund Newell document, "related to protecting the
firm or its shareholders from *abuse by the employee*—for example, by
failing to protect confidential information."[68] Goldman's code even
featured language as obvious and uninspiring as "We do not seek competitive advantages through illegal or unethical business practices."[69]

In January 2011, Goldman changed course, revamping its code
to state that "'compliance' with the law is the minimum standard to
which we hold ourselves."[70] Diversity and inclusion took on a new
prominence, appearing in the third sentence of Blankfein's introductory remarks. "In recent years," he stated, "we have expanded [our] vision to reflect the value we place on diverse opinions, experiences and
backgrounds, and to adapt to the changing needs of an increasingly
interconnected world."[71] Everything that follows in the code details

the ethics and norms the company required to achieve this "vision" and prosper in the new world. Among the company's new business values was the importance of diversity and inclusion: "We value diversity as an important asset that enhances our culture, helps us serve clients well and maximizes return for shareholders. For us to excel, we must create for our people an inclusive environment that welcomes and supports differences and encourages input from all perspectives."[72] Goldman Sachs still has a long way to go in improving its reputation and regaining investor and public trust, but thanks to Blankfein's strong ethical leadership, the company is on its way.

WHEN DIVERSITY AND ETHICS ALIGN: HIGHMARK HEALTH

Once you've articulated an ethical code, you have to bring that code alive by acting on it. David Holmberg, CEO of Pittsburgh-based Highmark Health, harnesses the power of diversity and inclusion to create an innovative and influential health-care powerhouse.[73] Valued at $18.5 billion, Highmark is the country's second-largest integrated delivery and finance operation, serving approximately forty million people in all fifty states.[74] In 2015, when David took the organization's top job, Highmark reported $565 million in losses. The following year, its operating profits soared to $64 million.[75] When I interviewed David and asked him about the key to the organization's turnaround, he mentioned the marketplace, health-care innovations, changing profit models, and new standards of patient care. But as we talked further, he described the especially vital roles played by diversity, inclusion, and ethical behavior.

Prior to joining Highmark, David learned about the imperative of diversity and inclusion while running Texas-based Visionworks, an optical company with approximately seven hundred retail locations. "Diversity is as close as the bridge of your nose," David told me in our interview. As he explained, the placement of the bridge of your nose depends on your broader facial structure. When you are selling eyewear, understanding the contours of different cheek bones and nose shapes can help you secure the optimal fit. Asian, Hispanic, African American,

and Caucasian people all have different facial features, and his diverse workforce attended to these differences while serving the company's clientele. Further, working with Hispanic opticians taught David that color combinations mattered when it came to eyewear, while working with African Americans sensitized him to the importance of temple length and eyewear. As David came to understand, the optical business is all about mass customization. Companies in the industry thus depend upon a diverse and inclusive group of people in order to succeed.

After taking the helm of Highmark in 2014, David turned to diversity and inclusion to deliver a level of mass customization similar to that which he had achieved in the optics business. Highmark's mission statement and code of ethics were already geared toward respecting individual differences, seeking to improve the outcomes, experiences, and solutions for each person the company served. "A diverse and inclusive workforce ensures Highmark Inc.'s capacity to serve all communities and to reach new and emerging markets," declares the company's code.[76] On the basis of these principles and his experience in retail, David knew he needed his workforce to mirror the larger marketplace. "I looked at what our markets were," he told me, "what businesses we were in, who we were serving, and then I looked at our own team, and I asked myself, 'Do we emulate the people that we're serving?'" As it turned out, the organization he'd inherited didn't resemble the larger marketplace as well as it might have. To increase his organization's competitiveness, David would need to diversify.

He decided to institute the Rooney Rule. It was no coincidence that he gravitated to this model—he was inspired by Dan Rooney's adoption of the rule when Rooney worked for the Pittsburgh Steelers, the health-care company's locally based NFL football team. But Highmark's strategic move wasn't a geographical coincidence. David gravitated to the Rooney Rule because, in his view, it wasn't bureaucratic, complicated, or human-resources driven. It represented a business strategy simple and decisive enough to convey to his forty thousand employees. "It started with me," David recalled. "I articulated that not only was [the Rooney Rule] the right thing to do, but that diverse inclusion was a corporate priority to be a successful company in the future, instead of the past."

After linking diversity and inclusion to the company's long-term success, David created a talented team that started to track the company's progress. "I was less concerned about the outcome and more concerned about teaching and training our people to have a different thought process or critical-thinking skill as it related to hiring," he recalls. Since 2015, diverse candidates have filled roughly 61 percent of the organization's director-level positions and 46 percent of the vice president vacancies. As this book goes to press, the company is almost 67 percent female, with women occupying one-third of executive positions. David also extended the Rooney Rule to his company's supplier program. In 2016, 8.3 percent of the company's spending, or $110 million in orders, was channeled through suppliers that were owned by people of color or women.

While the Rooney Rule helps Highmark increase its pipeline of diverse talent, a culture of inclusiveness helps it to retain that talent. I came to understand the implications for retention while having coffee with Evan Frazier, the company's senior vice president of community affairs.[77] Evan described how he was attracted to Highmark because of its longstanding reputation in the community and because of its mission-driven focus. He recalled reading the mission statement— dedicated to helping people live longer, healthier lives—and feeling really impressed. An executive of color reached out to him in 2009; this individual was leaving the organization but still consulting for it, committed to recruiting diverse talent. Evan's recruiters convinced him he could thrive and grow at the organization. And they were right. As the director of community impact programming, Evan has an opportunity to give back to the community, investing in diversity and sustainability initiatives throughout Pennsylvania and the larger region.[78] He's given back to the workforce as well. After joining the company's Black Network, he spearheaded the creation of a mentorship program to help develop younger diverse staffers in the organization so that they could build their careers and achieve their personal and professional goals. After eight years at the company, the longest Evan has worked in one place, he has no desire to leave. "The leadership of David Holmberg," he reflects, "has given me renewed faith in the direction of our organization, from a business standpoint but also

in terms of the direction we're moving as far as diversity and inclusion within our organization."

David Holmberg also mobilizes his diverse employee groups to help him make decisions. Highmark has a series of "business resource groups" focused on the LGBTQ community, African Americans, Hispanics, women, and the military. Understanding the value such groups bring to the business, Highmark has renamed these "business groups" and has actively drawn on them during difficult times. "When some of the events happened around the country in the last year or so, I was able to reach out to the various groups and get their advice on what our public position should be and what our policy decisions should be," he told me.

David refers to the summer of 2017, when white nationalists devastated Charlottesville. Trying to determine the best course of action given the implicit language about diversity and inclusion in the company's code of ethics, David solicited advice from his African American business group. He understood that he wasn't in the business of politics, but rather in the business of providing health care coverage. Ultimately, David joined the chorus of CEOs who publicly disavowed the tragic events and the president's response to them. When delivering these remarks before the organization, David stood side by side with the head of the African American business resource group. "It was empowering not only for the business resource group, but for everyone to realize that we mean what we say, and we say what we mean," David recalls.

It's clear that a diverse organization helps Highmark make better decisions, design better product solutions, and navigate a rapidly changing health-care landscape. A diverse workforce is helping Highmark stride confidently into a new era of value-based medicine, a dominant market trend in which health-care organizations are moving away from a fee-for-service business model in favor of a personalized, holistic model of care. In order to deliver this personalized care, David has done everything possible, from diversifying his leadership and suppliers to ensuring that he intimately knows his marketplace. And that's precisely why he joined other CEOs from around the country in defending human dignity in the wake of Charlottesville. These

troubling events ran contrary to the spirit of honoring human difference that he espouses at his company. Some might regard his decision
to speak out as an instance of excessive "CEO activism." But I don't
see the need for that label. His was a decision based on moral conviction and consistency, and it conformed to the company's code of
ethics. It was both the smart and the right thing to do.

PRINCIPLE *AND* PROFIT

Your company can take strong ethical positions in favor of diversity,
positioning it for growth, innovation, profitability, and popularity. But
it pays to follow several basic guidelines. First, when drafting your
ethical positions, especially your company's code of ethics, don't rely
solely on your human resources department and don't approach the
exercise as one of "compliance." Instead, follow David's lead and frame
ethics as a business opportunity. Develop your diversity strategy with
business goals such as better performance and sustainability in mind.
That way any diversity and inclusion initiatives that you enact, like the
Rooney Rule, a diversity supplier program, or the creation of business resource groups, become readily comprehensible and defensible
within the frame of that larger objective and vision.

Second, don't forget to include middle managers and secure their
buy-in. Dr. Beverly Edgehill, my friend and predecessor as CEO at
The Partnership, has focused her business research on the role of
middle managers and organizational performance.[79] "Middle managers have to be leaders too," Beverly told me, especially when it comes
to diversity and inclusion. As her research and business experience
have revealed, middle managers are the receivers of strategy and organizational initiatives, and are responsible for interpreting and trans-
lating such strategies to their direct reports, the bulk of a company's
workforce. As boundary players, middle managers serve as linchpins
between vision and action, and can be an extraordinary asset to organizations. But middle managers often receive diversity and inclusion initiatives that lack specific measurement goals and performance
targets. They often aren't averse to such initiatives but find them
too abstract and have difficulty appreciating their value. That must

change. If you include middle managers in the planning process of foundational documents such as codes of ethics, and if you link inclusion to performance reviews, bonus compensation, and long-term organizational goal achievement, middle management will take ownership of diversity and inclusion, ensuring that noble commitments emanating from the executive ranks are spread throughout the entire organization. In 2014, for example, Jay Hooley, chairman and CEO of the Boston-headquartered financial services company State Street, established ambitious targets to increase diversity in his company's leadership ranks by the end of 2017. To ensure such targets were reached, he made them an important component of every manager's annual performance review. In honor of his inclusivity and vision, The Partnership awarded him the inaugural Bennie Wiley CEO Diversity Award in 2015.

Third, your company's executive leadership must heed your ethical code and act with conviction even when it seems risky. "Just like anything else in leadership," affirms David Holmberg, "people will hear your words but will watch for your deeds." When David initiated the Rooney Rule at Highmark, he didn't encounter significant resistance. Instead, his workforce waited, watching to see whether he was serious. When David began holding executives accountable, the entire organization came on board. Howard Schultz has embodied a similar posture, not simply speaking out against health-care inequities, but concretely providing health care to his part-time workers, at considerable expense to the company. Goldman Sachs didn't simply affirm it supported people of difference. It included gender-reassignment surgery in its health-care offerings and alleviated the tax burdens of employees who had to pay extra for their partner's benefits.

IT'S ABOUT LEADERSHIP

In February 2017, Apple's CEO, Tim Cook, received an honorary doctorate from Scotland's University of Glasgow.[80] During the ceremony, Cook encouraged recent graduates to prioritize passion over profits. "You have to find the intersection of doing something you're passionate about and at the same time something that is in the service

of other people," Cook said. "If you don't find that intersection, you're not going to be very happy in life." Although such idealism is a staple of such graduation speeches, it was a striking message coming from the leader of the globe's most financially powerful company. During the ceremony, and at the fireside chat that followed, Cook reiterated many of his prior public statements about human dignity and diversity and inclusion. He registered his displeasure with Donald Trump's travel ban, discussing how vital immigrants were to his industry, and how his company's legendary founder, Steve Jobs, was actually the child of a Syrian immigrant.

During the question-and-answer session, a student approached the podium and asked Cook two questions. His first was a joke: would Cook give him a job? The crowd laughed. His second question was serious. He asked the chief executive about his company's "next big thing." But by that he didn't mean product innovation or technological breakthrough. "In terms of activism," the student clarified. Cook was uncomfortable with the "activist" label and responded that he didn't identify as such but instead espoused ethical principles and followed through on them. And here he joins ranks with other CEOs in this country. Whether it comes to immigration policy, gay rights, or outbursts of white supremacy in this country, CEOs are not playing for political points but rather simply exercising moral courage and speaking out against discrimination and in favor of human difference. Young people the world over look to Howard Schultz, Tim Cook, Lloyd C. Blankfein, Ken Chenault, Lynne Doughtie, and David Holmberg for leadership—not just business leadership but moral and ethical leadership. Employees and stakeholders look to us for that leadership as well. We must make sure that we exercise it, in times of crisis but also as we adopt the specific practices described in this book. We'll help create truly diverse, inclusive companies, ones that will be poised to win in today's economy.

EPILOGUE

IN DECEMBER 2017, as I was writing this book, the *Boston Globe* published a seven-part Spotlight series titled "Boston. Racism. Image. Reality." A tour de force of investigative journalism, the series addressed a perennial question posed by Bay State residents: does Boston deserve its racist reputation?

To a large extent, the answer appears to be yes. In 2017, four decades after the city's struggles over forced integration and busing, Boston is a bastion of higher education, biomedical innovation, and liberalism—a place associated with equal opportunity and possibility. But the Spotlight investigation provided a sobering assessment of the city's racially based wealth, education, and opportunity gaps. African Americans, the journalists revealed, were nearly absent from the city's middle-class neighborhoods, colleges, sports stadiums, political offices, newsrooms, media organizations, and boardrooms. African Americans made up just 1 percent of all board members in the state's publicly traded firms, and a grand total of two African Americans (Governor Deval Patrick and US Senator Edward Brooke) had assumed statewide office in fifty years. The number of African Americans in Boston's celebrated institutions of higher learning had barely budged in three decades.

This lack of representation and opportunity contributed to stunning differences in net worth and quality of life. Spotlight journalists cited the Federal Reserve Bank of Boston study *The Color of Wealth in Boston*, which noted that the average median net worth of white

families in the city was $247,500, while for nonimmigrant black families it was $8.[1] That meant white Bostonians possessed, on average, almost *31,000* times more wealth than their African American counterparts.

Many found these bleak data points startling, particularly the *Globe's* white readership. The $8 statistic was so shocking that some thought it was a typo. As someone who grapples with this data daily at The Partnership, I wasn't so easily startled. But as I spoke to my colleagues and community members in Boston and surveyed discussions on social media, I discovered that reaction to the series was decidedly mixed, especially in the African American community. Activist Kevin Peterson pointed to an ambivalence many felt when he said, "The *Globe's* voluminous reporting deserves a Pulitzer. But it was all words with few answers—straight reporting containing no substantive recommendations."[2] His observation is astute, for there are many Boston-based institutions and initiatives actively addressing these alarming statistics.

Today, I see far more millennials of color than diverse baby boomers, and I see the NAACP, the Massachusetts Black Lawyer's Association, the black church, and other institutions abuzz with youthful diverse energy, committed to changing the racial status quo. Despite persistent discrepancies in opportunity, I also see business development initiatives—such as Massport's Supplier Inclusion Initiative, Eastern Bank's Business Equity Initiative, the Greater Boston Chamber of Commerce's Pacesetter Initiative, and Hack.Diversity—making bold strides in overcoming the racial inequities plaguing our region, one business opportunity at a time. And I see diversity stalwarts like The Partnership, which have provided four thousand business leaders of color during the last three decades with professional leadership development and networking opportunities to effect change in the city and larger region.

In the months following the *Globe's* seven-part series, I've witnessed the emergence of a galvanized black and white public, determined to act. Fifteen years prior, this would have been impossible—the city was too polarized. Perhaps Boston, now a majority-minority city, is finally ready. Numerous businesses and community organizations have

contacted the *Globe*'s Spotlight Team, asking it to present discussion forums with their reporters alongside other change agents, such as Massachusetts Port Authority CEO Tom Glynn and board member Duane Jackson.

As of this writing, more than a hundred of these forums have taken place across the city. Immediately following the Spotlight series' publication, *Boston Globe* president Vinay Mehra, a longtime executive committee member of The Partnership as well as a member of our C-Suite Program, asked talented Partnership senior executive consultant Pratt Wiley and me to collaborate on a special forum at the John F. Kennedy Library, scheduled to coincide with Black History Month in February 2018. Hundreds of people attended the forum with leading organizations, such as the Hyams Foundation, National Grid, Blue Cross Blue Shield of Massachusetts, and the Boston Foundation, providing stewardship and sponsorship.

This would be the first of many *Boston Globe* initiatives focused on bringing diversity to the fore in Boston and enabling solutions to emerge. The Partnership continues to collaborate with the *Globe*, as we seek not merely to foster discussions on diversity but to be a part of meaningful change regarding this important issue. And we are so cognizant that in order for statistics and hard data to change the realities on the ground, attitudes and perceptions of race must change first.

As I've underscored throughout this book, the United States will soon approximate America's major metropolitan areas, such as Boston and Chicago, in achieving majority-minority status. This demographic transformation will revolutionize the way we conduct and structure our businesses. Our country's best business organizations, some of which I've spotlighted in these chapters, have followed younger generations in embracing diversity and inclusion. They understand that welcoming differences of all kinds makes us more innovative, versatile, in touch with consumers, and resistant to marketplace disruption. Diversity and inclusion, they believe, will make us better, financially and as a society.

Dr. Martin Luther King Jr. challenged America to value diversity in its truest form by judging individuals according to the content of their character and not the color of their skin. Today we know the

work of diversity and inclusion is never over. While the country has made considerable progress since King's era, current racial inequalities—as showcased in the Spotlight series—demonstrate how far we have yet to go. The same holds true for organizations everywhere. Your group might have made progress on diversity. You might have hired more leaders from underrepresented groups, increased your diverse supplier spending, or enacted community-based social-impact programming. But even with such noteworthy accomplishments, I hope you'll resist the urge to declare victory. Increasing diversity remains an ongoing challenge, and our organizations must constantly measure, reassess, recalibrate, and nurture their efforts. Only if we recommit ourselves to inclusion and treat it as a permanent project can we truly unleash diversity's full promise. Then, and only then, will our companies, and our society, succeed.

ACKNOWLEDGMENTS

I MUST FIRST GIVE CREDIT to all the African American predecessors who acted with selfless courage and sacrifice so that their descendants might be able to walk the path of freedom, justice, and dignity. One of the best ways to honor their sacrifice is to continue their struggle, as well as to help other disenfranchised groups advance. I have chosen to champion the causes of diversity and inclusion, as so many others have helped me along the way. And whatever I have achieved, I have not achieved alone.

This book has been a long journey, bringing together new partners and collaborators as well as long-cherished friends, colleagues, and family members. And I am better for our journey together. Seth Schulman and Rachel Gostenhofer so artfully helped capture the stories in this book, shaping the text and opening themselves up to the reality of what it is like to be diverse in America today. My editor, Helene Atwan of Beacon Press, has served as a guiding light, illuminating the entire voyage. I also wish to thank my beloved agent, Helen Rees who passed away. Her spirit will always remain with us, as her son Lorin nobly carries on the Rees family tradition.

My family's faith in me, particularly from my brother Paris and his wife, Maureen, has always been a buoy. My stepchildren, Deanna, Rachael, and Cyrus, with their intelligence and wit, always give me hope for the future. I am deeply indebted to their father, Bernie, whose strong foundation of intellect, integrity, and service enables them—and me—to soar. Bernie has championed this book from the very start and is a constant source of inspiration and support.

All people should have the opportunity to assemble their own personal board of advisors to support them in their professional and personal journey. I wish to extend thanks to the co-chairmen of my advisory board, Wayne Budd and Ralph Martin, as well as the members of my personal board of advisors, Bennie Wiley, Deborah Jackson, Diane Patrick, and Karen Morton. They have been by my side for decades.

I have also had the opportunity to grow throughout the years because so many CEOs and executives have provided me with opportunities. These individuals include Jim Coppersmith, Paul LaCamera, David D'Alessandro, Donald Guloien, John DesPrez, Elizabeth Cook, and Jim Gallagher, among many others.

And of course I owe a huge debt of gratitude to The Partnership Inc., our fearless board chair, Marcy Reed, our visionary board, and our talented staff. But perhaps there is no one at The Partnership to whom I owe more than Roseann Carbone, my assistant of seventeen years. Roseann and I are the epitome of diversity at work, and she is a treasured colleague who has helped to make my efforts at The Partnership, as well as at John Hancock, so rich and wonderful.

NOTES

INTRODUCTION

1. That culture has since continued under beloved civic leader and subsequent president Paul LaCamera and, thereafter, under the astute and equitable businessman Bill Fine.

2. For this discussion, I am indebted to Keenen Grooms (assistant director for strategic partnerships at the State Treasurer's Office of Massachusetts) and Scott Martin (then digital marketing and social media manager for the Greater Boston YMCA), interview with author, November 13, 2017.

3. Andrew Ryan, Adrian Walker, and Todd Wallack, "For Blacks in Boston, a Power Outage," *Boston Globe*, December 15, 2017.

4. Ibid.

5. Akilah Johnson, "Boston. Racism. Image. Reality: The Spotlight Team Takes On Our Hardest Question," *Boston Globe*, December 10, 2017.

6. Ryan, Walker, and Wallack, "For Blacks in Boston, a Power Outage."

7. For this section, I am indebted to Dawn Frazier-Bohnert (senior vice president and chief diversity and inclusion officer at Liberty Mutual Insurance Co.), interview with author, November 27, 2017.

8. "Liberty Mutual Receives 100 Percent Rating on Human Rights Campaign Foundation's 16th Annual Scorecard on LGBTQ Workplace Equality," Business Wire, November 9, 2017, https://www.businesswire.com/news/home/20171109005969/en /Liberty-Mutual-Receives-100-Percent-Rating-Human.

9. "Missing Pieces Report: The 2016 Board Diversity Census of Women and Minorities on Fortune 500 Boards," Alliance for Board Diversity, February 6, 2017, (11).

10. Both as of 2016: *Leading with Intent: 2017 National Index of Nonprofit Board Practices* (BoardSource, 2017), 10, 58; Rick Seltzer, "The Slowly Diversifying Presidency," *Inside Higher Ed*, June 20, 2017, https://www.insidehighered.com/news/2017/06/20 /college-presidents-diversifying-slowly-and-growing-older-study-finds.

11. Po Bronson with Ashley Merryman, "Are Americans Suffering Diversity Fatigue?," *Time*, May 31, 2016, http://content.time.com/time/nation/arti-cle/0,8599,1199702,00.html.

12. Except for France: Thomas Barta, Markus Kleiner, and Tilo Neumann, "Is There a Payoff from Top-Team Diversity?," *McKinsey Quarterly*, April 2012, https:// www.mckinsey.com/business-functions/organization/our-insights/is-there-a-payoff-from -top-team-diversity.

13. *Global Diversity and Inclusion: Fostering Innovation Through a Diverse Workforce* (New York: Forbes Insights, July 2011), 5, https://www.forbes.com/forbesinsights /innovation_diversity.

14. Sylvia Ann Hewlett, Melinda Marshall, and Laura Sherbin, "How Diversity Can Drive Innovation," *Harvard Business Review*, December 2013, https://hbr.org/2013/12 /how-diversity-can-drive-innovation.

15. Moises Velasquez-Manoff, "What Biracial People Know," *New York Times*, March 4, 2017, https://www.nytimes.com/2017/03/04/opinion/sunday/what-biracial -people-know.html.

16. "Transcript: Illinois Senate Candidate Barack Obama," *Washington Post*, July 27, 2004, http://www.washingtonpost.com/wp-dyn/articles/A19751–2004Jul27.html.

CHAPTER 1: FROM "NICE TO HAVE" TO "DO OR DIE"

1. For details of Trump's order, see "Fact Sheet: Protecting the Nation from Foreign Terrorist Entry to the United States," US Department of Homeland Security, released January 29, 2017, https://www.dhs.gov/news/2017/01/29/protecting-nation-foreign -terrorist-entry-united-states.

2. Perry Stein, "Restaurants, Schools Close in 'Day Without Immigrants' Protest," *Washington Post*, February 16, 2016, https://www.washingtonpost.com/local/restaurants -schools-close-in-day-without-immigrants-protest/2017/02/16/ac2af2f8-f44c-11e6-a9b0 -ecee7ce475fc_story.html?utm_term=.0e82c7f3adce.

3. Murad Ahmed and Madhumita Murgia, "US Hotels and Airlines Slash Prices as Trump Policies Hit Tourism," *Financial Times*, March 31, 2017, https://www.ft.com /content/d8d3402a-1540–11e7-b0c1–37e417ee6c76.

4. For all of these corporate reactions, see "Starbucks, Exxon, Apple: Companies Challenging (or Silent on) Trump's Immigration Ban," *New York Times*, January 30, 2017, https://www.nytimes.com/interactive/2017/business/trump-immigration-ban-company -reaction.html?_r=0.

5. Seth Fiegerman, "Uber CEO Defends Trump Relationship to Employees," *CNN Tech*, January 25, 2017, http://money.cnn.com/2017/01/25/technology/uber-ceo-trump.

6. Faiz Siddiqui, "Uber Triggers Protests for Collecting Fares During Taxi Strike against Refugee Ban," *Washington Post*, January 29, 2017, https://www.washingtonpost .com/news/dr-gridlock/wp/2017/01/29/uber-triggers-protest-for-not-supporting-taxi -strike-against-refugee-ban/?utm_term=.7981ccab9038; Adam Chandler, "Lyft and Uber's Public-Relations Battle over the Immigration Ban," *Atlantic*, January 29, 2017, https:// www.theatlantic.com/business/archive/2017/01/lyft-and-ubers-immigration-ban/514889.

7. Tracey Lien, "As Uber Deals with Crises, Lyft Raises $500 Million," *Los Angeles Times*, April 6, 2017, http://www.latimes.com/business/technology/la-fi-tn-lyft-funding -500m-20170406-story.html; Mike Isaac, "What You Need to Know about #DeleteUber," *New York Times*, January 31, 2017, https://www.nytimes.com/2017/01/31/business/delete -uber.html?_r=0.

8. Elizabeth Weise and Marco della Cava, "Lyft Faces Its Big Moment to Leap Ahead of Uber," *USA Today*, March 8, 2017, https://www.usatoday.com/story/tech/news /2017/03/08/lyft-uber-travis-kalanick-john-zimmer/98799804.

9. Marco della Cava, "Uber Has Lost Market Share to Lyft During Crisis," *USA Today*, updated June 14, 2017, https://www.usatoday.com/story/tech/news/2017/06/13 /uber-market-share-customer-image-hit-string-scandals/102795024.

10. Weise and della Cava, "Lyft Faces Its Big Moment." I don't mean to suggest that it was only the travel ban that influenced these numbers. In February, Susan Fowler blogged about her experiences with sexism at Uber, which also damaged the company.

11. Chandler, "Lyft and Uber's Public-Relations Battle over the Immigration Ban."

12. Lien, "As Uber Deals with Crises."

13. "Valerie Jarrett Joins Lyft Board of Directors," *Lyft Blog*, July 31, 2017, https:// blog.lyft.com/posts/jarrett-lyft-bod.

14. Greg Bensinger, "Lyft Adds Former Obama Adviser Valerie Jarrett to Board," *Wall Street Journal*, July 31, 2017, https://www.wsj.com/articles/lyft-adds-former-obama -adviser-valerie-jarrett-to-board-1501509601.

15. Siddiqui, "Uber Triggers Protest."

16. Chandler, "Lyft and Uber's Public-Relations Battle over the Immigration Ban."

17. Katie Benner and Kenneth Chang, "SpaceX Is Now One of the World's Most Valuable Privately Held Companies," *New York Times*, July 27, 2017, https://www .nytimes.com/2017/07/27/technology/spacex-is-now-one-of-the-worlds-most-valuable -privately-held-companies.html.

18. Amanda Holpuch, "'No More Brilliant Jerks'—Arianna Huffington Ushers in the New Uber," *Guardian*, July 30, 2017; Sam Levin, "Uber Hires Eric Holder to Investigate Sexual Harassment Allegations," *Guardian*, February 20, 2017, https://www.theguardian.com/technology/2017/feb/21/uber-hires-eric-holder-to-investigate-sexual-harassment-allegations; William D. Cohan, "Is Arianna Huffington Worse for Uber Than Travis Kalanick?," *Vanity Fair*, July 20, 2017, https://www.vanityfair.com/news/2017/07/is-arianna-huffington-worse-for-uber-than-travis-kalanick.

19. Michal Lev-Ram, "How Lyft Could Defeat Uber," *Fortune*, July 19, 2017, http://fortune.com/2017/07/19/uber-vs-lyft-race.

20. Ibid.

21. For background on this, see Thomas Maffai, "A 40-Year Friendship Forged by the Challenges of Busing," *Atlantic*, November 17, 2016, https://www.theatlantic.com/education/archive/2016/11/a-40-year-friendship-forged-by-the-challenges-of-busing/502733/; Renee Graham, "Yes, Boston, You Are Racist," *Boston Globe*, March 29, 2017, https://www.bostonglobe.com/opinion/2017/03/28/yes-boston-you-are-racist/yMd7u1evwC5g6XhGAHMdyH/story.html.

22. Remarks delivered by Dr. Beverly Edgehill, "30 Years of Impact Report," June 10, 2017.

23. Remarks delivered by chairman, president, and CEO Marillyn A. Hewson, Department of Energy Minorities in Energy First Anniversary Forum, November 18, 2014, http://www.lockheedmartin.com/us/news/speeches/1118-hewson-minorities-in-energy.html.

24. Hannah Kuchler, "Airbnb's Gender Diversity Efforts Put Uber in Shade," *Financial Times*, April 6, 2017, https://www.ft.com/content/6ae56540-0f62-11e7-b030-768954394623.

25. Liza Mundy, "Why Is Silicon Valley So Awful to Women?," *Atlantic*, April 2017, https://www.theatlantic.com/magazine/archive/2017/04/why-is-silicon-valley-so-awful-to-women/517788.

26. Adrienne LaFrance, "Tallying Female Workers Isn't Enough to Make Tech More Diverse," *Atlantic*, August 11, 2014, https://www.theatlantic.com/technology/archive/2014/08/what-good-is-all-this-tech-diversity-data-anyway/375829.

27. Grace Donnelly, "Only 3% Of Fortune 500 Companies Share Full Diversity Data," *Fortune*, June 7, 2017, http://fortune.com/2017/06/07/fortune-500-diversity.

28. The amount of data each of the tech companies chose to reveal varied.

29. Vindu Goel, "Yahoo Reveals Work Force Data, Joining Tech's Small Diversity Parade," *New York Times*, June 17, 2014, https://bits.blogs.nytimes.com/2014/06/17/yahoo-reveals-workforce-data-joining-techs-small-diversity-parade/?_r=0; LaFrance, "Tallying Female Workers Isn't Enough."

30. LaFrance, "Tallying Female Workers Isn't Enough."

31. Rupert Neate, "Twitter Employs Only 49 African Americans Despite Diversity Pledges," *Guardian*, July 1, 2015, https://www.theguardian.com/technology/2015/jul/01/twitter-staff-african-american-diversity.

32. Ibid.

33. African American numbers taken from the 2010 US Census report, while Latino ones taken from 2014 census report: Kia Kokalitcheva, "Google's Diversity Efforts Fall Flat," *Axios*, August 9, 2017, https://www.axios.com/googles-diversity-efforts-are-making-little-progress-2470784457.html; Neate, "Twitter Employs Only 49 African Americans Despite Diversity Pledges"; "Facts for Features: Hispanic Heritage Month 2015," US Census Bureau, September 14, 2015, https://www.census.gov/newsroom/facts-for-features/2015/cb15-ff18.html.

34. Frank Dobbin and Alexandra Kalev, "Why Diversity Programs Fail," *Harvard Business Review*, July–August 2016, https://hbr.org/2016/07/why-diversity-programs-fail.

35. Bethany McLean, "Wall Street Diversifies Itself," *Atlantic*, March 2017, https://www.theatlantic.com/magazine/archive/2017/03/wall-street-diversifies-itself/513851.

36. Figures as of 2012: Michael Shulman, "Shakeup at the Oscars," *New Yorker*, February 27, 2017, http://www.newyorker.com/magazine/2017/02/27/shakeup-at-the-oscars.

37. Anna Wiener, "Why Can't Silicon Valley Solve Its Diversity Problem?," *New Yorker*, November 26, 2016, http://www.newyorker.com/business/currency/why-cant -silicon-valley-solve-its-diversity-problem.

38. Ibid.

39. Dobbin and Kalev, "Why Diversity Programs Fail."

40. Tessa L. Dover, Brenda Major and Cheryl R. Kaiser, "Diversity Policies Rarely Make Companies Fairer, and They Feel Threatening to White Men," *Harvard Business Review*, January 4, 2016, https://hbr.org/2016/01/diversity-policies-dont-help-women -or-minorities-and-they-make-white-men-feel-threatened.

41. Mundy, "Why Is Silicon Valley So Awful."

42. Ibid.

43. Ibid.

44. Per Mundy's interpretation of the study: "Why Is Silicon Valley So Awful."

45. Glenn Llopis, "5 Reasons Diversity and Inclusion Fails," *Forbes*, January 16, 2017, https://www.forbes.com/sites/glennllopis/2017/01/16/5-reasons-diversity-and -inclusion-fails/#1aac4e6a50df.

46. Dobbin and Kalev, "Why Diversity Programs Fail."

47. Dover, Major, and Kaiser, "Diversity Policies Rarely Make Companies Fairer."

48. Lauren B. Edelman, "When Organizations Rule: Judicial Deference to Institutionalized Employment Structures," *American Journal of Sociology* 117 (2011).

49. For the information detailed in the following paragraphs illuminating structural bias and the tech companies that are working to overturn unconscious bias, I am indebted to Javier Barrientos (then senior manager of community, content, and marketplace diversity at Amazon), interview with author, September 5, 2017.

50. Shankar Vedantam, *The Hidden Brain: How Our Unconscious Minds Elect Presidents, Control Markets, Wage Wars, and Save Our Lives* (New York: Spiegel & Grau, 2010), 237.

51. Nicholas Kristof, "Our Biased Brains," *New York Times*, May 7, 2015, https:// www.nytimes.com/2015/05/07/opinion/nicholas-kristof-our-biased-brains.html.

52. Ibid.

53. Michael Stephan, "Say Hello to the Cognitive Recruiter," *Wall Street Journal*, April 12, 2017, http://deloitte.wsj.com/cio/2017/04/12/say-hello-to-the-cognitive -recruiter.

54. Ibid.

55. Ibid.

56. All these data taken from Talent Sonar's white paper, "Bad Hire Cost Calculator," available for download at talentsonar.com.

57. Stephan, "Say Hello."

58. Cavan Sieczkowski, "Jimmy Kimmel Hilariously Mocks Hollywood's Diversity Problem in Emmys Opener," *Huffington Post*, September 18, 2016, http://www .huffingtonpost.com/entry/jimmy-kimmel-emmys-diversity_us_57df2ce3e4b04a1497b50f7e.

59. David Carr, "Why the Oscars' Omission of 'Selma' Matters," *New York Times*, January 18, 2015, https://www.nytimes.com/2015/01/19/business/media/why-the-oscars -omission-of-selma-matters.html?_r=0.

60. Brandon Griggs, "Jada Pinkett Smith, Spike Lee to Boycott Oscars Ceremony," *CNN*, updated January 19, 2016, https://www.cnn.com/2016/01/18/entertainment/oscars -boycott-spike-lee-jada-pinkett-smith-feat/index.html.

61. Schulman, "Shakeup at the Oscars."

62. Lisa Respers France, "Study Finds #OscarsSoAgeist," *CNN Entertainment*, February 17, 2017, http://www.cnn.com/2017/02/17/entertainment/study-ageism-oscars.

63. Schulman, "Shakeup at the Oscars."

64. Georgia Wells, "Facebook Blames Lack of Available Talent for Diversity Problem," *Wall Street Journal*, July 14, 2016, https://www.wsj.com/articles/facebook-blames -lack-of-available-talent-for-diversity-problem-1468526303.

65. Kathleen Chaykowski, "Mark Zuckerberg Gives Facebook a New Mission," *Forbes*, June 22, 2017, https://www.forbes.com/sites/kathleenchaykowski/2017/06/22 /mark-zuckerberg-gives-facebook-a-new-mission/#b2cffea1343b.

66. Wells, "Facebook Blames Lack of Available Talent for Diversity Problem."

67. Kaya Thomas, "Invisible Talent," *NewsCo Shift* (personal blog), July 14, 2016, https://shift.newco.co/invisible-talent-409a085bee9c#.5tuy4u5v6.

68. Stav Ziv, "Starbucks Ends Phase One of Race Together Initiative After Grande Fail," *Newsweek*, March 23, 2015, http://www.newsweek.com/starbucks-ends-phase-one -race-together-initiative-after-grande-fail-316043.

69. Ibid.

70. For a video of the advertisement, see Daniel Victor, "Pepsi Pulls Ad Accused of Trivializing Black Lives Matter," *New York Times*, April 5, 2017, https://www.nytimes .com/2017/04/05/business/kendall-jenner-pepsi-ad.html?_r=0.

71. Ibid.

72. Ibid.

73. Mark Kaplan and Mason Donovan, *The Inclusion Dividend: Why Investing in Diversity & Inclusion Pays Off* (Boston: Bibliomotion, 2013), 9.

74. For these data points and the analysis of the causes driving them, see Vivian Hunt, Dennis Layton, and Sara Prince, *Diversity Matters*, McKinsey, February 2, 2015, as well as the abridged version of their study *Why Diversity Matters*, published in January, 2015. I consult both for these data.

75. Hunt, Layton, and Prince, *Diversity Matters*, 9.

76. Deborah L. DeHaas, Brent Bachus, and Eliza Horn, "Unleashing the Power of Inclusion | Attracting and Engaging the Evolving Workforce," Deloitte and the Billie Jean King Leadership Initiative, 2017, 4 and throughout the publication.

77. Ibid., 1.

78. Ibid., 4.

79. Ibid., 1, 4.

80. Ibid., 4; "Employee Engagement in U.S. Stagnant in 2015," Gallup, January 13, 2016, http://news.gallup.com/poll/188144/employee-engagement-stagnant-2015.aspx.

81. DeHaas, Bachus, and Horn, "Unleashing the Power of Inclusion," 6.

82. Ibid., 11.

83. Grooms and Martin, interview with author.

84. *2016 Hollywood Diversity Report: Busine$$ as Usual?* (Los Angeles: UCLA Ralph J. Bunche Center for African American Studies, February 2016), 56.

85. Ibid., 2.

86. Ibid., 55.

87. Jessica Guynn and Elizabeth Weise, "Lack of Diversity Could Undercut Silicon Valley," *USA Today*, June 26, 2014, http://www.usatoday.com/story/tech/2014/06/26 /silicon-valley-tech-diversity-white-asian-black-hispanic-google-facebook-yahoo /11372421.

88. Ibid.

89. Robinson Meyer, "On a Scale of 1 to 10, Silicon Valley's Lack of Racial Diversity Is a 7," *Atlantic*, November 1, 2015, https://www.theatlantic.com/technology/archive /2015/11/on-a-scale-of-1-to-10-silicon-valleys-lack-of-racial-diversity-is-a-7/412903.

90. Elizabeth MacBride, "A Diversity Problem," *Investment News*, December 14, 2015, http://www.investmentnews.com/article/20151214/FEATURE/151209979/a -diversity-problem.

91. Ibid.

92. Bethany McLean, "Wall Street Diversifies Itself," *Atlantic*, March 2017, https:// www.theatlantic.com/magazine/archive/2017/03/wall-street-diversifies-itself/513851.

93. Ibid.

94. Ibid.

95. Ibid.

96. Paul Sullivan, "In Fledgling Exchange-Traded Fund, Striking a Blow for Women," *New York Times*, March 4, 2016, https://www.nytimes.com/2016/03/05/your -money/in-fledgling-exchange-traded-fund-striking-a-blow-for-women.html.

97. Ibid.

98. Ibid. For more on these charitable endeavors, see "SHE Impacts: A Charitable Fund to Support Gender-Diverse Leadership," State Street Global Advisers, 2017, https:// www.ssga.com/investment-topics/general-investing/2017/SHE-Impacts-One-Pager.pdf.

99. For this profile I am indebted to Lisa D. Cook (associate professor of economics and international relations at Michigan State University), interview with author, October 13, 2017.

100. Jon Hilsenrath and Kristina Peterson, "Federal Reserve 'Doves Beat 'Hawks' in Economic Prognosticating," *Wall Street Journal*, July 29, 2013, http://www.pulitzer.org /files/2014/national-reporting/hilsenrath/01hilsenrath2014.pdf.

101. Aaron Klein, "The Fed's Striking Lack of Diversity and Why It Matters," *Brookings*, August 1, 2016, https://www.brookings.edu/opinions/the-feds-striking-lack-of -diversity-and-why-it-matters.

102. Ibid.

103. Lisa D. Cook and Chaleampong Kongcharoen, "The Idea Gap in Pink and Black," Working Paper 16331, National Bureau of Economic Research, September 2010, http://www.nber.org/papers/w16331.

104. Paul Taylor, *The Next America: Boomers, Millennials and the Looming Generational Showdown* (New York: Public Affairs, 2014), 71.

105. Ibid., 8.

106. Joel Kotkin, *The Next Hundred Million: America in 2050* (New York: Penguin, 2010), 144.

107. Taylor, *The Next America*, 70.

108. Ibid., 7.

109. Kotkin, *The Next Hundred Million*, 145.

110. Taylor, *The Next America*, 87.

111. Ibid., 4.

112. Ibid., 71.

113. Kotkin, *The Next Hundred Million*, 141.

114. Taylor, *The Next America*, 69.

115. Kotkin, *The Next Hundred Million*, 143.

116. Ibid., 144.

117. Taylor, *The Next America*, 11.

118. Kotkin, *The Next Hundred Million*, 146.

119. Taylor, *The Next America*, 74.

CHAPTER 2: RECRUITING LIKE ROONEY

1. For information on his career and insights about football and business, I am indebted to Arnold Garron (former NFL player, coach, and founder and managing director of APG Organizational Consulting, LLC), interview with author, June 7, 2017.

2. Greg Beacham, "LA Chargers Hire Anthony Lynn as Head Coach a Day After Move," *Seattle Times*, January 13, 2017, http://www.seattletimes.com/sports/the-chargers -have-hired-anthony-lynn-as-head-coach.

3. Connor Orr, "NFL Makes Sarah Thomas First Full-time Female Official," NFL .com, April 8, 2015, http://www.nfl.com/news/story/0ap3000000484154/article/nfl -makes-sarah-thomas-first-fulltime-female-official.

4. For more details on the story, see N. Jeremi Duru, *Advancing the Ball: Race, Reformation, and the Quest for Equal Coaching Opportunity in the NFL* (New York: Oxford University Press, 2011).

5. Ibid., 15–18.

6. Ibid., 11–12.

7. Ibid., 6.

8. Andrew Golding, "How the NFL Got the Rooney Rule," *Gelf Magazine*, January 3, 2011, http://www.gelfmagazine.com/archives/how_the_nfl_got_the_rooney_rule.php.

9. Thomas George, "Pro Football: Inside the N.F.L.; N.F.L. Pressured on Black Coaches," *New York Times*, October 6, 2002, http://www.nytimes.com/2002/10/06/sports /pro-football-inside-the-nfl-nfl-pressured-on-black-coaches.html.

10. Golding, "How the NFL Got the Rooney Rule"; Douglas C. Proxmire, "Coaching Diversity: The Rooney Rule, Its Application and Ideas for Expansion," *American Constitution Society for Law and Policy* (December 2008): 2.

11. Proxmire, "Coaching Diversity," 3.

12. Ashley Fox, "How the Rooney Rule Succeeds . . . and Where It Falls Short," ESPN.com, April 14, 2015, http://www.espn.com/nfl/story/_/id/12867233/rooney-rule -opened-doors-minority-head-coaching-candidates-do-more.

13. Ibid.

14. Proxmire, "Coaching Diversity," 3.

15. Mark Maske, "Super Bowl's Black Coaches Indicative of 'Great Strides,'" *Washington Post*, January 30, 2007, http://www.washingtonpost.com/wp dyn/content/article /2007/01/29/AR2007012901409.html.

16. Fox, "How the Rooney Rule Succeeds."

17. Maske, "Super Bowl's Black Coaches."

18. Mark Maske, "Steelers' Stability Under Dan Rooney Is a Lesson for NFL Teams," *Chicago Tribune*, April 17, 2017, http://www.chicagotribune.com/sports/football /ct-nfl-steelers-dan-rooney-spt-20170417-story.html.

19. Associated Press, "Rooney Rule: 8 Minority Head Coaches for 2017," *USA Today*, January 13, 2017, https://www.usatoday.com/story/sports/nfl/2017/01/13/rooney -rule-8-minority-head-coaches-for-2017/96554502.

20. Rick Palmore, "A Call to Action—Diversity in the Legal Profession," published on the website of the Association of Corporate Counsel, October 2004, http://www.acc .com/vl/public/Article/loader.cfm?csModule=security/getfile&pageid=16074&recorded=1.

21. Cassandra Forin, "Are You Answering the Call to Action?" *For the Defense* (2011): 50; Linda Greenhouse, "The Supreme Court's Diversity Dilemma," *New York Times*, December 24, 2015, https://www.nytimes.com/2015/12/24/opinion/the-supreme -courts-diversity-dilemma.html.

22. For this profile, I am indebted to Wayne Budd (senior counsel at Goodwin Proctor, LLP), interview with author, November 1, 2017.

23. For these figures, I rely on E. Macey Russell (partner, Choate Hall & Stewart, LLP), "The Decline in African American Law Partners: A Wake Up Call," *Institute for Inclusion in the Legal Profession Review* (2014): 185.

24. Ibid., 185.

25. Claire Bushey, "Chicago's Top Law Firms Lack Diversity—and Clients Are Starting to Notice," *Crain's*, October 29, 2016, http://www.chicagobusiness.com/article /20161029/ISSUE01/310299994/chicagos-top-law-firms-lack-diversity-and-clients-are -starting-to-notice.

26. Russell, "The Decline in African American Law Partners," 189. Note, the in-house counsel figures are from a 2011 survey.

27. Bushey, "Chicago's Top Law Firms Lack Diversity."

28. Ibid.

29. Ibid.

30. For the following hypothetical scenario and analysis, I rely on Glenn Llopis, "Workforce Representation Is About Quotas, Not Growth: It's Time to Embrace Diversity with Inclusion," *Forbes*, May 6, 2017, https://www.forbes.com/sites/glennllopis/2017 /05/06/workforce-representation-is-about-quotas-not-growth-its-time-to-embrace -diversity-with-inclusion/#749b5fcd6f9e.

31. DeHaas, Bachus, and Horn, "Unleashing the Power of Inclusion," 6.

32. C. C. Dubois, "The Impact of the Rooney Rule: Far Beyond the NFL," *Pittsburgh Post-Gazette*, April 30, 2017, http://www.post-gazette.com/opinion/Op-Ed/2017/04/30 /The-impact-of-the-Rooney-Rule-far-beyond-the-NFL/stories/201704300145.

33. For this profile on Xerox, I rely on Paul Solman, "Making Sen$e: How Xerox Became a Leader in Diversity—and Why That's Good for Business," *PBS NewsHour*, September 15, 2014, http://www.pbs.org/newshour/making-sense/xerox-employees -arent-carbon-copies. In addition to Solman's story, the report contains two embedded videos in which public news correspondent Paul Solman visits Rochester, New York, in 1991, and then twenty years later, documenting the progress made within these two decades. I rely on these two valuable videos as well.

34. Robert Howard, "The CEO as Organizational Architect: An Interview with Xerox's Paul Allaire," *Harvard Business Review* (September–October 1992), https://hbr.org /1992/09/the-ceo-as-organizational-architect-an-interview-with-xeroxs-paul-allaire.

35. Earlier in 2018, Xerox was acquired by Fujifilm. During the time research was being conducted for this book, diversity was a large part of its success, however, given the disruption of the technology industry, Xerox, too, fell to acquisition.

36. Denise Lee Yohn, "How IKEA Designs Its Brand Success," *Forbes*, June 10, 2015, https://www.forbes.com/sites/deniselyohn/2015/06/10/how-ikea-designs-its-brand-success/#3376ffad6755.

37. Natalia Brzezinski, "Values-Based Leadership and Empowering Women: Interview with CEO of IKEA Group," *Huffington Post*, December 20, 2013, http://www.huffington post.com/natalia-lopatniuk-brzezinski/valuesbased-leadership-em_b_4479389.html.

38. Ibid.

39. Martha C. White, "Ikea Strategy Ditches the Dream Home for the Daily Grind," *New York Times*, October 30, 2016, https://www.nytimes.com/2016/10/31/business/media/ikea-strategy-ditches-the-dream-home-for-the-daily-grind.html?_r=0.

40. Ibid.

41. Ibid.

42. Arnold Garron, interview with author, June 7, 2017.

43. Kevin Seifert, "How American Football Is Becoming a Worldwide Sport," ESPN.com, May 5, 2016, http://www.espn.com/nfl/story/_/id/15273529/how-american-football-becoming-worldwide-sport-europe-china-beyond.

44. "Robert L. Johnson Urges U.S. Corporations to Establish a Version of the 'NFL Rooney Rule' to Increase Employment and Business Opportunities for African Americans," PR Newswire, October 2, 2011, https://www.prnewswire.com/news-releases/robert-l-johnson-urges-us-corporations-to-establish-a-version-of-the-nfl-rooney-rule-to-increase-employment-and-business-opportunities-for-african-americans-130952493.html.

45. Jannell Ross, "Robert Johnson, First Black American Billionaire, Proposes Plan to Reduce Black Unemployment," *Huffington Post*, October 11, 2011, https://www.huffingtonpost.com/2011/10/11/robert-johnson-bet-black-unemployment_n_1005260.html.

46. Dubois, "The Impact of the Rooney Rule."

47. White House, "Fact Sheet: President Obama Announces New Commitments from Investors, Companies, Universities, and Cities to Advance Inclusive Entrepreneurship at First-Ever White House Demo Day," press release, August 4, 2015, https://obamawhitehouse.archives.gov/the-press-office/2015/08/04/fact-sheet-president-obama-announces-new-commitments-investors-companies.

48. Laura Lorenzetti, "What Pinterest Is Learning from the Pittsburgh Steelers About Diversity," *Fortune*, July 30, 2015, http://fortune.com/2015/07/30/pinterest-diversity-initiative/.

49. Aarti Shahani, "Intel Discloses Diversity Data, Challenges Tech Industry to Follow Suit," *Morning Edition*, National Public Radio, February 3, 2016, http://www.npr.org/sections/alltechconsidered/2016/02/03/465270938/intel-discloses-diversity-data-challenges-tech-industry-to-follow-suit; White House, "Fact Sheet: President Obama Announces New Commitments from Investors." According to NPR's Aarti Shahani, Krzanich's goal of "full representation" is meant to "reflect the available talent pool" in America, as opposed to America itself. The White House's fact sheet, however, suggests that the goal is to "have a workforce that represents American demographics by 2020."

50. White House, "Fact Sheet: President Obama Announces New Commitments from Investors."

51. Valentina Zarya, "Why Is the "Rooney Rule" Suddenly Tech's Answer to Hiring More Women?," *Fortune*, August 10, 2015, http://fortune.com/2015/08/10/rooney-rule-diversity-in-tech/.

52. "Uber Founder Travis Kalanick Resigns after Months of Turmoil," *BBC News*, June 21, 2017, http://www.bbc.com/news/business-40351859.

53. "Uber Report: Eric Holder's Recommendations for Change," *New York Times*, June 13, 2017, https://www.nytimes.com/2017/06/13/technology/uber-report-eric-holders-recommendations-for-change.html?_r=0.

54. At least that is what they reported to the BBC: "Uber Chief Travis Kalanick May Face Bumpy Ride," *BBC News*, June 12, 2017, http://www.bbc.com/news/business -40242538.

55. Reid Wilson, "Racial Imbalance Exists All Across Local Governments, Not Just in Police Departments," *Washington Post*, August 14, 2014, https://www.washingtonpost .com/blogs/govbeat/wp/2014/08/14/racial-imbalance-exists-all-across-local-governments -not-just-in-police-departments/?utm_term=.474192ba390a.

56. Dubois, "The Impact of the Rooney Rule."

57. "Advancing Diversity in City Recruitment and Hiring," Executive Order, City of Pittsburgh Office of the Mayor, April 19, 2017, http://apps.pittsburghpa.gov/mayorpeduto /4.19.17_-_Advancing_Diversity_in_City_Recruitment_and_Hiring.pdf.

58. Don Bell, "Only 5 Percent of Senate Staffers Are Black. Congress Needs the 'Rooney Rule,'" *Washington Post*, April 25, 2017, https://www.washingtonpost.com/post everything/wp/2017/04/25/only-5-percent-of-senate-staffers-are-black-congress-needs -the-rooney-rule/?tid=a_inl&utm_term=.526fc4f535fa.

59. Ibid.

60. Kristen Bialik and Jens Manuel Krogstad, "115th Congress Sets New High for Racial, Ethnic Diversity," *Pew Research Center*, January 24, 2017, http://www.pewresearch .org/fact-tank/2017/01/24/115th-congress-sets-new-high-for-racial-ethnic-diversity/.

61. David Waldenstein, "Success and Shortfalls in Effort to Diversify N.F.L. Coach-ing" *New York Times*, January 20, 2015, https://www.nytimes.com/2015/01/21/sports /football/jets-hiring-of-todd-bowles-leaves-nfl-far-short-of-goal-on-diversity.html.

62. Earl Butch Graves Jr., "Why the NFL's Rooney Rule Is a Sham," *Black Enter-prise*, February 5, 2013, http://www.blackenterprise.com/nfl-rooney-rule-is-a-sham/.

63. Waldenstein, "Success and Shortfalls."

64. Associated Press, "Rooney Rule."

65. Waldenstein, "Success and Shortfalls."

CHAPTER 3: BUILDING A BETTER BOARD—AND A LARGER,
MORE VIBRANT ORGANIZATION

1. For this profile I am indebted especially to Ellen Joan Pollock, "Cypress CEO Blasts Sister Who Asked for Diverse Board," *Wall Street Journal*, July 15, 1996, https:// www.wsj.com/articles/SB837379519825209500; Colman McCarthy, "Lesson for a Nun," *Washington Post*, July 20, 1996, https://www.washingtonpost.com/archive/opinions/1996 /07/20/lesson-for-a-nun/a33e58a1-ae8b-42e2-83c7-9390174fcee9/?utm_term =.9dfd35dcadac.

2. The full text of Sister Doris Gormley's letter is available at the *Wall Street Journal*, updated July 15, 1996, https://www.wsj.com/articles/SB837202547303758500.

3. Pollock, "Cypress CEO Blasts Sister."

4. Ibid.

5. Richard Brandt, "The Bad Boy of Silicon Valley," *Bloomberg*, December 9, 1991, https://www.bloomberg.com/news/articles/1991-12-08/the-bad-boy-of-silicon-valley.

6. Pollock, "Cypress CEO Blasts Sister."

7. McCarthy, "Lesson for a Nun."

8. Pollock, "Cypress CEO Blasts Sister."

9. "Commonsense Corporate Governance Principles," http://www.governanceprin-ciples.org, accessed February 28, 2018; Ross Kerber, "U.S. CEOs Back Board Diversity, GAAP Adherence in Reform Push," Reuters, July 21, 2016, http://www.reuters.com /article/us-companies-management-idUSKCN10122T.

10. Catalyst, *Why Diversity Matters* (July 2013), 2, http://www.catalyst.org/system /files/why_diversity_matters_catalyst_0.pdf.

11. Ibid.

12. Rachel Feintzeig, "More Companies Say Targets Are the Key to Diversity," *Wall Street Journal*, September 30, 2015, https://www.wsj.com/articles/more-companies-say -targets-are-the-key-to-diversity-1443600464; Eric Pfanner, "Corporate Japan Looks for Outside Advice," *Wall Street Journal*, updated June 8, 2015, https://www.wsj.com /articles/corporate-japan-looks-for-outside-advice-1433789544.

13. "Podcast: Problems with Board Diversity Are Getting Worse, Nonprofit Leader Says," *Chronicle of Philanthropy*, December 8, 2017, https://www.philanthropy.com /article/Podcast-Problems-With-Board/242010.

14. *Leading with Intent*, 12.

15. Ibid.

16. Jim McAlpin and Michael Shumaker, "The Link Between Board Diversity and Smart Business," BankDirector.com, July 17, 2015, https://www.bankdirector.com /committees/governance/the-link-between-board-diversity-and-smart-business.

17. *Diversity in Leadership: Minority and Female Representation on Fortune 250 Boards and Executive Teams* (Russell Reynolds Associates, September 2014), 7, http://www.russell reynolds.com/insights/thought-leadership/minority-female-representation-on-fortune -250-boards-executive-teams.

18. See the company website: "Immigration Nonprofits Receive $1.5M from Eastern Bank Charitable Foundation," Eastern Bank, October 19, 2017, https://www.eastern bank.com/immigration-nonprofits-receive-15m-eastern-bank-charitable-foundation.

19. Deirdre Fernandes, "Eastern Bank Gets to $10 Billion Mark," *Boston Globe*, July 28, 2016, https://www.bostonglobe.com/business/2016/07/28/eastern-bank-gets-billion -mark/tAbhNubxecDr5YkLVPBrjI/story.html

20. Kurt Badenhausen, "America's Best Banks 2016," *Forbes*, January 7, 2016, https:// www.forbes.com/sites/kurtbadenhausen/2016/01/07/americas-best-banks-2016/#38f2b 9b63c45.

21. "Biggest US Banks by Asset Size (2018)," https://www.mx.com/moneysummit /biggest-banks-by-asset-size-united-states

22. "Embracing Diversity," Eastern Bank, https://www.easternbank.com/site/about _us/pages/diversity.aspx.

23. Jim McAlpin and Michael Shumaker, "The Link Between Board Diversity and Smart Business," BankDirector.com, July 17, 2015, https://www.bankdirector.com /committees/governance/the-link-between-board-diversity-and-smart-business.

24. For this explanation of Eastern's three-tiered leadership structure and its diversification, I am indebted to Bob Rivers (chairman and CEO of Eastern Bank), interview with author, May 12, 2017

25. Rivers, interview with author.

26. Wendell J. Knox (former president and CEO of Abt Associates, Inc., and director of Eastern Bank), interview with author, July 11, 2017.

27. Deborah C. Jackson (president of Cambridge College and director of Eastern Bank), interview with author, June 10, 2017.

28. See "Believe," Eastern Bank, https://www.easternbank.com/believe; Beth Healy, "Businesses Call Defense of Marriage Act Unfair," *Boston Globe*, February 28, 2013, https://www.bostonglobe.com/business/2013/02/28/nearly-businesses-ask-supreme -court-strike-down-defense-marriage-act/KwETbPZkdyVklCvwTu6tmM/story.html.

29. Rivers, interview with author.

30. "Top Largest Employers for 2017 in Greater Boston," *Boston Globe*, November 16, 2017, https://www.bostonglobe.com/business/specials/top-places-to-work/2017/11 /16/top-largest-employers-for-greater-boston/P3Xb3FceEyi7voozeIf1TJ/story.html; "Believe," Eastern Bank.

31. Rivers, interview with author.

32. Deirdre Fernandes, "Ads Show Eastern Bank's True Colors on Social Issues," *Boston Globe*, March 7, 2017, https://www.bostonglobe.com/business/2017/03/06 /ads-show-eastern-bank-true-colors-social-issues/qRopPYLYmNTbxi5HkB1WBI /story.html.

33. Karen M. Kroll, "Eastern Bank: Join Us For Good," *ABA Bank Marketing*, December 4, 2017, https://ababankmarketing.com/insights/eastern-bank-join-us-good/.

34. Cynthia M. Krus, Lisa A Morgan, and Terri Ginsberg, "Board Diversity: Who Has a Seat at the Table," *Corporate Governance Advisor* 20 (2012): 2.

35. Ibid.

36. Doris Kearns Goodwin, "Defeat Your Opponents. Then Hire Them," *New York Times*, August 3, 2008, http://www.nytimes.com/2008/08/03/opinion/03goodwin.html.

37. Todd Purdum, "Team of Mascots," *Vanity Fair*, July 2012, accessed August 31, 2016, http://www.vanityfair.com/news/2012/07/obama-cabinet-team-rivals-lincoln.

38. Christopher Bennett and Richard Crisp, "The Missing Link Between Diversity and Creativity in Companies?," Conference Board of Human Capital Exchange, May 31, 2016, https://hcexchange.conference-board.org/blog/post.cfm?post=5198.

39. Sheen S. Levine and David Stark, "Diversity Makes You Brighter," *New York Times*, December 9, 2015, http://www.nytimes.com/2015/12/09/opinion/diversity-makes-you-brighter.html.

40. Ibid.

41. Boris Groysberg and Deborah Bell, "Dysfunction in the Boardroom," *Harvard Business Review*, June 2013, https://hbr.org/2013/06/dysfunction-in-the-boardroom.

42. Ibid.

43. Catalyst, *Why Diversity Matters*.

44. Knox, interview with author.

45. Rivers, interview with author.

46. "#1 SBA Small Business Lender," Eastern Bank, https://www.easternbank.com/1-sba-small-business-lender, accessed June 21, 2018.

47. Eastern Bank, "Celent Names Eastern Bank the 'Model Bank of the Year' for 2016," press release, April 14, 2016, https://www.easternbank.com/site/about_us/newsroom/2016Archive/Pages/release04142016.aspx.

48. Knox, interview with author.

49. Rivers, interview with author.

50. Caroline Fairchild, "How Macy's Quietly Created One of America's Most Diverse Boards," *Fortune*, February 18, 2015.

51. Rivers, interview with author.

52. Jackson, interview with author.

53. Rivers, interview with author.

54. For this concluding section, I rely on the reflections of Bennie Wiley, Bob Rivers, and Ralph C. Martin II, at the Bennie Wiley CEO Award Presentation, Seaport World Trade Center, Boston, December 12, 2017.

CHAPTER 4: CONNECTING WITH COMMUNITY AT JOHN HANCOCK

1. "1998 US Embassies in Africa Bombings Fast Facts," CNN.com, http://www.cnn.com/2013/10/06/world/africa/africa-embassy-bombings-fast-facts/index.html, updated August 9, 2017.

2. Gregory Warner, "How One Kenyan Tribe Produces the World's Best Runners," *All Things Considered*, National Public Radio, November 1, 2013, http://www.npr.org/sections/parallels/2013/11/01/241895965/how-one-kenyan-tribe-produces-the-worlds-best-runners; Adharanand Finn, "Young, Barefoot and Fiercely Competitive: Kenya's Future Athletes," *Guardian*, February 22, 2011, https://www.theguardian.com/lifeandstyle/2011/feb/22/running-fitness-iten-kenya-school.

3. For more, please see Mary Brophy Marcus, "What Makes Kenya's Marathon Runners the World's Best?," *Goats and Soda*, National Public Radio, November 4, 2014, http://www.npr.org/sections/goatsandsoda/2014/11/04/361403249/what-makes-kenyas-marathon-runners-the-worlds-best.

4. "Catherine Ndereba First Woman to Win Boston Fourth Time," *BMW-Berlin 44th Marathon News*, April 20, 2005, http://skating.bmw-berlin-marathon.com/en/news-and-media/news/2005/04/20/catherine-ndereba-first-woman-to-win-boston-fourth-time.html.

5. David Vogel, "CSR Doesn't Pay," *Forbes*, October 16, 2008, https://www.forbes.com/2008/10/16/csr-doesnt-pay-lead-corpresponso8-cx_dv_1016vogel.html.

6. Susan McPherson, "6 CSR Trends to Watch in 2017," *Forbes*, January 19, 2017, https://www.forbes.com/sites/susanmcpherson/2017/01/19/6-csr-trends-to-watch-in-2017/#429f3d41b1cc.

7. Katrin Hansen and Cathrine Seierstad, *Corporate Social Responsibility and Diversity Management: Theoretical Approaches and Best Practices* (Switzerland: Springer International Publishing, 2017), 2.

8. All figures provided by Tom Crohan (assistant vice president and counsel, Corporate Responsibility and Government Relations at John Hancock), interview with author, July 25 and August 4, 2017.

9. Michael E. Porter and Mark R. Kramer provide an excellent overview of the topic, which I draw from in this paragraph. Please see their "Strategy and Society: The Link Between Competitive Advantage and Corporate Social Responsibility," *Harvard Business Review*, December 2006, https://hbr.org/2006/12/strategy-and-society-the-link -between-competitive-advantage-and-corporate-social-responsibility.

10. Adam Vaughan, "Shell Begins Huge Task of Decommissioning Brent Oil Rigs," *Guardian*, February 6, 2017, https://www.theguardian.com/business/2017/feb/06/shell -decommissioning-brent-oil-rigs.

11. John H. Cushman Jr., "International Business: Nike Pledges to End Child Labor and Apply U.S. Rules Abroad," *New York Times*, May 13, 1998, http://www.nytimes.com /1998/05/13/business/international-business-nike-pledges-to-end-child-labor-and -apply-us-rules-abroad.html.

12. Jeffrey Hollender and Bill Breen, *The Responsibility Revolution: How the Next Generation of Businesses Will Win* (San Francisco: Jossey-Bass, 2010).

13. As this book goes to press, another rebranding is under way, with CSR departments shifting their language from "responsibility" to "social impact." For one CSR expert, such a change "reflects a growing consensus that the key driver for a company's pro-social program should be not some generic standard of responsibility or as penance for perceived negative effects, but rather unique, measurable, positive impact—human, environmental, societal, and financial" (McPherson, "6 CSR Trends to Watch in 2017").

14. And it's not just multinational outfits that assume responsibility. In 2013, Tom Douglas came to symbolize such a trend for America's small and medium-size enterprises (SMEs) and local businesses. Douglas, the owner of fourteen Seattle-based restaurants and bakeries, made international headlines for voluntarily increasing the minimum wage for cooks at his restaurants to $15 per hour. Douglas did it because it was the right thing to do: "We're literally committing one-third of our profits to this. But, you know, I'm 25 years in. I feel like now I own my car, you know, I own my house, I own my farm. Now, instead of buying more toys, I just feel like this is the way I want to pay back a bit of the incredible luck that I've had over the years, and the incredible hard work that many, many, many people have put in over the years" ("Why a Seattle Restaurant Owner Is Against 'Living Wage' Laws," *Morning Edition*, National Public Radio, August 29, 2013, http://www.npr.org/2013/08/29/216720753/seattle-restaurant-owner-on-living -wage-laws.

15. All figures taken from *2017 Cone Communications Research Study*, Boston, www .conecomm.com.

16. Jeffrey Hollender and Bill Breen, "Six Obstacles on the Road to Corporate Responsibility," *Huffington Post*, May 15, 2010, http://www.huffingtonpost.com/jeffrey -hollender/six-obstacles-on-the-road_b_493813.html.

17. Ibid.

18. Aaron Chatterji, "When Corporations Fail at Doing Good," *New Yorker*, August 29, 2013, http://www.newyorker.com/business/currency/when-corporations-fail-at -doing-good.

19. Jesse Eisinger, "How Mark Zuckerberg's Altruism Helps Himself," *New York Times*, December 3, 2015, https://www.nytimes.com/2015/12/04/business/dealbook /how-mark-zuckerbergs-altruism-helps-himself.html.

20. Tracey Keys, Thomas W. Malnight, and Kees van der Graaf, "Making the Most of Corporate Social Responsibility," *McKinsey*, December 2009, http://www.mckinsey .com/global-themes/leadership/making-the-most-of-corporate-social-responsibility.

21. Stuart Elliott, "The Media Business: Advertising; Brands that Shaped Marketing in the 20th Century, and Some with Promise in the 21st," *New York Times*, December 13, 1999, http://www.nytimes.com/1999/12/13/business/media-business-advertising-brands -that-shaped-marketing-20th-century-some-with.html?scp=1&sq=most%20powerful %20brands%20of%20the%2020th%20century&st=cse.

22. For much of the material in this chapter on CSR at John Hancock, as well as other valuable insights, I am indebted to Tom Crohan, interviews with author, July 25 and August 4, 2017.

23. Melissa Berczuk, "Boston Teens Earn Nearly $10M over 10 Years Through John Hancock's MLK Summer Scholars Program," John Hancock/PRNewswire, January 12, 2017, https://www.johnhancock.com/news/corporate-social-responsibility-/2017/01/boston-teens-earn-nearly—10m-over-10-years-through-john-hancock-s-mlk-summer-scholars-program.html.

24. For more, see Best Buddies, https://www.bestbuddies.org/.

25. John Hancock, "2015 Best Buddies Challenge," YouTube video, published May 22, 2015, https://www.youtube.com/watch?v=6btxAWOn2CM.

26. For personal information about Dudley, I relied on "Meet Dudley Williams III," Best Buddies, https://www.bestbuddies.org/blog/2015/01/02/meet-dudley-williams-iii/.

27. Craig Welton, "Dudley Williams III—2015 Employee of the Year," YouTube video, published December 27, 2015, https://www.youtube.com/watch?v=qyl-8Amm4Sg.

28. Ibid.

29. Taruka Srivastav, "Creative Agencies Pitch Inclusion of 'Intellectually Disabled' Candidates to the Advertising Community in Latest Film," *Drum*, September 17, 2017. Creative Spirit is an Australian-based nonprofit, and it's unclear whether Rossi was speaking about Australia specifically or in more global terms. The Special Olympics committee in the United States commissioned a national study showing how unemployment rates among the intellectually disabled are more than twice those in the workforce in general: "Unemployment of People with Intellectual Disabilities More Than Twice as High as General Population," PR Newswire, February 17, 2014, https://www.prnewswire.com/news-releases/unemployment-of-people-with-intellectual-disabilities-more-than-twice-as-high-as-general-population-245835281.html.

30. Jean Case, "The Business of Doing Good: How Millennials Are Changing the Corporate Sector," *Forbes*, June 18, 2014, https://www.forbes.com/sites/jeancase/2014/06/18/millennials2014/#7373d0984c34.

31. For this profile, I am indebted to Micho Spring (chair of global corporate practice and president of Weber Shandwick New England), interview with author, August 25, 2017.

32. Carol Morello and Ted Mellnik, "Minorities Become a Majority in Washington Region," *Washington Post*, August 31, 2011, https://www.washingtonpost.com/local/minorities-become-a-majority-in-washington-region/2011/08/30/gIQADobxqJ_story.html?utm_term=.c8e63f749ad9. As this report details, whites made up 64 percent of the Washington region's population in 1990 and 55 percent of the population in 2000.

33. For more, please explore the venture's website, https://angel.co/coin-8.

34. David F. D'Alessandro, *Brand Warfare: 10 Rules for Building the Killer Brand* (New York: McGraw-Hill, 2001), 37–38.

35. Berczuk, "Boston Teens Earn Nearly $10M."

36. "Giving Children Brighter Futures Through Better Nutrition," Hershey Company, https://www.thehersheycompany.com/en_us/responsibility/nourishing-minds.html, accessed February 28, 2018.

37. T. W. Burger, "Milton Hershey School Evolves from Small Industrial School to Diverse Educational Experience," Pennlive.com, September 13, 2009, http://www.pennlive.com/midstate/index.ssf/2009/09/milton_hershey.html.

38. "Our Journey to Nourish One Million Minds," Hershey Company, https://www.thehersheycompany.com/en_us/news-center/blog/doing-well-by-doing-good-our-journey-to-nourish-one-million-minds.html.

39. Matilda Steiner-Aseidu and Firibu Kwesi Saalia, "A Pilot Study to Determine the Efficacy of Consuming a Highly Fortified Groundnut Nutritional Supplement on the Nutritional Status of School Children," Hershey Company, December 2016, https://www.thehersheycompany.com/content/dam/corporate-us/documents/information/nurishing-minds-pilot-study.pdf.

40. "The Hershey Company to Launch Hershey's Cookie Layer Crunch," Hershey Company, https://www.thehersheycompany.com/en_us/news-center/news-detail.html ?2209005&, accessed February 28, 2018.

41. Burger, "Milton Hershey School Evolves."

CHAPTER 5: MARKETING OUTSIDE THE BOX

1. For this profile, I am indebted to Patrick Smith (executive vice president at KeyBank and former head of customer experience strategy at Liberty Mutual Insurance), interview with author, August 23, 2017.

2. Lynnley Browning, "A Bank for the Masses Reaches for the Elite," *New York Times*, October 3, 2007, http://www.nytimes.com/2007/10/03/business/media/03adco.html.

3. Ibid.

4. Ibid.

5. Samantha Masunaga, "Target Takes Aim at Latinos with New Marketing Campaign," *Los Angeles Times*, April 18, 2015, http://www.latimes.com/business/la-fi-target -latino-marketing-20150418-story.html.

6. Associated Press, "Hispanics to Pass Blacks in Buying Power," *NBC News*, September 1, 2006, http://www.nbcnews.com/id/14623151/ns/ business-stocks_and_economy/t/hispanics-pass-blacks-buying-power/#.WcJgP8iGPIU.

7. Marc De Swaan Arons, "How Brands Were Born: A Brief History of Modern Marketing," *Atlantic*, October 3, 2011, https://www.theatlantic.com/business/archive /2011/10/how-brands-were-born-a-brief-history-of-modern-marketing/246012/#slide1.

8. Clint C Wilson, II, Félix Gutiérrez, and Lena M Chao, *Racism, Sexism, and the Media: Multicultural Issues into the New Communications Age* (Thousand Oaks, CA: SAGE Publications, 2013), 151.

9. Lenika Cruz, "'Dinnertimin' and 'No Tipping': How Advertisers Targeted Black Consumers in the 1970s," *Atlantic*, June 7, 2015, https://www.theatlantic.com /entertainment/archive/2015/06/casual-racism-and-greater-diversity-in-70s-advertising /394958/; Michelle Castillo, "Turning an Athlete into a Brand: Today's Formula," CNBC.com, February 2, 2016, https://www.cnbc.com/2016/02/02/turning-an-athlete -into-a-brand-todays-formula.html.

10. As quoted in Cruz, "'Dinnertimin' and 'No Tipping.'"

11. "Made-to-Order: The Rise of Mass Personalisation," *Deloitte Consumer Review* (2015): 4.

12. Ibid.

13. Hua Hsu, "The End of White America?," *Atlantic*, January/February 2009, https://www.theatlantic.com/magazine/archive/2009/01/the-end-of-white-america /307208/.

14. For this profile, I am indebted to Donna Latson Gittens (founder and CEO at MORE Advertising), interview with author, November 17, 2017.

15. Burt Helm, "Ethnic Marketing: McDonald's Is Lovin' It," *Bloomberg Businessweek*, July 8, 2010, https://www.bloomberg.com/news/articles/2010-07-08/ethnic -marketing-mcdonalds-is-lovin-it.

16. Ibid.

17. For this paragraph, I rely on Masunaga, "Target Takes Aim at Latinos."

18. Jeff Beer, "This Ad Agency Has Launched a Collaborative Plan to Make the Creative Class More Diverse," *Fast Company*, September 21, 2017, https://www.fast company.com/40471370/this-ad-agency-has-launched-a-collaborative-plan-to-make -the-creative-class-more-diverse.

19. Sapna Maheshwari, "Brands to Ad Agencies: Diversify or Else," *New York Times*, September 30, 2016, https://www.nytimes.com/2016/10/01/business/media/brands-to -ad-agencies-diversify-or-else.html?_r=0.

20. Sydney Ember, "Accusations of Sexism and Racism Shake Ad Agency and Industry," *New York Times*, March 18, 2016, https://www.nytimes.com/2016/03/19/business /j-walter-thompson-gets-new-chief-after-departure-over-suit.html.

21. Maheshwari, "Brands to Ad Agencies."

22. This paragraph relies on Maheshwari, "Brands to Ad Agencies."

23. All executive quotes from Maheshwari, "Brands to Ad Agencies."

24. Timothy Stenovec, "Ford India Ad: Car Company, Ad Agency Apologize for Figo Ad Showing Gagged & Bound Women," *Huffington Post*, March 24, 2013, http://www.huffingtonpost.com/2013/03/24/ford-india-figo-ad-bound-and-gagged-women_n_2941297.html, updated December 6, 2017.

25. "Chevy 'Fu Manchu' Ad Pulled After Commercial for Chevrolet Trax Deemed 'Offensive,'" *Huffington Post*, May 2, 2013, http://www.huffingtonpost.com/2013/05/02/chevy-fu-manchu-ad-pulled-offensive_n_3200843.html.

26. Robert Allen, "'See Detroit Like We Do' Ad with Mostly White People Sparks Outrage," *USA Today*, July 24, 2017, https://www.usatoday.com/story/news/nation-now/2017/07/24/detroit-sign-mostly-white-people-putrage/504737001/.

27. Alan Sherter, "Quicken Loans Founder: We 'Screwed Up' on Detroit Display Sign," *CBS News*, July 24, 2017, https://www.cbsnews.com/news/quicken-loans-dan-gilbert-detroit-display-sign/.

28. Emma Winowiecki, "Mostly White 'See Detroit Like We Do' Ad Draws Backlash and Apologies," Michiganradio.org, National Public Radio, July 24, 2017, http://michiganradio.org/post/mostly-white-see-detroit-we-do-ad-draws-backlash-and-apologies.

29. Allen, "'See Detroit Like We Do.'"

30. Michelle Castillo, "Study: Americans Want More Diversity in Ads," CNBC.com, updated March 7, 2016, https://www.cnbc.com/2016/03/07/study-americans-want-more-diversity-in-ads.html.

31. *Taking a Stand: Brands, Social Good & Consumer Expectations* (YouGov, March 15, 2016), https://d25d2506sfb94s.cloudfront.net/cumulus_uploads/document/ur242bgmos/Holmes%20Report-YouGov-Brands,%20Social%20Good%20&%20Consumer%20Expectations%20.pdf.

32. Stephanie Capparell, *The Real Pepsi Challenge: The Inspirational Story of Breaking the Color Barrier in American Business* (New York: Wall Street Journal Books, 2007).

33. Ibid., ix. Please note that in some formats, the page numbers in the preface are missing.

34. Ibid., xi.

35. Ibid., 11.

36. Ibid., 21.

37. Ibid., x–xi.

38. David A. Thomas and Stephanie J. Creary, "Meeting the Diversity Challenge at PepsiCo: The Steve Reinemund Era," *Harvard Business Review*, August 17, 2009, 5.

39. Bennie Wiley (former president and CEO of The Partnership and director on the boards of the Dreyfus/Laurel Funds), interview with author, August 23, 2017.

40. For this background on Pepsi, I am indebted to Dr. David Thomas (president of Morehouse College), interview with author, October 16, 2017.

41. Claudia H. Deutsch, "A Woman to Be Chief at PepsiCo," *New York Times*, August 15, 2006, http://www.nytimes.com/2006/08/15/business/15pepsi.html?ref=topics.

42. Thomas and Creary, "Meeting the Diversity Challenge," 6.

43. Ibid., 7.

44. Thomas, interview with author.

45. Ibid.

46. Thomas and Creary, "Meeting the Diversity Challenge," 5, 9.

47. Ibid., 6–7.

48. Ibid., 7.

49. Thomas, interview with author.

50. Ibid.

51. Thomas and Creary, "Meeting the Diversity Challenge," 12–13.

52. Deutsch, "A Woman to Be Chief at PepsiCo."

53. Ibid.; Katrina Brooker, "How Pepsi Outgunned Coke," *CNN Money*, February 1, 2006, http://money.cnn.com/2006/02/01/news/companies/pepsi_fortune/.

54. Holly Lebowitz Rossi, "7 CEOs with Notably Devout Religious Beliefs," *Fortune*, November 11, 2014, http://fortune.com/2014/11/11/7-ceos-with-notably-devout

-religious-beliefs/. Nooyi consistently ranks among the top handful of Fortune's most powerful women: "Most Powerful Women: Indra Nooyi," *Fortune*, 2017, http://fortune .com/most-powerful-women/indra-nooyi-2/.

55. "PepsiCo Names Larry D. Thompson General Counsel; Succeeds David R. Andrews, Who Retires in February," *Bevnet*, August 23, 2004, https://www.bevnet.com /news/2004/08–24–2004-pepsico_larry_d_thompson_general_counsel.asp.

56. Deutsch, "A Woman to Be Chief at PepsiCo."

57. Capparell, *The Real Pepsi Challenge*; Brooker, "How Pepsi Outgunned Coke."

58. Brooker, "How Pepsi Outgunned Coke."

59. Ibid.

60. Dan Schawbel, "Indra Nooyi: Achieving Both Financial Growth and Purpose at PepsiCo," *Forbes*, November 21, 2017, https://www.forbes.com/sites/danschawbel/2017/11 /21/indra-nooyi-achieving-both-financial-growth-and-purpose-at-pepsico/#5fb2947eeaa6.

61. As a 2015 *Harvard Business Review* profile noted, "The company has enjoyed steady revenue growth during her [Nooyi's] nine years in the top job, and Pepsi's stock price is rising again after several flat years" (Adi Ignatius, "How Indra Nooyi Turned Design Thinking into Strategy: An Interview with PepsiCo's CEO," *Harvard Business Review*, September 2015, https://hbr.org/2015/09/how-indra-nooyi-turned-design -thinking-into-strategy). For the company's growth under Nooyi, see Jackie Wattles, "Pepsi CEO Indra Nooyi Gets Big Pay Bump," *CNN Money*, March 18, 2017, http:// money.cnn.com/2017/03/18/news/companies/pepsi-indra-nooyi/index.html.

62. David Firestone, "While Barbie Talks Tough, G. I. Joe Goes Shopping," *New York Times*, December 31, 1993, http://www.nytimes.com/1993/12/31/us/while-barbie -talks-tough-g-i-joe-goes-shopping.html?mcubz=1. Visit Feminist Hacker Barbie at https://computer-engineer-barbie.herokuapp.com/.

63. Eliana Dockterman, "A Barbie for Every Body," *Time*, February 8, 2016. See also Paul Ziobro, "Mattel to Add Curvy, Petite, Tall Barbies," *Wall Street Journal*, January 28, 2016, https://www.wsj.com/articles/mattel-to-add-curvy-petite-tall-barbies-1453991134.

64. Ziobro, "Mattel to Add Curvy, Petite, Tall Barbies"; Ann Hart, "Introducing the New, Realistic Barbie: 'The Thigh Gap Has Officially Gone,'" *Telegraph*, January 28, 2016, http://www.telegraph.co.uk/news/shopping-and-consumer-news/12112027 /Introducing-the-new-realistic-Barbie-The-thigh-gap-has-officially-gone.html.

65. Dockterman, "A Barbie for Every Body"; Hart, "Introducing the New, Realistic Barbie."

66. Shan Li, "Mattel's Holiday Wish: To Get Its Toys on More Children's Wish Lists," *Los Angeles Times*, November 27, 2014, http://www.latimes.com/business/la-fi -mattel-barbie-20141128-story.html; Dockterman, "A Barbie for Every Body."

67. Emily Peck, "Barbie's Surprising Comeback Has Everything to Do with Race," *Huffington Post*, March 2, 2017, http://www.huffingtonpost.com/entry/barbie-diversity_us _58b5debde4b060480e0c7aa2.

68. Eliana Dockterman, "How You Buy the New Barbies," *Time*, January 28, 2016, http://time.com/4194206/new-barbies-how-to-buy-them/.

69. Hart, "Introducing the New, Realistic Barbie."

70. Dockterman, "A Barbie for Every Body."

71. Some news stories identify different numbers of eye colors, hair styles, and other facial features. I take these figures from Dockterman, "A Barbie for Every Body."

72. "Mattel Wins Toy of the Year Award for Barbie Fashionistas in the Doll of the Year Category," PR Newswire, February 21, 2017, http://www.prnewswire.com/news -releases/mattel-wins-toy-of-the-year-award-for-barbie-fashionistas-in-the-doll-of-the -year-category-300410981.html.

73. Quoted in *Global Diversity and Inclusion: Fostering Innovation Through a Diverse Workforce*, 6.

74. Hart, "Introducing the New, Realistic Barbie."

75. Erik Oster, "Tom Burrell Becomes the First African American Inducted into the One Club Creative Hall of Fame," *AdWeek*, September 19, 2017, http://www.adweek .com/agencies/tom-burrell-becomes-first-african-american-inducted-into-one-club -creative-hall-of-fame/.

76. Hart, "Introducing the New, Realistic Barbie"; Peck, "Barbie's Surprising Comeback"; "After Backlash, Computer Engineer Barbie Gets New Set Of Skills," *All Things Considered*, National Public Radio, November 22, 2014, http://www.npr .org/2014/11/22/365968465/after-backlash-computer-engineer-barbie-gets-new-set -of-skills.

77. Emily Peck, "Mattel Finally Nails It with Game Developer Barbie," *Huffington Post*, June 17, 2016, http://www.huffingtonpost.com/entry/game-developer-barbie_us _57642e6de4b0853f8bf0ae75.

78. Ibid.

79. Mahita Gajanan, "Mattel Just Launched a New Line of Ken Dolls and One of Them Has a Dad Bod," *Fortune*, June 20, 2017, http://fortune.com/2017/06/20/mattel -barbie-ken-doll-dad-bod-man-bun/.

80. Peck, "Barbie's Surprising Comeback."

81. Specifically, $971.8 million (Peck, "Barbie's Surprising Comeback").

82. For this profile, I am indebted to Yvonne Garcia (senior vice president of investment manager services at State Street Corporation), interview with author, September 7, 2017.

83. Beer, "This Ad Agency Has Launched."

84. 72andSunny, *Expand and Diversify the Creative Class*, April 2018, https://assets .contentful.com/1l8uxi2exlw4/11xKpgjdQiaguAai6OAoC4/cd49451061179329505405 ddd1c9c156/72andSunny_Mission_Playbook.pdf.

85. Ibid., 23.

86. Ibid., 25–26.

87. Ibid., 14.

88. Ibid., 20, 29.

89. Beer, "This Ad Agency Has Launched."

90. D'Alessandro, *Brand Warfare*, 128.

CHAPTER 6: INNOVATING A MORE COLORFUL COMPANY

1. For this section, I rely on Jean Paul Kambazza (software engineer), interview with author, August 24, 2017.

2. For the background on Hack.Diversity, as well as many other insights about technology, I rely on Jody Rose (president of the New England Venture Capital Association), interview with author, August 31, 2017.

3. "GE's New Headquarters: More Innovation Than HQ," *Boston Globe*, May 3, 2017, https://www.bostonglobe.com/business/2017/05/03/new-headquarters-more -innovation-than/afgDVdU4XMTywfMZROldLL/story.html.

4. Vauhini Vara, "Why Doesn't Silicon Valley Hire Black Coders?" *Bloomberg*, January 21, 2016, https://www.bloomberg.com/features/2016-howard-university-coders/.

5. Many studies point to the predominance in the venture capital space of white men, who disproportionately choose to fund other white, male businesses. One study in 2016, "the first comprehensive look at the demographics of venture capital," revealed that "women make up 45% of the venture capital work force, mostly in administrative roles, but just 11% of investment partners, or the equivalent, on venture investment teams. African Americans make up 3% and Latinos 4% of the venture capital workforce. None of the 217 firms with more than 2,500 employees had an African-American investment partner" (Jessica Guynn, "Venture Capital Is Overwhelmingly White and Male," *USA Today*, December 15, 2016, https://www.usatoday .com/story/tech/news/2016/12/15/national-venture-capital-association-deloitte -diversity-survey/95453926/).

6. Ben Schiller, "Why Venture Capitalists Aren't Funding the Businesses We Need," *Fast Company*, September 28, 2017, https://www.fastcompany.com/40467045/why -venture-capitalists-arent-funding-the-businesses-we-need.

7. "This. Is not. Charity," *Medium*, March 31, 2017, https://medium.com/hack -diversity-movement/this-is-not-charity-40340a7f6256.

8. Both quotations from "This. Is not. Charity."

9. "This. Is not. Charity." The study actually discussed at the event was a 2016 Vision Project study that included data from this report, *The Degree Gap: Fourth Annual*

Report on the Vision Project to the People of Massachusetts (Boston: Massachusetts Department of Higher Education, June 2016), 8, http://www.tbf.org/videos/2016/june/~/media/TBFOrg/Files/Reports/Vision%20Project%20Annual%20Report%20616.pdf.

10. *The Degree Gap*, 17.

11. "This. Is not. Charity."

12. Tyler Cowen, *The Great Stagnation: How America Ate All the Low-Hanging Fruit of Modern History, Got Sick, and Will (Eventually) Feel Better* (New York: Dutton, 2011).

13. "Has the Ideas Machine Broken Down?," *Economist*, January 12, 2013, https://www.economist.com/news/briefing/21569381-idea-innovation-and-new-technology-have-stopped-driving-growth-getting-increasing.

14. Ibid. The *Economist* also credits this expression to Thiel's fellow partners and colleagues at the Founders Fund venture capital group.

15. Fareed Zakaria, "Why Is the Number of US Start-Ups Falling?" *Washington Post*, May 19, 2016, https://www.washingtonpost.com/opinions/why-is-the-number-of-us-start-ups-falling/2016/05/19/53fe8e04-1ded-11e6-9c81-4be1c14fb8c8_story.html?utm_term=.e2597308b9ff; Ryan A. Decker et al., "Where Has All the Skewness Gone? The Decline in High-Growth (Young) Firms in the US," Working Paper no. 21776, National Bureau of Economic Research, December 2015.

16. Ian Hathaway and Robert E. Litan, *Declining Business Dynamism in the United States: A Look at States and Metros* (Washington, DC: Brookings Institution, May 2014), abstract and p. 3, https://www.brookings.edu/wp-content/uploads/2016/06/declining_business_dynamism_hathaway_litan.pdf.

17. Steve Denning, "Why U.S. Entrepreneurship Is Dying," *Forbes*, May 27, 2016, https://www.forbes.com/sites/stevedenning/2016/05/27/why-us-entrepreneurship-is-dying/#7cce29ed7d74.

18. Danny Vinik, "America's Innovation Crisis," *Politico*, October 14, 2016, http://www.politico.com/agenda/story/2016/10/americas-innovation-crisis-000222.

19. Reenita Das, "Ten Top Technologies That Will Transform the Healthcare Industry," *Forbes*, October 11, 2016, https://www.forbes.com/sites/reenitadas/2016/10/11/healthcare-2025-ten-top-technologies-that-will-transform-the-industry/#4fce31ae3e18.

20. "Has the Ideas Machine Broken Down?"

21. Regina E. Herzlinger, "Why Innovation in Health Care Is So Hard," *Harvard Business Review*, May 2006, https://hbr.org/2006/05/why-innovation-in-health-care-is-so-hard.

22. Michael Horn, "Disruptive Innovations in Higher Ed Emerging from outside Mainstream," *Forbes*, July 23, 2015, https://www.forbes.com/sites/michaelhorn/2015/07/23/disruptive-innovations-in-higher-ed-emerging-from-outside-mainstream/#9816f5764 1a2.

23. Michael Horn, "Disruptive Innovation and Education," *Forbes*, July 2, 2014, https://www.forbes.com/sites/michaelhorn/2014/07/02/disruptive-innovation-and-education/#c9c30ea3c6e1.

24. Bill Coplin, "The Real Problem with Our Education System," CNBC.com, June 11, 2015, https://www.cnbc.com/2015/06/11/the-real-problem-with-our-education-system-commentary.html.

25. See, for example, Nick Bilton, "Is the Silicon Valley Dynasty Coming to an End?," *Vanity Fair*, April 21, 2017, https://www.vanityfair.com/news/2017/04/is-the-silicon-valley-dynasty-coming-to-an-end.

26. Matt Stoller, "The Evidence Is Piling Up—Silicon Valley Is Being Destroyed," *Business Insider*, April 19, 2017, http://www.businessinsider.com/the-evidence-is-piling-up-silicon-valley-is-being-destroyed-2017-4.

27. "Has the Ideas Machine Broken Down?"

28. Ibid.

29. David Auerbach, "Venture Capitalists Are Not a Disease: They're Only a Symptom of What's Ailing Silicon Valley," *Slate*, July 9, 2014, http://www.slate.com/articles/technology/bitwise/2014/07/silicon_valley_innovation_venture_capital_is_not_the_problem.html.

30. "Has the Ideas Machine Broken Down?"

31. *Deloitte Business Confidence Report 2016: The Bold Organization—Innovate, Lead, Attract* (Deloitte, 2016), 4.

32. Lynne Doughtie, "Innovation Is About More Than the Next Big Thing," *Forbes*, March 1, 2017, https://www.forbes.com/sites/kpmg/2017/03/01/innovation-is-about-more-than-the-next-big-thing/#178df3c91512.

33. Soren Kaplan, "How One Insurance Firm Learned to Create an Innovation Culture," *Harvard Business Review*, August 15, 2017, https://hbr.org/2017/08/how-one-insurance-firm-learned-to-create-an-innovation-culture.

34. Bharat Kapoor, Kevin Nolan, and Natarajan (Venkat) Venkatakrishnan, "How GE Appliances Built an Innovation Lab to Rapidly Prototype Products," *Harvard Business Review*, updated July 21, 2017, https://hbr.org/2017/07/how-ge-built-an-innovation-lab-to-rapidly-prototype-appliances; Arjun Kharpal, "Google's Larry Page Disguised Himself During a Driverless Car Race to Hire the Founder of His Moonshot Lab," CNBC.com, May 11, 2017, https://www.cnbc.com/2017/05/11/google-larry-page-moonshot-lab.html; Barb Darrow, "Microsoft Is Building Its Own AI Hardware with Project Brainwave," *Fortune*, August 23, 2017, http://fortune.com/2017/08/23/microsoft-project-brainwave-ai/. For background on the origins of Google X, see Jon Gertner, "The Truth About Google X: An Exclusive Look Behind the Secretive Lab's Closed Doors," *Fast Company*, April 15, 2014, https://www.fastcompany.com/3028156/the-google-x-factor#1.

35. Kaplan, "How One Insurance Firm Learned."

36. *Waiter, is that inclusion in my soup? A New Recipe to Improve Business Performance* (Deloitte Australia/ Victorian Equal Opportunity and Human Rights Commission, May 2013), 2.

37. Ibid., 25.

38. *Global Diversity and Inclusion: Fostering Innovation Through a Diverse Workforce*, 5.

39. Amy C. Edmondson, *Teaming: How Organizations Learn, Innovate, and Compete in the Knowledge Economy* (San Francisco: Jossey-Bass, 2012).

40. Carla Harris (vice chairman and managing director at Morgan Stanley Wealth Management), interview with author, September 8, 2017.

41. Hae-Jung Hong and Yves L. Doz, "L'Oréal Masters Multiculturalism," in *On Managing Across Cultures* (Boston: Harvard Business Review Press, 2016), 36.

42. Ibid., 38.

43. Ibid., 38.

44. Ibid., 41.

45. Katherine W. Phillips and Denise Lewin Loyd, "When Surface and Deep-Level Diversity Collide: The Effects on Dissenting Group Members," *Organizational Behavior and Human Decision Processes* 99 (2006): 143.

46. As the study argues, "Surface-level diverse groups (with two similar and one dissimilar individuals) were perceived as more positive and accepting, fostered more persistent and confident voicing of dissenting perspectives, and displayed greater task engagement than surface-level homogeneous groups (containing all similar individuals)" (Phillips and Loyd, "When Surface and Deep-Level Diversity Collide," 143).

47. Phillips and Loyd, "When Surface and Deep-Level Diversity Collide," 158.

48. William D. Cohan, "The Last Stand of Ken Chenault," *Fortune*, June 8, 2016, http://fortune.com/ken-chenault-american-express/.

49. Ibid.

50. For an up-to-date list of the Fortune 500, please see http://fortune.com/fortune500/.

51. For this profile on Biogen, I am indebted to Javier Barrientos (senior manager of community, content, and marketplace diversity at Amazon), interview with author, September 5, 2017.

52. For this section, I am indebted to Farah Pandith (diplomat and adjunct senior fellow for the Council on Foreign Relations), interview with author, August 31, 2017.

53. Queena Kim, "Google Hopes to Hire More Black Engineers by Bringing Students to Silicon Valley," *NPREd*, National Public Radio, March 28, 2017, http://www.npr.org/sections/ed/2017/03/28/521737097/google-hopes-to-hire-more-black-engineers-by-bringing-students-to-silicon-valley.

54. *Global Diversity and Inclusion: Fostering Innovation Through a Diverse Workforce*, 14. I should note that this profile suggests that the company changed its structure to enable the Edge program in 2009, but the program might have come after that time.

55. Harris, interview with author.

56. Patrick Smith, interview with author, August 23, 2017.

57. Robert Livingston (lecturer of public policy at the Harvard University Kennedy School), interview with author, August 22, 2017.

58. For this background, I am indebted to Darren Donovan (office managing principal of Boston, New England, and Update New York at KPMG), interview with author, November 8, 2017.

59. Twentieth Annual Rosoff Awards ceremony, Ad Club, May 2, 2016, http://www.adclub.org/widget/event-2192067.

CHAPTER 7: SUPPLYING FOR SUCCESS

1. For the background on Massport, I am indebted to Duane Jackson (vice chairman of the Massachusetts Port Authority and managing member of Alinea Capital Partners, LLC), interview with author, November 1, 2017.

2. This information is taken from National Public Radio's interview with Richard Taylor: "CityLine: The Omni Hotel Precedent," WCVB, updated May 31, 2017, http://www.wcvb.com/article/cityline-the-omni-hotel-precedent/9957474; Jon Chesto, "Politicians, Business Leaders Welcome Omni Hotels to Seaport," *Boston Globe*, May 16, 2017, https://www.bostonglobe.com/business/2017/05/15/politicians-business-leaders-welcome-omni-hotels-seaport/5jBEywaUchVcuU5Dna8aOP/story.html.

3. Jule Pattison-Gordon, "Black Firms Tackle Fourth Largest Hotel Project in Boston," *Bay State Banner*, April 19, 2017, http://baystatebanner.com/news/2017/apr/19/black-firms-tackle-fourth-largest-hotel-project/.

4. Ibid.

5. Andrew Ryan, "A Brand New Boston, Even Whiter Than the Old," *Boston Globe*, December 11, 2017, http://apps.bostonglobe.com/spotlight/boston-racism-image-reality/series/seaport/.

6. "CityLine: The Omni Hotel Precedent."

7. Jon Chesto, "Hotel Bids Add Minority Partners," *Boston Globe*, April 29, 2015, https://www.bostonglobe.com/business/2015/04/28/developers-assemble-minority-investors-for-seaport-hotel-project/QuANmxPcSXopn5MFUZLu6I/story.html.

8. Ibid.

9. Pattison-Gordon, "Black Firms Tackle Fourth Largest Hotel Project."

10. Ryan, "A Brand New Boston."

11. Nik DeCosta-Klipa, "Boston Is the No. 1 City in America for Income Inequality, Which Is Not Good," Boston.com, January 14, 2016, https://www.boston.com/news/local-news/2016/01/14/boston-is-the-no-1-city-in-america-for-income-inequality-which-is-not-good.

12. This figure, which calculated all assets and subtracted all forms of debt, applied to African Americans who were nonimmigrants: Ryan, "A Brand New Boston."

13. Ibid.

14. According to the *Boston Globe*, "Lenders have issued only three residential mortgages to black buyers in the Seaport's main census tracts, out of 660 in the past decade" (Ryan, "A Brand New Boston"). The Spotlight series, of which this article forms part, was published in December 2017, and so I construe "in the past decade" to refer to 2007–2017.

15. Akilah Johnson, "The Spotlight Team Takes On Our Hardest Question," *Boston Globe*, December 10, 2017.

16. Ibid.

17. Ryan, "A Brand New Boston."

18. Ibid.

19. Pattison-Gordon, "Black Firms Tackle Fourth Largest Hotel Project."

20. Ibid.

21. Parija Kavilanz, "Best Cities for Black Entrepreneurs," *CNN Money*, February 23, 2015, http://money.cnn.com/2015/02/23/smallbusiness/best-cities-for-black-entrepreneurs-georgia/index.html.

22. Pattison-Gordon, "Black Firms Tackle Fourth Largest Hotel Project."

23. "Most Supplier Diversity Programs Fail to Deliver," *Material Landing & Logistics*, May 17, 2010, http://www.mhlnews.com/global-supply-chain/most-supplier-diversity-programs-fail-deliver.

24. Ibid.

25. National Minority Supplier Development Council, *How To Guide to a Corporate Minority Business Development Program* (New York: NMSDC, 2015), 4, http://www.nmsdc.org/wp-content/uploads/How-To-2015edited.pdf.

26. Orlando C. Richard et al., "Do External Diversity Practices Boost Focal Firm Performance? The Case of Supplier Diversity," *International Journal of Human Resource Management* 26, no. 17 (2015): 2230, doi: 10.1080/09585192.2014.985324.

27. NMSDC, *How To Guide to a Corporate Minority Business Development Program*, 4.

28. Ian Worthington et al., "Researching the Drivers of Socially Responsible Purchasing: A Cross-National Study of Supplier Diversity Initiatives," *Journal of Business Ethics* 79 (May 2008): 322.

29. Mayank Shah and Monder Ram, "Supplier Diversity and Minority Business Enterprise Development: Case Study Experience of Three US Multinationals," *Supply Chain Management* 11, no. 1 (2006): 76.

30. Hesun Park-Poaps and Kathleen Rees, "Stakeholder Forces of Socially Responsible Supply Chain Management Orientation," *Journal of Business Ethics* 92 (2010), doi: 10.1007A10551–009–0156–3.

31. Ibid., 305–6.

32. Worthington et al., "Researching the Drivers of Socially Responsible Purchasing," 323. In the case of construction contracts, the threshold was $1 million.

33. Joe T. Darden and Richard W. Thomas, *Detroit: Race Riots, Racial Conflicts, and Efforts to Bridge the Racial Divide* (East Lansing, MI: Michigan State University Press, 2013).

34. James C. McKinley Jr., "New York Reviving Quota Regulations for Minority Firms," *New York Times*, August 18, 1992, http://www.nytimes.com/1992/08/18/us/new-york-reviving-quota-regulations-for-minority-firms.html.

35. For the larger context of these individual initiatives, see Worthington et al., "Researching the Drivers of Socially Responsible Purchasing," and Darden and Thomas, *Detroit*.

36. Worthington et al., "Researching the Drivers of Socially Responsible Purchasing," 324.

37. Both data points taken from the US Department of Commerce's Minority Business Development Agency, "U.S. Minority-Owned Firms," fact sheet, January 2016, https://www.mbda.gov/sites/mbda.gov/files/migrated/files-attachments/2012SBO_MBE FactSheet02o2216.pdf.

38. Worthington et al., "Researching the Drivers of Socially Responsible Purchasing," 324.

39. Ibid.

40. National Minority Supplier Development Council, *The Year of Impact, 2015: Annual Report* (New York: NMSDC, 2015), http://www.nmsdc.org/wp-content/uploads/2015-NMSDC-Annual-Report-Digital-1.pdf; Shah and Ram, "Supplier Diversity and Minority Business Enterprise Development," 76.

41. "The Business Case for Minority Business Enterprises: Fueling Economic Growth," White Paper, National Minority Supplier Development Council, 5, http://www.nmsdc.org/wp-content/uploads/v3Alt-Wht-8.5-x11-Single.pdf.

42. Ibid.

43. See the company's website at Billion Dollar Roundtable, https://www.billiondollarroundtable.org/.

44. "Supplier Diversity," Ford, https://corporate.ford.com/microsites/sustainability-report-2016–17/people-communities/people/supplier-diversity.html, accessed February 28, 2018.

45. Shah and Ram, "Supplier Diversity and Minority Business Enterprise Development," 77.

46. Ibid., 76–78.

47. Ibid., 78.

48. Ibid., 79.

49. Ibid., 78.

50. All information about succession taken from "Succession Planning for MBE/ WBE/VBEs," webinar video (09:33), http://www.fordsdd.com/sdd_program/supplier _dev_prog.html.

51. "Tier 2 Program," Ford Supplier Diversity Development, http://www.fordsdd .com/tier2/tier2.html.

52. Shah and Ram, "Supplier Diversity and Minority Business Enterprise Development," 79.

53. "Tier 2 Program."

54. "Ford Motor Company Announces $1.1 Billion Spend with Veteran Owned Businesses," *U.S. Veterans Magazine*, June, 8, 2017, https://www.usveteransmagazine .com/2017/06/08/ford-motor-company-partner-veteran-owned-businesses/.

55. Shah and Ram, "Supplier Diversity and Minority Business Enterprise Development," 79.

56. "Ford's Award-Winning Supplier Diversity Development Program Exceeds Minority-Owned Business Spending Goals," *Digital Dealer*, March 14, 2013, https:// www.digitaldealer.com/fords-award-winning-supplier-diversity-development-program -exceeds-minority-owned-business-spending-goals/; "Tier 2 Program."

57. "Tier 2 Program."

58. "Vinnie Johnson, Piston Group Founder, Chairman & CEO," Piston Group, http://www.pistongroup.com/who-we-are/founder/, accessed February 28, 2018.

59. For this profile I am indebted to "Automotive," Case Studies, Morris Anderson, October 17, 2011, http://www.morrisanderson.com/resource-center/entry/Auto-supplier -jumps-into-IT-Piston-Group-sells-data-storage-to-Ford/.

60. "Ford's Award-Winning Supplier Diversity Development Program."

61. Adrianna Samaniego et al., "How They Did It: Google's Innovative Approach to Supplier Diversity," *Supply Chain Management Review*, July 5, 2017, http://www.scmr .com/article/how_they_did_it_googles_innovative_approach_to_supplier_diversity.

62. Ibid.

63. Ibid.

64. Ibid.

65. Ibid.

66. Ibid.

67. Ibid.

68. Ibid.

69. Ibid.

70. Ibid.

71. Ibid.

72. Ibid.

73. "Google Inc.," Shalimar Media Group, http://www.shalimarmedia.com/google -inc/.

74. Samaniego et al., "How They Did It."

75. See Google's YouTube channel for an articulation of this vision, as well as a series of success stories: "Accelerate with Google," YouTube, https://www.youtube.com /user/acceleratewithgoogle, accessed April 2, 2018.

76. Information taken from company website: "Small Business Supplier Diversity," Google, https://www.google.com/diversity/suppliers/, accessed February 28, 2018.

77. "Digital Coaches Program," YouTube, 2.41, https://www.youtube.com/watch ?v=e7CMsXi2cqI#action=share.

78. "Introducing the Business Equality Initiative (BEI)," Eastern Bank, https://www .easternbank.com/BEI, accessed February 28, 2018.

79. See Eastern Bank's website for more: https://www.easternbank.com/about-us.

80. For this profile, I am indebted to Jim Rooney (president and CEO at the Greater Boston Chamber of Commerce), interview with author, December 5, 2017.

81. Stephen Smith, "'Mississippi Burning' Murders Resonate 50 Years Later," *CBS News*, June 20, 2014, https://www.cbsnews.com/news/mississippi-burning-murder s-resonate-50-years-later/.

82. Camila Domonoske, "Officials Close Investigation into 1964 'Mississippi Burning' Killings," *The Two-Way*, National Public Radio, June 21, 2016, https://www.npr .org/sections/thetwo-way/2016/06/21/482914440/officials-close-investigation-into-1964 -mississippi-burning-killings.

83. Richard L. Taylor, "Oak Bluffs Town Column: Oct. 13," *Vineyard Gazette*, October 12, 2017, https://vineyardgazette.com/news/2017/10/12/oak-bluffs-town-column -oct-13.

CHAPTER 8: A NEW AGE OF BUSINESS ETHICS

1. Joe Ruiz and Doreen McCallister, "Events Surrounding White Nationalist Rally in Virginia Turn Fatal," *The Two-Way*, National Public Radio, August 12, 2017, https:// www.npr.org/sections/thetwo-way/2017/08/12/542982015/home-to-university-of -virginia-prepares-for-violence-at-white-nationalist-rally; Joe Heim et al., "One Dead as Car Strikes Crowds Amid Protests of White Nationalist Gathering in Charlottesville; Two Police Die in Helicopter Crash," *Washington Post*, August 13, 2017, https://www .washingtonpost.com/local/fights-in-advance-of-saturday-protest-in-charlottesville /2017/08/12/155fb636-7f13-11e7-83c7-5bd5460fod7e_story.html.

2. Rachel Lewis, "These 18 CEOs Had Strong Words for President Trump's Charlottesville Response," *Fortune*, August 8, 2017, http://fortune.com/2017/08/17/ceos -trump-charlottesville-criticized/.

3. Ibid.

4. David Gelles, "The Moral Voice of Corporate America," *New York Times*, August 19, 2017, https://www.nytimes.com/2017/08/19/business/moral-voice-ceos.html?hp &action=click&pgtype=Homepage&clickSource=story-heading&module=first-column -region&region=top-news&WT.nav=top-news&_r=0.

5. Lewis, "These 18 CEOs Had Strong Words for President Trump's Charlottesville Response."

6. Gelles, "The Moral Voice of Corporate America"; Lewis, "These 18 CEOs Had Strong Words for President Trump's Charlottesville Response."

7. Lewis, "These 18 CEOs Had Strong Words for President Trump's Charlottesville Response."

8. Ibid.

9. Lynne Doughtie, "KPMG CEO Lynne Doughtie: Standing United Behind Our Culture and Values," *Diversity Inc.*, August 17, 2017, http://www.diversityinc.com/news /kpmg-ceo-lynne-doughtie-standing-united-behind-culture-values.

10. Jena McGregor and Elizabeth Dwoskin, "The Cost of Silence: Why More CEOs Are Speaking Out in the Trump Era," *Washington Post*, February 17, 2017, https://www.washingtonpost.com/news/on-leadership/wp/2017/02/17/the-cost-of -silence-why-more-ceos-are-speaking-out-in-the-trump-era/?utm_term=.e55b29bb6f82.

11. Gelles, "The Moral Voice of Corporate America."

12. "A Challenge We Need to Act On Together," CEO Action for Diversity & Inclusion, https://www.ceoaction.com/about/, accessed February 28, 2018.

13. McGregor and Dwoskin, "The Cost of Silence."

14. Jerry Davis, "What's Driving Corporate Activism," *New Republic*, September 27, 2016, https://newrepublic.com/article/137252/whats-driving-corporate-activism.

15. Michele Norris, "The Woolworth Sit-In That Launched a Movement," *All Things Considered*, National Public Radio, February 1, 2008, https://www.npr.org/templates /story/story.php?storyId=18615556.

16. Ibid.

17. Davis, "What's Driving Corporate Activism."

18. Eric Owles, "How Nestlé Expanded Beyond the Kitchen," *New York Times*, June 27, 2017, https://www.nytimes.com/2017/06/27/business/dealbook/nestle-chocolate-milk -coffee-history.html; Associated Press, "Hugo Boss Acknowledges Link to Nazi

Regime," *New York Times*, August 15, 1997, http://www.nytimes.com/1997/08/15/business
/hugo-boss-acknowledges-link-to-nazi-regime.html.

19. Laura Wagner, "'Republicans Buy Sneakers, Too,'" *Slate*, July 28, 2016, http://
www.slate.com/articles/sports/sports_nut/2016/07/did_michael_jordan_really_say
_republicans_buy_sneakers_too.html; David S. Broder, "Jesse Helms, White Racist,"
Washington Post, originally published August 29, 2001, and reposted July 7, 2008, http://
www.washingtonpost.2008/07/content/article/2008/07/06/AR2008070602321.html.

20. Though some have questioned whether he actually said this: Wagner, "'Republicans Buy Sneakers, Too.'" According to some accounts, Jordan said, "Republicans buy
shoes, too."

21. "Air Jordan Brand History," Air Jordan, December 24, 2014, http://airjordan
shoeshq.com/air-jordan-brand-history/.

22. See, for example, "Hugo Boss Apology for Nazi Past as Book Is Published," *BBC
News*, September 21, 2011, http://www.bbc.com/news/world-europe-15008682.

23. "Disney Co. Will Offer Benefits to Gay Partners," *New York Times*, October 8,
1995, http://www.nytimes.com/1995/10/08/us/disney-co-will-offer-benefits-to-gay
-partners.html.

24. Jeff Truesdell, "How Gay Day Pushed Disney out of the Closet," *Orlando Weekly*,
May 31, 2000, https://www.orlandoweekly.com/orlando/how-gay-day-pushed-disney
-out-of-the-closet/Content?oid=2262655.

25. Davis, "What's Driving Corporate Activism"; M. Alex Johnson, "Southern Baptists End 8-Year Disney Boycott," *NBC News*, June 22, 2005, http://www.nbcnews.com
/id/8318263/ns/us_news/t/southern-baptists-end—year-disney-boycott/#.Wg3nPkqnHIU.

26. Truesdell, "How Gay Day Pushed Disney out of the Closet."

27. James Surowiecki, "The Trump-Era Corporate Boycott," *New Yorker*, January 9,
2017, https://www.newyorker.com/magazine/2017/01/09/the-trump-era-corporate-boycott.

28. Brayden G. King, "The Tactical Disruptiveness of Social Movements: Sources
of Market and Mediated Disruption in Corporate Boycotts," *Social Problems* 58, no. 4
(2011), doi: 10.1525/sp.2011.58.4.491.

29. James Surowiecki, in "The Trump-Era Corporate Boycott," for example, suggests that concessions were won in "more than a third" of all instances, while Northwestern University's Kellogg School of Management suggested that was true "about 25
percent" of the time ("Boycotts and the Bottom Line," press release, Northwestern University, November 16, 2011, http://www.kellogg.northwestern.edu/news_articles/2011
/boycotts.aspx).

30. "NBC Says It Will Hold Universal Studios Responsible for Advertising Losses
on Program," *Journal of the American Family Association* (November/December 1991): 1,
https://afajournal.org/1991/11-1291AFAJ.pdf.

31. According to the show's executive producer, Donald P. Bellisario: Bill Carter,
"NBC Defends Move on 'Quantum Leap,'" *New York Times*, October 1, 1991, http://
www.nytimes.com/1991/10/01/news/nbc-defends-move-on-quantum-leap.html.

32. "NBC Says It Will Hold Universal Studios Responsible for Advertising Losses
on Program," 24.

33. Carter, "NBC Defends Move on 'Quantum Leap.'"

34. See also Brayden King and Sarah A. Soule, "Social Movements as
Extra-Institutional Entrepreneurs: The Effect of Protest on Stock Price Returns," *Administrative Science Quarterly* 52, no. 3 (2007).

35. *CEO Activism in 2017: High Noon in the C-Suite* (Weber Shandwick & KRC
Research, 2017), 5–6, http://www.webershandwick.com/uploads/news/files/ceo-activism
-in-2017-high-noon-in-the-c-suite.pdf.

36. Ibid., 7.

37. Ibid., 13.

38. "Measuring the Return on Character," *Harvard Business Review*, April 2015,
https://hbr.org/2015/04/measuring-the-return-on-character.

39. Fred Kiel, *Return on Character: The Real Reason Leaders and Their Companies Win*
(Boston: Harvard Business Review Press, 2015); "Measuring the Return on Character."

40. "Measuring the Return on Character."

41. Sapna Maheshwari, "Statement on Trump Puts New Balance Shoe Company in Cross Hairs," *New York Times*, November 15, 2016, https://www.nytimes.com/2016/11/16/business/statement-on-trump-puts-new-balance-shoe-company-in-cross-hairs.html.

42. Ibid.

43. Sapna Maheshwari, "Advertisers Delete Tweets Around Calls to Boycott Sean Hannity," *New York Times*, November 14, 2017, https://www.nytimes.com/2017/11/14/business/media/sean-hannity-advertisers.html.

44. Sapna Maheshwari, "Pizza Is Partisan, and Advertisers Are Still Adjusting," *New York Times*, November 19, 2017, https://www.nytimes.com/2017/11/19/business/media/advertisers-partisan-politics.html.

45. Clifford Krauss, "Shell, to Cut Carbon Output, Will Be Less of an Oil Company," *New York Times*, November 28, 2017, https://www.nytimes.com/2017/11/28/business/energy-environment/shell-carbon-oil.html.

46. Tom Braithwaite, "Why Can't San Francisco's Tech Culture Solve the City's Social Problems?," *Financial Times*, December 1, 2017, https://www.ft.com/content/262e2b2c-d423–11e7–8c9a-d9c0a5c8d5c9; Cornell Barnard, "Salesforce CEO Aims to End Family Homelessness in San Francisco," *ABC 7 News*, December 9, 2016, http://abc7news.com/society/salesforce-ceo-aims-to-end-family-homelessness-in-sf/1648823/.

47. Lynn S. Paine et al., "Up to Code: Does Your Company's Conduct Meet World-Class Standards?," *Harvard Business Review*, December 2005, https://hbr.org/2005/12/up-to-code-does-your-companys-conduct-meet-world-class-standards.

48. "The Good, the Bad, and Their Corporate Codes of Ethics: Enron, Sarbanes-Oxley, and the Problems with Legislating Good Behavior," *Harvard Law Review* 116 (May 2003): 2123; Paine et al., "Up to Code."

49. Paine et al., "Up to Code."

50. *Business Codes of the Global 200: Their Prevalence, Content and Embedding* (KPMG/Erasmus University, 2008), 6, http://www.ethicsmanagement.info/content/Business%20codes%20Fortune%20200.pdf.

51. See "Our Mission," Starbucks website, https://www.starbucks.com/about-us/company-information/mission-statement, accessed February 28, 2018.

52. David Kesmodel and Ilan Brat, "Why Starbucks Takes On Social Issues," *Wall Street Journal*, March 23, 2015, https://www.wsj.com/articles/why-starbucks-takes-on-social-issues-1427155129.

53. Andrew Ross Sorkin, "Howard Schultz to Step Down as Starbucks Chief Next Year," *New York Times*, December 1, 2016, https://www.nytimes.com/2016/12/01/business/dealbook/starbucks-chief-howard-schultz-to-step-down-next-year.html.

54. Ibid.

55. Ibid.; Candice Choi, "Starbucks CEO Defends 'Race Together' After Backlash," Associated Press, March 18, 2015, https://apnews.com/163703e9d8544702ac45202eea3041f4.

56. Howard Schultz, introductory comments, *Business Ethics and Compliance: Standards of Business Conduct*, Starbucks Coffee Company, 2011, https://businessconduct.eawebline.com/SoBC-English.pdf.

57. Starbucks, *Business Ethics and Compliance*, 10.

58. David Yanofsky, "Here's Our Estimate for the Sales Starbucks Will Lose Because of Racial-Bias Training," *Quartz*, May 29, 2018, https://qz.com/1290071/heres-our-estimate-for-the-sales-starbucks-will-lose-because-of-racial-bias-training.

59. Sorkin, "Howard Schultz to Step Down"; Tanza Loudenback and Shana Lebowitz, "Starbucks CEO Howard Schultz Is Stepping Down—Here's His Incredible Rags-to-Riches Story," *Business Insider*, December 1, 2016, http://www.businessinsider.com/biography-howard-schultz-starbucks-step-down-ceo-2016-12.

60. Nathaniel Popper, "A Gay, Latino Partner Tests Goldman's Button-Down Culture," *New York Times*, April 1, 2016, https://www.nytimes.com/2016/04/03/business/dealbook/goldmans-tech-chief-pushes-the-bank-to-be-more-open-like-him.html.

61. Ibid.

62. Matt Taibbi, "The Great American Bubble Machine," *Rolling Stone*, April 5, 2010, http://www.rollingstone.com/politics/news/the-great-american-bubble -machine-20100405.

63. Susanne Craig, "Blankfein to Speak Out for Same-Sex Marriage," *New York Times*, February 5, 2012, https://dealbook.nytimes.com/2012/02/05/blankfein-to-speak -out-for-same-sex-marriage/.

64. Ibid.

65. Ibid.

66. Ibid.

67. Patrick McGeehan, "Two Giants of Finance Will Release Diversity Data," *New York Times*, April 15, 2012, http://www.nytimes.com/2012/04/16/nyregion/goldman -sachs-and-metlife-to-disclose-staff-diversity-data.html.

68. John N. Reynolds and Edmund Newell, *Ethics in Investment Banking* (New York: Palgrave Macmillan, 2011), 45 (emphasis mine).

69. Ibid., 45.

70. "Our Shared Responsibility to Our Clients, Colleagues and Communities: Code of Business Conduct and Ethics," Goldman Sachs, 3, http://www.goldmansachs.com /investor-relations/corporate-governance/corporate-governance-documents/revise-code -of-conduct.pdf.

71. Ibid., 2.

72. Ibid., 6.

73. For this section, I am indebted to David Holmberg (president and CEO of Highmark Health), interview with author, October 6, 2017.

74. "David L. Holmberg: President and CEO, Highmark Health and Chairman of the Board, Highmark Inc.," Highmark, https://www.highmark.com/hmk2/bios/holmberg .shtml, accessed February 28, 2018.

75. Steve Twedt, "Highmark Health Sees Return to Profitability," *Pittsburgh Post-Gazette*, March 17, 2017, http://www.post-gazette.com/business/healthcare-business /2017/03/17/highmark-financial-profit-health-insurance-allegheny-health-network /stories/201703170236.

76. *Working with Integrity: Code of Business Conduct* (Highmark Health, 2017), 5, 19, https://www.highmark.com/hmk2/pdf/Code_of_Conduct_508.pdf.

77. For this section, I am indebted to Evan Frazier (senior vice president of commu- nity affairs at Highmark Health), interview with author, November 6, 2017.

78. For an overview, please see "Corporate Responsibility," Highmark Health, https://www.highmark.com/hmk2/responsibility/commitment.shtml, accessed February 28, 2018.

79. For this section, I am indebted to Dr. Beverly Edgehill (vice president of orga- nizational development at TJX Companies, Inc.), interview with author, November 13, 2017.

80. For this section, I rely on McGregor and Dwoskin, "The Cost of Silence," and Feliz Solomon, "Apple CEO Tim Cook Tells Students: If You Work Only for Money, You Will Never Be Happy," *Washington Post*, February 10, 2017, http://fortune.com /2017/02/10/apple-ceo-tim-cook-career-advice-job-money.

EPILOGUE

1. Ana Patricia Munoz et al., *The Color of Wealth in Boston* (Boston: Federal Reserve Bank, March 25, 2015), https://www.bostonfed.org/publications/one-time-pubs/color -of-wealth.aspx.

2. Kevin C. Peterson, "Boston Globe Race Series Not News to City's Blacks, Shocks White Readers," *Huffington Post*, December 19, 2017, https://www.huffingtonpost.com /entry/boston-globe-racism-series-not-news-to-citys-blacks_us_5a395c11e4bocebf48 e9f812.

INDEX

Abe, Shinzo, 59
Academy of Motion Picture Arts and
  Sciences, 19–20, 25–26
Ad Club (Boston), 140
advertising industry, 101–3, 105–6, 117
affirmative-action policies, 149
African Americans: in advertising
  industry, 105; black capitalism, 148;
  in Boston, 18, 145, 181, 206n14; in
  Detroit, 107; in NFL, 39–41; parity
  of, 6; PepsiCo marketing to, 108–9;
  Starbucks and, 171; venture capital
  and, 34–35, 121, 203n5; in the work-
  force, 20; at Xerox, 48
Agnefjäll, Peter, 50
Airbnb, 18
Albertson, Kurt, 147
Alexander, Paul, 66
Ali, Mohamad, 122
American Express, 132–33
American Family Association (AFA),
  165–66
Apple, 18
Arnold, Damika, 53
Asians, 35, 105
Association of Latino Professionals for
  America (ALPFA), 114–15

Banaji, Mahzarin, 23
banking. See finance and banking
  industry
Bank of America (BOA), 98–101, 117
Banks, Aerica, 156
Barbie dolls, 111–14
Barr, Roseanne, 172

Barrientos, Javier, 22–24, 133–34
Bedrock company, 106–7, 117
Bell, Deborah, 69
Bell, Don, 54
Benioff, Marc, 168
Bennett, Christopher, 67
Berlusconi, Silvio, 106
Best Buddies Challenge bicycle ride,
  89–91
Beydoun, Khaled, 107
Biogen, 133–34
Black Panther (movie), 31
blacks. See African Americans
Black Twitter, 19
Blankfein, Lloyd C., 172–73
boards of directors: diversity on, 57–76;
  business benefits of, 67–70; conclu-
  sions on, 74–76; of Eastern Bank,
  60–66, 74; introduction to, 57–60;
  lack of, 9; talent acquisition and,
  71–74
BoardSource, 59
Boston, 6, 17, 142–43, 145, 157–59,
  181–84
Boston Globe, 6, 144, 145, 182, 183
Boston Marathon Kenya Project (John
  Hancock), 78–82, 97
Boston Women Build in the Bayou,
  83–84
Botus, Stacy, 88–89
boycotts, 165–66, 210n29
branding, 86–94, 101–2
Braswell, Sarah, 92
Breen, Bill, 83, 85–86
Brewer, Roz, 171

Brooke, Edward, 181
Brookings Institution, 34, 124, 145
Brown, Reggie, 32
Budd, Wayne, 43–44, 45
Burrell, Tom, 113
Business Equality Initiative (BEI, Eastern Bank), 74, 157
businesses. *See* diversity; *individual companies*
business ethics, new age of, 161–80; codes of ethics, creation of, 168–73; codes of ethics, guidelines for, 178–79; ethical corporations, 164–68; Highmark Health, 174–78; introduction to, 161–64; leadership and, 179–80

Calderón-Rosado, Vanessa, 64–65
California Public Employees' Retirement System (CalPERS), 67
California State Teachers' Retirement System (CalSTRS), 33, 67
Capparell, Stephanie, 108–9
Catalyst Research Center, 59
CEO activism, 161–66
chambers of commerce, 158–59
Chaney, James, 159
Charlottesville, Virginia, 161–63, 177–78
Chatterji, Aaron, 86, 163
Che, Michael, 145
City of Richmond v. Croson, 149
Club Bootcamp, 117
Cochran, Johnnie, 39–40, 42
codes of ethics, 168–73, 178–79
cognitive functions, impact of diversity on, 67–68
COIN (socially conscious investment startup), 94
Coke, comparison with PepsiCo, 108, 111
community impact programming, 77–97; best practices, 94–96; brand enhancements, 86–94; conclusions on, 97; corporate–community relationships, 83–86; introduction to, 77–83
companies. *See* diversity; *individual companies*
Cone Communications, 84–85
Cook, Lisa, 34, 35
Cook, Tim, 179–80

Coplin, Bill, 125
Coppersmith, Jim, 1
corporate social responsibility (CSR) programs, 80–86, 92–94, 148, 198n13. *See also* community impact programming
Cowen, Tyler, 123
Creative Spirit, 199n29
Credit Suisse, 136
Crisp, Richard, 67–68
Crohan, Tom, 88, 93, 94
CSAA Insurance Group, 127–28

D'Alessandro, David, 87, 95, 117
Dartmouth College, Tuck School of Business, 154
deep-level diversity, 131
Deloitte, 29–30, 127, 129
Detroit, African Americans in, 107
Dimon, Jamie, 162
dissent, presence of diversity and, 131
diversity: of boards of directors, 57–76; business ethics, new age of, 161–80; community impact programming, 77–97; deep-level diversity, 131; growing importance of, 14–38; innovation and, 119–41; introduction to, 1–13; leadership diversity, 39–56; in marketing, 98–118; in supply chains, 142–60
diversity, growing importance of, 14–38; age of diversity, dawning of, 17–24; business impact of diversity, 28–35; conclusions on, 37–38; demography as destiny, 35–37; introduction to, 14–17; mainstream diversity programs, failures of, 25–28; surface-level diversity, 131, 205n46

Dobbin, Frank, 21–22
Dodd, Chris, 15
Donovan, Darren, 139
Dormitory Authority, 146
Doughtie, Lynne, 127, 162
Douglas, Tom, 198n14
Doz, Yves L., 131
Dreyer, John, 165
Dubois, Cynthia (C.C.), 47
duBrowa, Corey, 27
Duguid, Michelle M., 21

Duke University, wealth disparity study, 145
Dungey, Channing, 171–72
Dungy, Tony, 39, 42
Dzanis, Marie, 33

Eastern Bank, 60–66, 69, 71–74, 157
Eastern Insurance Group, 61
Economist, on stagnation in innovation, 126
Edgehill, Beverly, 18, 178
Edmondson, Amy, 129–30
employee resource groups (ERGs), 116, 137, 139, 177
employee turnover, 24
entertainment industry: codes of ethics in, 171–72
entertainment industry, lack of diversity in, 19–20, 25–26, 30–31
entrepreneurialism, stagnation in, 123–24, 126
Epstein, Esta, 3
ethics. *See* business ethics
exchange-traded funds (ETFs), 32–34
Express Business Loans, 71–72

Facebook, 26, 86
Fanuele, Michael, 105–6
Federal Reserve Bank of Boston, 145, 181–82
Ferguson, Missouri, police diversity, 53
finance and banking industry: Bank of America, 98–101, 117; Eastern Bank, 60–66, 69, 71–74, 157; exchange-traded funds, 32–34; lack of diversity in, 19
Fine, Bill, 187n1
Fletcher, Corie, 139
Forbes, Insights study, 10, 129
Ford Motor Company, 106, 150–53, 155
Fowler, Susan, 188n10
Frazier, Evan, 176–77
Frazier, Kenneth C., 162
Frazier-Bohnert, Dawn, 7–8
Freedom Summer, 159
Friedman, Rob, 89
Fulp, Carol: career, 2–4, 11–12; D'Alessandro and, 87; influence of, 68; influences on, 159; at Kennedy Library forum, 183; summer camp

experiences, 128; in Tanzania, 77; unconscious bias against, 70
Fulp, C. Bernard, 60, 77, 159

Gantt, Harvey, 164–65
Garcia, Yvonne, 114–15
Garron, Arnold, 39–40, 51
General Electric, 121
General Mills, 105–6
General Motors, 106
Gibbons, David, 143
Gilbert, Dan, 106
Gittens, Donna Latson, 3, 103, 117
glass ceiling, 9, 21
Glynn, Tom, 143, 183
Goldberg, Deborah, 4–5
Golden, Neil, 104
Goldman Sachs, 172–74, 179
Gomez, Rick, 104–5
Goodell, Roger, 42
Goodman, Andrew, 159
Goodwin, Doris Kearns, 67
Google, 18, 19, 153–57
Gormley, Doris, 57, 60
Graves, Earl, Sr., 110
Graves, Earl "Butch," Jr., 54–55
Greater Boston Chamber of Commerce, 157–59
Green, Ernest, 146
Green, Logan, 15
Grooms, Keenen, 4–5
Grover, Owen, 32
Groysberg, Boris, 69
Grutter v. Bollinger, 43
Gulliver, Robert, 42

Hack.Diversity, 119–23
Hairston, Leslie, 45
Hands, Darrin, 153
Hansen, Katrin, 81
Harris, Carla, 130, 136–38
health care industry, 124–25
Helms, Jesse, 164–65
Hershey, Milton and Catherine, 96
Herzlinger, Regina E., 125
Hewson, Marillyn A., 18
Highmark Health, 174–78
Hill Holliday advertising firm, 98
hiring. *See* recruitment and hiring
Hispanics, 35, 44, 105. *See also* Latinos
Hobson, Mellody, 171

Holder, Eric, 16, 53
Hollender, Jeffrey, 83, 85–86
Holmberg, David, 174–75, 176, 179
homophily, 138
Hong, Hae-Jung, 131
Hooley, Jay, 179
Hopcroft, Tom, 122
Horn, Michael, 125
Hudnell, Rosalind, 129
Huffington, Ariana, 16
Hugo Boss company, 164

IKEA, 49–51
immigration, 35–36
innovation, 119–41; at American
    Express, 132–33; at Biogen, 133–34;
    conclusions on, 140–41; diver-
    sity as engine for, 97, 127–31; at
    Eastern Bank, 71–72; guidance on
    improving, 135–40; importance of,
    123–27; introduction to, 119–23;
    at Lockheed Martin, 18; in public
    sector, 134–35
insurance industry, women in, 61
Intel, 18, 52–53, 129
intellectual development disabilities
    (IDD), individuals with, 89–91,
    199n29

Jackson, Deborah, 65, 69, 70, 74
Jackson, L. Duane, 143, 146, 156,
    159–60, 183
Jackson, Jesse, 19
Jarrett, Valerie, 15
Jobs, Steve, 180
John Hancock, 78–82, 87–89, 93–95, 97
Johnson, Robert, 52
Johnson, Vinnie, 152
Johnston, Norm, 168
Jones, Jeff, 104–5
Jordan, Michael, 165
J. Walter Thompson, 105

Kalanick, Travis, 15, 16, 53
Kalev, Alexandra, 21–22
Kambazza, Jean Paul, 119–20
Kaplan, Soren, 127
Kapor, Mitch, 31–32
Kelly, Eric, 32
Kesoglou, Niki, 136
Kiel, Fred, 167

Kimmel, Jimmy, 25
King, Bernice, 28
King, Brayden, 165
King, Martin Luther, Jr., 183
Knight, Phil, 83
Knowles, Jeremy, ix
Knox, Wendell, 64, 65, 71, 72, 73
Kotkin, Joel, 35–36, 37
KPMG, 127, 139
Kramer, Mark R., 198n9
KRW International, 166–67
Krzanich, Brian, 18, 53, 194n49

LaCamera, Paul, 187n1
large purchasing organizations (LPOs),
    149
Latinos, 20, 99, 104, 121, 203n5
leadership diversity, 39–56; at IKEA,
    49–51; introduction to, 39–43; lack
    of, 43–47; Rooney Rule, applications
    of, 51–56; at Xerox, 47–49, 51
LeBretton, Matt, 167
legal field, lack of diversity in, 43–45
Lego, 112
Leiden, Jeff, 122
Levine, Sheen, 68
LGBTQ individuals, Eastern Bank and,
    61, 62, 63, 65–66
Liberty Mutual, 7–8, 115
Lincoln, Abraham, 67
Livingston, Robert, 130, 136, 138–39
Llopis, Glenn, 21, 46
Lockheed Martin, 18
L'Oréal, 130–31
Loyd, Denise Lewin, 131
lunch counter sit-ins, 164
Lyft, 15–16

MacBride, Elizabeth, 32
Mack, Walter S., Jr., 108–9
Macri, Jill, 18
Madison Avenue. See advertising
    industry
Mahaney, Mark, 16
Manulife, 93
Mariana (BOA team member), 99–101
marketing, diversity in, 98–118;
    conclusions on, 117–18; guidance
    on improving, 115–17; at IKEA,
    50–51; impact of, 30; introduction
    to, 98–101; models for, 107–15; new

voices in marketing, 101–7; Pepsi ad campaign, 27–28
Martha's Table, 92
Martin, Scott, 4, 5, 30
Martinez, Gustavo, 105
Massachusetts, Department of Public Health, 103
Massachusetts Port Authority (Massport), 142–44, 146, 156, 159–60
Mattel, 111–14
McAuliffe, Terry, 161
McDonald's, 102, 104
McIlwain, Charlton, 102
McKay, Rich, 41
McKinsey, 10, 28, 29, 59
McKnight, Lisa, 112
Mehra, Vinay, 183
Mehri, Cyrus, 39–40, 42
Merrill Lynch, 32, 98
middle managers, importance of, 178–79
millennials, 29, 46, 51, 91, 107–8, 166, 182
Miller, Quincy, 74
MLK Scholars program, 87–89, 91, 94, 95–96, 97
Moore, Roy S., 167
Moses, Matthew, 155
Mulcahy, Anne, 48
Mundy, Liza, 21

NAACP, 159
Nadella, Satya, 162
National Football League (NFL), 38, 39–41, 51–52, 54–55
National Minority Supplier Development Council (NMSDC), 147, 149–50, 151, 157
NBC, 165–66
Ndereba, Catherine, 80
Nestlé, 164
NetApp company, 152–53
Newell, Edmund, 173
New York City, taxi system strike, 14, 15
Nike, 83, 84, 165
Nixon, Richard, 148
Nooyi, Indra K., 11, 110–11, 202n54, 202n61

Obama, Barack, 11, 52, 67
Ogletree, Charles, 55
Omni Hotels & Resorts, 142, 144

Pandith, Farah, 134–35, 137
The Partnership, Inc., 11, 17–18, 74–75, 179, 182, 183
patents, gender diversity and, 35
Patrick, Deval L., ix–x, 143, 181
Pattison-Gordon, Jule, 146
Payzant, Tom, 78
Peck, Emily, 114
Peduto, Bill, 53–54
people of color/difference. See African Americans; Asians; Hispanics; Latinos
PepsiCo, 27–28, 108, 109–11, 117, 202n61
Peterson, Kevin, 182
Phillips, Katherine W., 131
Pinterest, 52
Piston Automotive, 152–53
Pittsburgh, use of Rooney Rule, 53–54
Porter, Michael E., 198n9
Preston, Carla, 153
psychological safety, 129–30
Public Law 95–907 (1978), 148–49
public sector, innovation and diversity in, 134–35
Pymetrics, 23–24

Ram, Monder, 150–51
recruitment and hiring, 23–24, 29, 71–74
Reinemund, Steve, 109–11
responsibility revolution, 148
return on character (ROC), 167
returns on equity (ROE), 10
Reynolds, John N., 173
Rivers, Robert "Bob," 62–64, 65, 67, 69, 71, 72–74
RLJ rule, 52
Rodgers, Thurman John "T.J.," 58
Rooney, Dan, 41
Rooney, Jim, 143, 157–58
Rooney Rule, 38, 41–42, 46–47, 51–56, 137, 176
Rose, Jody, 120–22
Rossi, Laurel, 90
Royal Dutch Shell, 168

Samaniego, Adrianna, 153–54, 155
Samoluk, Tom, 93
Sarbanes-Oxley Act (2002), 169
Scannell, Robert, Jr., 95–96
Schultz, Howard, 170–71, 172
Schwerner, Michael, 159

Scott, Gunner, 65
Scotti, Diego, 106
Seaport (Boston), 142–46, 206n14
Seierstad, Cathrine, 81
Settles, Darryl, 144
72andSunny (marketing and advertising company), 116
72U, 117
Shah, Mayank, 150–51
Shah, Niraj, 122
Shahani, Aarti, 194n49
SHE (ETF), 33
Shriver, Anthony, 89
Siddiqui, Faiz, 15
Signer, Michael, 161
Silicon Valley. *See* technology industry
Simmons, David, 113
Smith, Patrick, 98–101, 117, 137
Spring, Micho, 91–92
Stager, Nancy, 75
Starbucks, 27, 170–71
Stark, David, 68
structural biases, 22–23
supply chains, diversity in, 142–60; conclusions on, 159–60; at Ford Motor Company, 150–53, 155; at Google, 153–55; guidance on improving, 156–59; introduction to, 142–47; supplier diversity, origins of, 148–50
surface-level diversity, 131, 205n46
Surowiecki, James, 165, 210n29
Sutton, Rebecca, 61

talent acquisition. *See* recruitment and hiring
Talent Sonar, 23
Target, 104–5
Taylor, Paul, 36
Taylor, Richard, 144
technology industry, 20, 26–27, 31–32, 116, 119–23, 125–26
Thiel, Peter, 123, 126
Thomas, David, 110
Thomas, Kaya, 26
Thomas-Hunt, Melissa C., 21
Thompson, Sue, 33
Time magazine, 9
Toyota, 85–86
transgender individuals, 65
Trump, Donald, 14, 37, 161–62
Tuck School of Business (Dartmouth College), 154

Turner, Kenn, 143, 146
2014 Millennial Impact report, 91
2042 (year), significance of, 8
Twitter, 19

Uber, 15–17, 53, 188n10
UCLA, Department of African American Studies, 30–31
unconscious biases, 20–23, 70
University of Georgia, study on Hispanic buying power, 99
US Congress and congressional staff, lack of diversity in, 54
US State Department, 134–35, 137
US Supreme Court cases, 43, 149

Velasquez-Manoff, Moises, 12
venture capital field, 34–35, 203n5
Vertex Pharmaceuticals, 145

Waldstein, David, 54
Walker, Darren, 163
Wallestad, Anne, 59
Wall Street Journal, 26
Walmart, 22
Walt Disney Company, 165
Ward, Karen Holmes, 2
Wayfair, 119–20, 122
WCVB, 1–4
Weatherup, Craig, 73
Weber Shandwick, 91–92, 166
White, Martha C., 50
whites, 9, 35, 45, 59, 62
Wiener, Anna, 26
Wildmon, Donald E., 166
Wiley, Bennie, 17–18, 74, 109, 110
Wiley, Pratt, 183
Wilkins, David, 44–45
Williams, Dudley, III, 91
Williams, Maxine, 26
Wilson, Joe, 47
Wilson Rule, 53
Witzke, Michael, 151
women: in advertising industry, 105, 116; Airbnb and, 18; at Biogen, 133; on boards of directors, 59, 61–62, 69–70; in finance industry, 61–62, 136; at Highmark Health, 176; at IKEA, 50; in insurance industry, 61; in leadership roles, 19, 138–39; as Mattel advisors, 113; in NFL, 39, 42; at Starbucks, 171;

venture capital and, 35, 121, 203n5;
  wealth disparities of, 35; at Xerox,
  48–49
Woolworth's, 164
Wooten, John, 55
"A World of Difference" public service
  campaign, 2–3
Worthington, Ian, 149

Xerox, 47–49, 51, 53, 194n35

Yellen, Janet, 34
YMCA of Greater Boston, 5
YouGov media firm, 107–8

Zimmer, John, 15
Zuckerberg, Mark, 86

ABOUT THE AUTHOR

CAROL FULP is president and CEO of The Partnership, Inc., New England's premier organization dedicated to enhancing regional competitiveness by attracting, developing, retaining, and convening multicultural professionals. She created The Partnership's C-Suite Program, which brings together the highest level of multicultural executives in the Commonwealth of Massachusetts. Prior to joining The Partnership, Fulp served as senior vice president of corporate responsibility and brand management at John Hancock Financial, director of community programming and human resources for WCVB (the ABC-TV Boston affiliate), and corporate employee relations manager for the Gillette Company. Fulp is also active in Massachusetts politics and serves on many boards and foundations. President Barack Obama appointed her a representative of the United States to the sixty-fifth session of the United Nations' General Assembly. She has earned many awards and accolades for her excellence in business leadership and public service, including three honorary graduate degrees. She lives with her husband, C. Bernard ("Bernie") Fulp, in Boston.